THE BLOCKADERS

By the same author:

Just An Old Navy Custom
The Secret Navies
On Hazardous Service
The Royal Navy Since 1945
Royal Sailors
Lilliput Fleet
Armed with Stings
Phantom Fleet
They Called it Accident

THE BLOCKADERS

A. Cecil Hampshire

WILLIAM KIMBER · LONDON

First published in 1980 by
WILLIAM KIMBER & CO. LIMITED
Godolphin House, 22a Queen Anne's Gate,
London, SW1H 9AE

Typeset by Jubal Multiwrite Limited
and printed and bound in Great Britain by
Redwood Burn Limited, Trowbridge and Esher

Contents

List of Illustrations

Foreword and acknowledgements

During the two great wars of the twentieth century, British sea power was employed to maintain an economic blockade of our principal enemy, first Imperial, then Nazi, Germany.

In the 1914—18 war the British blockade became a stranglehold which contributed in no small measure to the defeat of the Central Powers. Because of the changed course of the second world conflict its effects were less drastic; nevertheless, it constituted an important and much feared strategic weapon of war.

The blockade was exerted by little advertised units of the Royal Navy patrolling the northern approaches to the North Sea, from the Orkney Islands to the coast of Greenland, to prevent the flow of contraband goods to and from the enemy. The ships were very vulnerable to air, surface warship and submarine attacks, and for the most part they had to operate under the most appalling weather conditions.

For help in rounding out the full story of the blockaders I owe special thanks to, among others Mr S.D. Sandes, Lieutenant W.O. Carr RN (Rtd), J.C.W. Last, Esq. (former Commodore P & O SN Company), Mr I. Jamieson, Mr A.J. Smith, Mr H. Mattinson, Lieutenant-Commander T.H. Maxted, DSO, RD, RNR (Ret), Mr W. McLennan, Mr M. Massie, Mr C. Griffiths, Mr J.H. King, MI Mar, E, and Mr J. Foley.

A.C.H.

CHAPTER ONE

Checkmate

One cold grey November morning a solitary freighter was steaming slowly northwards through the Denmark strait. This bleak stretch of water which runs between Iceland and the eastern coast of Greenland is one of the world's most inhospitable seaways at the best of times. Because of the presence of icebergs which continually drift down from the Arctic Ocean, the weather is often thick and foggy. In winter, frequent icy gales and blinding snow blizzards, which can quickly whip up mountainous seas, are liable to scream down upon the luckless mariner with little warning.

Although these extreme conditions were for once temporarily absent, the freighter captain was nevertheless compelled to exercise the greatest care in navigation, for he had deliberately taken his ship as close as he dared to the edge of the icepack fringing the Greenland shore. There was another reason for the crew of the 3,600-ton *Borkum* to remain keyed up to an unusual state of alertness, for all hands knew that their long voyage from South America with a full cargo of grain had entered upon its most hazardous stage.

Although Dutch colours were painted upon her sides, the *Borkum* was not flying the national flag of that country, and in fact she was owned by the Norddeutscher Line of Bremen. The year was 1939, and since the previous September Nazi Germany had been at war with Britain and France. Captain Meyer of the *Borkum* had been ordered by the German Ministry of Transportation to use his best endeavours to elude British naval patrols and get his ship and its valuable cargo safely back to the Reich. For that reason he had elected to take the more difficult route round the north of Iceland, intending then to head across the North Sea and seek the shelter of Norwegian territorial waters to reach home.

He was not to succeed.

The hands of the bulkhead clock in the *Borkum's* charthouse were converging on noon when a strange vessel was sighted approaching at speed. At first glance she seemed to be another merchantman, albeit much larger than the *Borkum*. Apprehensively the freighter's deckhands clustered at the rails to watch, while the bridge staff trained their binoculars on her. As the vessel drew nearer a string of flag signals in the International Code broke out at her yardarms. 'Stop! Do not use your radio. I intend to board.' Her normal peacetime livery replaced by camouflage paint, the White Ensign streaming from her gaff proclaimed the newcomer to be a British warship.

Meyer turned to his chief officer. 'Quick! Send an SOS giving our position before they can jam us, and add that we are being stopped by a British auxiliary cruiser,' he snapped. As the latter sped aft to the wireless shack on his mission, Meyer took his time before ringing down 'Slow' on the engine room telegraph, then through his glasses resumed his scrutiny of the warship.

Maintaining a cautious position off the freighter's quarter, the latter was now zigzagging at slow speed. Meyer could see the guns on her foredeck and noted that these were fully manned and kept trained on his vessel. By now she had lowered a cutter which was being rowed towards the *Borkum*. In less than ten minutes the boat was alongside, and two naval officers and several armed sailors swarmed up the jumping ladder which had been reluctantly lowered for them.

While one of the officers led the bluejackets below to commence searching the ship, the other mounted to the bridge. But even before he glanced at the ship's papers, which had obediently been produced at his curt request, Lieutenant-Commander Bernard Moloney RNR knew that the intercepted vessel was German and not Dutch. By a curious oversight Meyer and his officers were still wearing their 'NDL' cap badges.

'You have become a prize of the British Navy, Captain,' Moloney told him. 'If you have made any arrangements to scuttle you had better tell me.'

Meyer shook his head in disgust. 'You got here too soon,' he grunted.

After a brief exchange of signals with the armed merchant cruiser, which in peacetime appeared in Lloyd's Register as the 17,000-ton Anchor liner *California*, her name now prefixed with the letters 'HMS' in the Navy List, Moloney was instructed to retain on board two of the *Borkum's* seamen, nine of her engine room staff and a cook, and send the officers and remaining crew members over to the *California*.

Within an hour or so the transfer had been completed, additional British officers and ratings being sent over as prize crew from the warship. Moloney was then ordered to make for a designated position off the coast of Iceland where he would receive wirelessed instructions as to the *Borkum's* final destination. Soon afterwards the two vessels parted company, the *California* to return to her patrol area. With him Moloney now had Sub-Lieutenant Russell RNVR and Midshipman Lister RNR as watchkeeping officers, and Sub-Lieutenant (E) Macfadzean RNVR to take charge of the freighter's engine room. A dozen British sailors formed the prize crew and armed guard.

The weather continued to remain reasonably fine, and the *Borkum* was able to maintain her normal, rather slow, speed of seven to eight knots. Although the Germans who had been retained on board went about their duties obediently enough, their demeanour remained sullen and uncommunicative. Then, towards midnight, the ship's speed began to slow down until it dropped to a mere two knots. When Moloney, pistol in hand, went below to investigate he found most of the German engine room ratings drunk. He ordered a thorough search of their quarters to be made, and some forty bottles of liquor were found in their berths. These were removed and thrown overboard.

Next day a further search was instituted, and two hundred more bottles were discovered hidden in a storeroom beneath some dirty linen. These, too, were summarily disposed of over the side. The ship's speed was found to have been slowed down by the pipeline leading to the engine room bilge pumps having become choked with grain — a deliberate attempt at sabotage. Macfadzean set the German firemen to work at clearing these, and after about twenty-four hours it was possible to resume normal speed.

Four days after parting company with the *California* the weather rapidly deteriorated, and between Iceland and the Fair Isle Channel heavy seas and poor visbility made conditions uncomfortable. Moloney had now received orders to take the ship into Leith, and despite the fact that few navigational instruments were available, he was optimistic of making a landfall without difficulty. Unhappily things were not to work out that way.

During the afternoon Sub-Lieutenant Russell, on watch on the bridge, was scanning the horizon through his glasses when he sighted a surfaced submarine some two miles off the ship's starboard quarter. He immediately informed Moloney, who quickly joined him. The submarine was obviously a U-boat, and as she began to overhaul the freighter a flag signal was seen to be flying from a short staff above her conning tower. It was an order to stop engines. Moloney's response was to ignore this, turn the stern of the *Borkum* to the U-boat and instruct Macfadzean to work up to the maximum speed possible.

'We've got a bloody Hun on our tail,' he told the young engineer officer.

Although he did not know it, the presence of the submarine was not simply an unlucky coincidence. It was the result of the radio message which had been successfully transmitted by the freighter shortly before she was boarded. Picked up by the German Consul at Reykjavik, in Iceland, it had been re-transmitted by him to German naval headquarters. The latter acted swiftly, and *U-33*, commanded by Kapitänleutnant von Dresky, on patrol in the north-west approaches, was ordered to try to intercept.

Von Dresky now hoisted the threatening signal, 'I am about to open fire!' at the same time increasing speed and moving round to the freighter's starboard bow. Moloney ordered Macfadzean to keep steaming at all costs, and told the petty officer of the armed guard to get his men and the Germans working on deck down below and out of sight. The U-boat then fired her first shot across the merchantman's bows.

This had no effect except that the *Borkum* abruptly altered course and made straight for the submarine with the obvious intention of ramming. Von Dresky was forced to take avoiding action, and U-boat and merchantman now began to circle around each other with their relative positions unchanged. The infuriated submarine captain ordered fire to be opened on the *Borkum* as soon as his guns would bear.

After several near misses, the U-boat finally managed to put a shell through the freighter's engine room skylight. This exploded on the platform, shattering the steam pipes and wounding a German fireman. His panic-stricken compatriots promptly ceased work and made for the upper deck. As the *Borkum* began to lose way the U-boat put another shell through her forepart, which penetrated to No 1 hold and set fire to the wheat cargo. Von Dresky then signalled her to abandon ship, but Moloney's defiant answer was to order Russell to hoist British colours over the German ensign. Then in his own words, 'The submarine took up a position off our port bow and really had at us.'

The crippled *Borkum* was hit by five salvoes in rapid succession. One shell killed two Germans who were trying desperately to lower the jolly boat; another blew away the after steering engine; a third set the ship's midship structure on fire, so that her bridge soon became enveloped in smoke. The telegraph between bridge and engine room was also put out of action, forcing Macfadzean himself eventually to come up to report that the situation below had become hopeless because of the burst steam pipes.

Moloney realised that there was nothing for it now but to abandon ship. Although he could no longer see the enemy, the doomed freighter was still taking punishment fore and aft. Soon she was completely ablaze, flames and smoke mingled with escaping steam rising in a funeral pyre high above her.

Russell took charge of the port lifeboat, which appeared to be undamaged. Crammed into it were seven members of the prize crew and seven Germans, one of whom had been badly wounded. Soon after it cast off two more Germans, who had earlier dived overboard, were picked up. But the boat was found to be leaking, and needed at least two men to bail continuously. The Germans were too exhausted for either rowing or bailing, and it was left to the British sailors to do all the work. Later that night the wounded man died, bringing the total casualties to four, all Germans. His body was put over the side.

Meanwhile Moloney, Macfadzean and the rest of the survivors had managed to get away from the ship in the starboard lifeboat, which was fortunately intact. During the night the two boats became separated, and all hands had an uncomfortable time in the heavy seas, but morale remained high. Bailing and rowing continuously, they managed to keep roughly on a south-easterly course.

Shortly before midnight the survivors in Russell's boat sighted two British trawlers, on patrol as armed boarding vessels, heading towards the blazing *Borkum* to investigate, and fired flares to attract their attention. These were seen, and the men picked up by one of the trawlers, which then proceeded to look for the second lifeboat. This, too, was found after some hours of searching.

After being landed at Kirkwall, Moloney was interviewed in due course by his admiral, the redoubtable Max Horton, subsequently to become Commander-in-Chief, Western Approaches during the forthcoming Battle of the Atlantic, who asked his motive for refusing to obey the U-boat captain's orders. Moloney explained that he had fully considered his action beforehand and thought there was an outside chance of being able to ram the U-boat despite the *Borkum's* slow speed if the submarine was badly handled. In any event, he added, he was sure that his action would so annoy the U-boat captain as to cause him to sink the freighter or damage her to such an extent that she would never be able to reach an enemy harbour.

Later Horton wryly recalled that, 'I had the lieutenant-commander to dinner, along with a well-known newspaper correspondent
as he had such a good story to tell. But despite my champagne —
or because or it — the young officer failed to make anything of
a wonderful yarn!'

Moloney was awarded an immediate DSO, but his opponent was
not so lucky. Less than three months after the destruction of the
Borkum the German Naval War Diary recorded that *U-33* had been
sunk by the British minesweeper *Gleaner*, leaving no survivors.

Moloney's armed merchant cruiser, HMS *California*, was a unit
of the Northern Patrol, which represented the revival by this
country of a strategic policy first used against a European dictator
in the Napoleonic wars. To find out how it operated in the first of
the two great world conflicts of the twentieth century, we must
hark back to the year of 1914.

CHAPTER TWO

Tenth Cruiser Squadron

Originally drawn up in 1904 and kept under constant revision, the British Admiralty's War Plan which visualised Germany as our principal antagonist in the event of future hostilities, included as an important part of our main strategy the exertion of economic pressure upon that country by cutting off her shipping from oceanic trade by patrolling cruisers supported by the main fleet. In the event this economic blockade was to become, at least in the early years of the first world conflict, the Royal Navy's only really offensive policy. In the opinion of Admiral Beatty, 'The squadron which enforced the blockade formed the one unit that could win us the war.'

Thus while the Dover Strait was guarded by an adequate naval force, and cruisers patrolled the western approaches to the Channel, the Irish Sea and the Atlantic trade routes, the northern exit of the North Sea was to be watched by a special group of warships designated 'Cruiser Force B', or Northern Patrol Force. It was later to be re-titled the Tenth Cruiser Squadron. Its functions were to intercept German merchant vessels, stop neutrals proceeding to German ports with contraband, take or destroy any men-of-war or armed merchant vessels passing in or out of the North Sea, and deny the anchorage in the Shetlands to the enemy. A subsidiary task was to obtain intelligence from passing vessels.

The squadron's principal fuelling base was to be Scapa Flow, to which captured vessels were to be sent. Between the Northern Patrol and enemy bases the main British Fleet would be cruising. In case of overriding necessity the Commander-in-Chief, Grand Fleet (originally called the Home Fleet) could call on Cruiser Force B for a particular service, but in general the latter would work independently.

The extent of the Force's patrol, while not strictly defined by latitude and longitude, covered the area between the Shetlands and Norway to the east, and the Shetlands and the coast of Scotland to the south. The passage between the Shetlands and the Orkney Islands is some 40 miles wide, while the distance from the

Shetlands to the nearest point in Norway in latitude 61 degrees north is about 150 miles. But the coast of Norway is so fringed with islands, which form the *Indreled*, or Inner Leads, that vessels seeking to avoid capture could stay in that country's territorial waters for hundreds of miles. In latitude 62 degrees north, however, ships making their way north or south along the Norwegian coast are compelled to emerge into the open sea, and the admiral commanding Cruiser Force B was warned that this would be a fruitful area to patrol.

However, the possibility that the enemy would make use of Scandinavian ports was not fully considered. It was expected that the expense of sending goods to Germany by this circuitous route, and the inadequacy of transport services between Scandinavia and Germany would confine traffic within narrow limits.

Curiously enough, in view of the developing importance of the blockade, the ships selected to compose Cruiser Force B were the oldest cruisers in the Navy List, maintained on a Third Fleet basis. The designations 'First', 'Second' and 'Third' Fleets used in the Royal Navy prior to the First World War to describe warships in home waters had no connection with the strategic dispositions or functions of squadrons: it referred only to the state of readiness for war in which the vessels were maintained.

Known as the *Edgar* class, there were eight of these vessels, all built between 1893 and 1894 under the Naval Defence Act of 1889, their names in addition to *Edgar,* being *Royal Arthur, Hawke, Endymion, Grafton, Crescent, Gibraltar,* and *Theseus.* All had been extensively refitted and re-armed. Displacing between 7000 and 7350 tons, they were fitted with either two 9.2-inch guns and ten 6-inch, or one 9.2-inch and twelve 6-inch. Coal-burning, their maximum speed was 17 knots.

Although on a Third Fleet basis, they had been employed as a boys' training squadron, and thus carried full nucleus crews and extra hands for training duties. But they could not be fully manned for war service until the order to mobilise the Naval Reserves was issued, and thus could not be on station until some days after the warning telegram.

When war appeared to be inevitable the Admiralty became worried that the enemy might try to land in the Shetlands. As early as 28th July 1914, therefore, four destroyers and a light cruiser were ordered to those islands. To add to the general apprehension in Whitehall, information was received on 3rd August that three German transports had passed out of the Baltic

The Edgar class cruiser *Crescent*, flagship of Cruiser Force 'B' in 1914

AMC *Alsatian*, flagship of the 10th Cruiser Squadron in the First World War

two days earlier. On learning this, the Admiralty ordered the Commander-in-Chief, Home Fleet to frustrate any attempt on the Shetlands, and he despatched five more of his modern cruisers at full speed to the islands, and backed them up by stationing battle cruisers south of Fair Isle. Although hostilities had not then actually broken out, the warships were authorised to use force to prevent any landings.

There was also reason to believe that the Germans would send out armed merchant cruisers to break into the Atlantic. Winston Churchill, then First Lord of the Admiralty, feared that, 'Forty-two fast German merchant cruisers needed only a breathing space to get loose.' Accordingly the Admiralty ordered the Commander-in-Chief to put to sea with the Grand Fleet and sweep to within a hundred miles of the Norwegian coast. The fleet duly sailed on 4th August and returned after three days without having sighted anything unusual. It had also been reported that the Germans had established one or more bases somewhere along the Norwegian coast north of latitude 62 degrees north. Further Grand Fleet sweeps were therefore carried out in that area until the Norwegian Government protested, when these had to cease. There were in fact no such enemy bases.

Meanwhile, however, a German armed merchant cruiser had already broken out. She was the fast North German Lloyd liner *Kaiser Wilhelm der Grosse*, 22,700 tons, which had been armed and commissioned in the Elbe. In the evening of 4th August she was ordered to sail and commence raiding. Her course took her northward within sight of the Norwegian coast, and when her captain considered that he had passed the British patrol line, he headed for the Atlantic round the north of Iceland. On his way up the North Sea he actually passed within forty miles of the Grand Fleet which had just finished searching the area. Had the Northern Patrol been in position they might well have met the raider. Fortunately the latter had been at large for only three weeks when she met the British cruiser *Highflyer* off the West African coast, and after a brief engagement was forced to scuttle herself. During that time she had sunk 10,400 tons of British shipping.

Four other potential raiders were also abroad, which the Germans speedily transformed into fighting units. They were the liners *Cap Trafalgar*, *Kronprinz Wilhelm* and *Prinz Eitel Friedrich*, and the steamship *Cormoran*. The *Cap Trafalgar* was in harbour at Buenos Aires at the outbreak of war when she was requisitioned by the German naval attaché, armed with guns transferred from the German gunboat *Eber* from West Africa, and commissioned as an auxiliary cruiser on 31st August. She was sunk a fortnight later by the British armed merchant cruiser *Carmania*. The *Kronprinz Wilhelm* in New York was ordered to rendezvous at sea with the German cruiser *Karlsruhe*, which transferred guns, ammunition, and officers and men to her; and the *Prinz Eitel Friedrich* was converted to armed raider at Tsingtao. The *Cormoran*, a Russian merchantman which had been captured by the Germans, was also converted to auxiliary warship at Tsingtao, to which port she had been taken by her captors.

At the time of mobilisation the ships of Cruiser Force B were at their respective home ports: the *Crescent, Edgar* and *Grafton* at Portsmouth; *Endymion, Theseus* and *Gibraltar* at Devonport; *Royal Arthur* at Chatham, and *Hawke* refitting at Queenstown. Rear-Admiral Dudley de Chair, who had formerly been in charge of the Training Squadron, was appointed to command Cruiser Force B.

In the afternoon of 1st August he was ordered to mobilise the force. He promptly hoisted his flag in the *Crescent*, and next day the order went out to mobilise the Naval Reserves. By working overtime in the dockyard and naval barracks the *Crescent, Grafton,* and *Edgar* were made ready by 3rd August, and de Chair sailed, hoping to be joined at sea by the Devonport ships. But they were still delayed, and he continued up the Irish Sea, capturing a small German steamer en route, and arriving at Scapa in the morning of the 6th. The Devonport vessels joined up soon afterwards, but it was not until 9th August that the patrol was in operation.

Except for the *Kaiser Wilhelm der Grosse*, however, few prizes had been missed. As early as 31st July all German merchantmen had been recalled to neutral ports, and in the next three days German ships in the North Sea ran for Norwegian ports to lay up. Most of them were small vessels, but in harbour at Tromso was the North German Lloyd liner *Prinz Friedrich Wilhelm* of 17,000 tons and 17½ knots speed. Since she was on our list of German liners which could be converted into auxiliary cruisers, and rumour had it that she was being armed, a close watch was kept on that port until it was reliably reported by our agents that she had been laid up for the winter.

Foreseeing our blockade measures, the enemy had concluded that we would maintain our patrol line across the North Sea and the Skagerrak, and establish our main force between it and the

German Bight. However, to check up on this, the Germans decided to carry out a reconnaissance, using ten submarines spaced seven miles apart in line abreast, to cruise as far as a line drawn from Scapa Flow to Bergen. From there they were to turn back to a line stretching from Scapa to Stavanger.

The U-boat flotilla set out before dawn on 6th August, and on the outward run saw nothing. When they arrived at the northern limit of the designated sweep the senior officer decided to send one boat up as far as the Shetlands-Norwegian line. But she also found nothing, and having no time to hang around, returned south. In fact the only British warships sighted by the U-boats were cruisers and destroyers of the Grand Fleet which were guarding the passage to France of the British Expeditionary Force. Two of the submarines were lost: *U-15* rammed by the cruiser *Birmingham* and *U-13* which unaccountably disappeared.

This sortie gave the enemy little idea of our methods of patrol and served only to confuse them. Their impression was that the Royal Navy would be permanently occupying a definite line of patrol, and as the only vessels they could reasonably consider capable of fulfilling this function were the light cruisers and destroyers which had been spotted by the U-boats, they thought this to be the blockade line.

On 10th August the *Hawke* and *Royal Arthur* joined up with de Chair's squadron, and he now organised his ships into two divisions. The *Crescent* (flag), *Grafton*, *Endymion* and *Theseus* formed the First Division; and *Edgar* (senior officer), *Royal Arthur*, *Gibraltar* and *Hawke* the Second Division. The First Division was allotted the southern, or Shetlands, end of the patrol, while the Second Division patrolled off Norway.

But at this stage of the war there was little work for them to do. The outbreak of hostilities had paralysed the shipping trade all over the world, although for financial reasons rather than the fear of capture, and it was some time before vessels of any nationality put to sea in any numbers. In the North Sea traffic had practically come to a standstill. Accordingly the Commander-in-Chief, Grand Fleet — now Admiral Jellicoe, who had taken over from Admiral Callaghan — called on the ships of Cruiser Force B to join his flag for operations in the North Sea.

It was suspected that the Germans had established a base in the Faroe Islands, and the admiral commanding the Sixth Cruiser Squadron — which at that time consisted only of his flagship the *Drake* — together with the *Endymion* and *Gibraltar*, was detached to investigate. But there was no such base. Except for trawlers, no German ship had visited the islands for two years. For a time the three cruisers continued to patrol between the Faeroes and Iceland.

On his next sweep into the North Sea Jellicoe ordered the *Crescent, Grafton, Theseus* and *Edgar* to patrol on his eastern flank in case enemy ships should emerge from the Skagerrak. *Hawke* and *Royal Arthur* remained on patrol off Norway. But the excursion put a heavy strain on the ageing engines of the *Edgars*, and they had to return to Lerwick to coal.

This sortie by the Grand Fleet coincided with a second German attempt to ascertain the position of our patrol line. This time they dropped the idea of sweeping up the North Sea with an extended line of U-boats: too many would be required, and few were capable of undertaking the long voyage. Instead, two of the best boats were ordered to sail up as far as Egersund, in Norway, then cross to Peterhead to gain as much information as possible.

One of the boats, *U-20* carrying the half-flotilla's senior officer, Kapitänleutnant Albert Gayer, encountered a British cruiser and destroyer off the Norwegian coast and was forced to submerge. When she did reach Egersund, four black buoys were seen which Gayer thought were navigational marks for the patrolling ships. Engine and compass defects then compelled *U-20* to return to Heligoland. Gayer thought that we were carrying out destroyer sweeps, which would make long voyages difficult for submarines. The second boat went up as far as Kinnaird Head, saw nothing and returned home. The Germans therefore concluded that the blockade line did not run from Peterhead to Egersund as they had thought, but they did not know where it was and accordingly abandoned all operations against the Grand Fleet for the time being.

The Admiralty, however, objected to the *Edgars* being taken away from their designated function, and told Jellicoe that it was considered important to maintain the Northern Patrol continuously to prevent ships getting in or out of the North Sea. 'Four armed merchant ships are being sent up as soon as ready to assist in making the Patrol more effective. The Patrol can spread in any direction you propose.' Consequently both the Norwegian and Shetlands patrols were reinstituted.

The Norwegian patrol line ran from a specified latitude and longitude about one hundred miles north of Bergen. From this point, steering a course slightly east of north, the ships of the Patrol maintained a line of bearing five miles apart. During darkness they turned sixteen points together at pre-arranged times to preserve the line of bearing, experiments having proved this to be the best formation against contraband runners.

The ships of the Shetlands patrol, however, steamed in line ahead between Muckle Flugga, the most northerly tip of the Shetlands, and the start position of the Norwegian patrol. Because they were to see a great deal of this lonely and forbidding outpost of the British Isles, the crews who manned the ships of the Northern Patrol dubbed themselves the 'Muckle Flugga Hussars'. This was later changed to the 'Terrible Tenth', not because of the fear they inspired so much as the harsh conditions under which they had to operate! Since they were aware that if confronted at any time by any heavy enemy surface unit their fate would be quick and decisive before help could reach them, they regarded themselves as being 'the cheese in the mousetrap'.

*

It is time now to look at the measures which were in force for stopping the flow of contraband goods to the enemy.

At the outset of the war the terms of the 1909 Declaration of London were adopted with certain modifications. Briefly, this treaty, which had not been ratified by the British Government, enacted that during time of war neutral nations were forbidden to supply either of the belligerents with certain commodities which could be used for warlike purposes. These goods were divided into three categories: *absolute contraband*, which included articles of an exclusively military character such as guns and explosives; *conditional contraband* — goods capable of both military and non-military uses such as fuel, clothing and foodstuffs, subject to seizure only if destined for the armed forces of an enemy State; and a *free list* of articles which could never be considered contraband, such as raw cotton, oil, copper and rubber. But the latter were four of the most important adjuncts to modern warfare! Thus the British Government insisted on drawing up its own list of contraband goods — although to avoid upsetting the United States cotton was excluded for a year. Thereafter we ourselves purchased it — at ever rising prices. Most neutral ships had therefore to be stopped and searched.

The German naval operational orders for the conduct of war in the North Sea included a ruthless minelaying campaign, and as early as 5th August a minefield was laid off the English coast north of the Thames by a converted German merchantman. This quickly brought results in the sinking of the British cruiser *Amphion* — ironically soon after the culprit had been caught by the cruiser and her accompanying destroyers. The Germans then extended their minelaying operations to the Tyne and Humber.

The British Admiralty now began to connect minelayers with contraband. It was thought — mistakenly as it turned out — that the Germans were using fishing craft and ordinary merchantmen, perhaps disguised as neutrals, for minelaying. Accordingly an order went out that all ships of the Fleet were to stop and search every vessel encountered. Foreign trawlers would be searched in British ports.

This order brought an immediate reaction from Admiral Jellicoe, who wanted the Admiralty instead to close all east coast ports to trade and prohibit fishing. But the Admiralty considered such a measure to be too drastic: fishermen were in fact discovering minelayers and minefields. Contraband carriers were unlikely to be found near the coast, and stoppage was a matter for the Grand Fleet cruisers and the Northern Patrol.

Admiral Beatty, who commanded the battle cruiser fleet, disagreed with this. Time, he said, did not permit of boarding all ships encountered. Boarding was a hindrance to operations, and because of the growing activities of U-boats, a danger to ships. Merchant traffic should be regulated from the shore. Ships in British ports could be examined there, and if cleared given a safe conduct and the Fleet informed. Consuls abroad should advise vessels bound for Scandinavia to put into Lerwick for the latest information, and ships trading regularly across the North Sea to British ports could be regarded as harmless and left to be inspected in port.

There now occurred a disaster which tragically underlined Beatty's warning about the danger of U-boats. In the early morning of 22nd September 1914 the submarine *U-9* torpedoed in succession the armoured cruisers *Aboukir*, *Hogue* and *Cressy* which were on patrol examining steamers and trawlers in the southern North Sea. Each had unwisely gone to the aid of an earlier victim, and all went down with considerable loss of life. The destruction of what had been dubbed the 'live bait squadron' brought among its repercussions the resignation of the then First Sea Lord, Admiral Prince Louis of Battenberg, father of the late Earl Mountbatten, and the return to this post of Admiral Fisher who had earlier retired.

The Admiralty had at first prohibited the use of armoured ships to stop and examine merchant vessels, or even patrolling off the east coast of Scotland. But as Jellicoe possessed so few unarmoured ships he could not hope to stop contraband. Eventually he was provided with a number of small craft for use as armed boarding vessels.

A sweep carried out by Grand Fleet cruisers at the end of September clearly showed that the methods then in force of trying to intercept contraband by boarding ships at sea were unsuccessful. A large number of neutral vessels, or ships flying neutral flags, were seen making eastwards towards the Skagerrak. None flew the flag previously agreed upon to show that they had been boarded, but nevertheless had to be allowed to pass without examination. Both Jellicoe and Beatty urged that the only method of securing control over contraband was to insist that all vessels call at a British port for examination and be given a secret signal without which any vessel encountered should be turned back.

But now the Admiralty went even further. On 5th November the whole of the North Sea was declared a military area, the reason given for this decision being that the Germans were scattering mines indiscriminately in its waters. Accordingly the warning was issued that ships passing a line drawn from the north-west of the Hebrides through the Faeroes to Iceland did so at their peril; and requiring all other vessels trading to Scandinavia to come through the English Channel for sailing directions.

At once the Scandinavian Powers protested. Following our institution of a War Channel along the east coast of Britain, and the mining of the Dover Strait, these neutral nations had diverted their routes northabout as being safer. Accordingly the concession was made that a limited number of liners belonging to each country would be allowed to use the northabout passage provided that due notice was given, and that the vessels called at Kirkwall on each voyage. This concession coincided with the announcement that a secret German minefield had been discovered off Tory Island, north-west of Ireland, in the track of Atlantic shipping; and that Smith's Knoll, off the Norfolk coast, until then considered safe, had also been mined by the enemy. This news helped to persuade the protesting countries to accept the drastic extension of our belligerent rights.

Permission was given to the eight most important Scandinavian shipping companies trading to America to use the northabout route provided that their ships called at Kirkwall for instructions on their eastward voyages. These directed that from Kirkwall they were to head directly for Bergen, then follow the Norwegian coast to their destination. Westbound ships were to make for a position in latitude 60 degrees north, longitude 3 degrees west, and from thence to keep north of 60 degrees north latitude until clear of the British Isles. All other ships were to proceed southabout.

When this announcement was made by the Admiralty, units of the Grand Fleet were operating with Cruiser Force B, now designated the Tenth Cruiser Squadron. While the latter patrolled north of the Shetlands, ships of the Third Battle Squadron cruised between the Shetlands and the Faeroes, with armed merchant cruisers covering both sides of the islands; and ships of the Sixth Battle Squadron patrolled west of the Barra Islands.

Jellicoe now asked the Admiralty whether or not he was forcibly to prevent all neutrals from entering the North Sea. He was told that force should not be used to turn back neutral vessels which had not received permission to use the northabout route and did not voluntarily call at Kirkwall, but that they should be brought into Kirkwall for examination, which should be made as exhaustive as possible. Discretion was to be used, since the object was to deter neutral vessels from using the northabout route, and in any case to induce them voluntarily to call at Kirkwall for examination.

*

Thus far the Tenth Cruiser Squadron had sighted no German ships on the Northern Patrol. Feeling that the Force was not being fully utilised, Jellicoe obtained the approval of the Admiralty to bring the ships south to replace the more valuable cruisers of the Grand Fleet which were watching off Kinnaird Head to cover the movements of vessels to and from Scapa Flow and Cromarty Firth. The three armed merchant cruisers which had been taken up would continue to patrol off the Shetlands.

Using Cromarty as their base, the *Edgars* now began to patrol a rectangular 'box' some thousand square miles in extent north and east of Kinnaird Head. Another cruiser squadron was detailed to work with them in such a way that there would always be eight vessels on patrol. Their duties were to intercept all trade; protect fleet bases against minelayers and submarines; examine areas where floating mines or other suspicious objects had been reported; and give notice of the approach of, and engage, enemy cruisers encountered. One ship, the *Theseus,* was detached to escort a

convoy of merchant ships to Archangel carrying coal and guns for
Russia, the first of a series of such convoys.

Then in October de Chair's squadron suffered its first loss.

On the 15th of that month five of the *Edgars* were steaming
along their patrol line at intervals of ten miles abreast in the order
Endymion, Hawke, Theseus, Edgar and *Grafton.* At 0930 the
Endymion and *Hawke* closed and stopped briefly while the
former, which had recently left harbour, transferred mails to the
latter before going on to do the same for the other ships. The
Hawke meanwhile resumed course at 13 knots.

Some four hours later lookouts on board the *Theseus* saw a
torpedo approaching on the starboard beam. This was successfully
avoided, and a warning signal immediately flashed to her consorts.
The senior officer present, who happened to be the captain of the
Edgar, promptly informed Jellicoe of the incident, and ordered
the patrolling ships to assemble in the northernmost corner of the
patrol area. Acknowledgments of the order were received from all
except the *Hawke* — which indicated that something untoward
had happened to her.

When all attempts to raise that vessel by wireless had failed,
Jellicoe despatched a division of destroyers, headed by the flotilla
leader *Swift,* in search. After spending the whole night scouring
the area in which the *Hawke* had last been reported, they eventually
came across a raft containing one officer and six ratings. Continuing
the search, the *Swift* sighted a submarine and was narrowly missed
by a torpedo fired at her. Despite this the hunt went on, and
another fourteen ratings were picked up. On her way back to
Scapa the *Swift* again sighted a U-boat and opened fire, forcing it
to dive.

Next day another officer and forty-nine ratings from the *Hawke*
were landed at Aberdeen from a British trawler. They had got
away in one of the only two lifeboats that had floated and been
picked up by a Norwegian steamer, which transferred them to the
trawler.

From these survivors it was learned that soon after receiving her
mails from the *Endymion* and resuming patrol, the *Hawke* had
been struck by a torpedo on the starboard side abreast the foremost funnel. She at once took on a severe list, and a few minutes
later turned bottom upwards. There had been no time to call for
help and none of her consorts was in sight. It was only by means
of the boats and such rafts as had floated off that the few survivors
were able to save themselves.

The submarine responsible was *U-9*, the same boat which had sunk the *Cressys*. Together with *U-17* she had left Heligoland two days earlier on a mission to discover the whereabouts of the Grand Fleet. After sinking the *Hawke*, the *U-9* had tried to torpedo the *Theseus* before continuing her voyage to the Orkneys. *U-17* remained behind near the scene of the sinking and later attempted to attack the *Swift* without success.

The torpedoing of the *Cressys* had come as an unpleasant revelation to many officers in the British Navy of the offensive capabilities of submarines. With the loss of the *Hawke* adding another 500 to the 1400 officers and men already drowned, Jellicoe decided to withdraw the whole of the Grand Fleet from the North Sea. The Tenth Cruiser Squadron now joined the older battleships of the Third Battle Squadron patrolling to the north-west of the Shetlands. When these ships were also temporarily withdrawn to Lough Swilly with the rest of the Grand Fleet, the Tenth Cruiser Squadron continued to maintain the patrol with the Third Cruiser Squadron.

But the Northern Patrol as such was still not fully in force, although by late October Jellicoe had instituted the following arrangements for stopping German trade and the passage of contraband in neutral vessels:

1. A cruiser force working north of the Shetlands and occasionally visiting the Norwegian coast.
2. One or two armed merchant cruisers patrolling south of the Faeroes;
3. A group of battleships stationed in the area between the Faeroes and the Orkneys to form a second line which had to be passed, and to act in the North Sea or elsewhere to intercept enemy armed vessels;
4. A squadron off the northernmost point of the Hebrides to intercept ships passing the Flannan islands;
5. Some ships stationed south of the Hebrides to intercept merchantmen passing north through the Minches;
6. Two or three minesweepers to intercept trade passing between Sule Skerry and the Orkneys

But reports had been received by the Admiralty and the Commander-in-Chief that large numbers of contraband runners were passing north of the Faeroes. Three armed merchant cruisers were supposed to be working in that area, but one of them had earlier been wrecked. Jellicoe now asked the Admiralty for at least two more.

To add to his worries about U-boats there was the growing threat of enemy minelaying. For at that period of the war, as Jellicoe saw it, there was no great disparity between the first-line strengths of the fighting fleets of Britain and Germany. There were occasions when he felt that the margin of British superiority over the Germans became dangerously narrow. One such occurred on 27th October when the modern battleship *Audacious*, a unit of the Grand Fleet's Second Battle Squadron, was mined and sunk off the north-west of Ireland during exercises.

While taking urgent steps to ascertain the extent of the mine-field — mentioned earlier as being near Tory Island — Jellicoe ordered the Third and Tenth Cruiser Squadrons to spread out and try to intercept the enemy vessel which had laid it. Unknown to him this was the 17,000-ton North German Lloyd liner *Berlin* which, disguised as a British ship, had left Wilhelmshaven on 16th October on a minelaying mission, and passed up the west coast of Ireland undetected.

On receipt of the Commander-in-Chief's signal Admiral de Chair ordered those of his ships on patrol, which included the *Edgar, Endymion, Theseus, Gibraltar* and *Royal Arthur*, to take up positions on a base line running north-east of Muckle Flugga. The inner ship was to be seven miles from that headland and the remainder 10 miles apart. They were to cross the base line steering south-east at midnight, and to alter course 16 points every two hours. The Third Cruiser Squadron was to prolong the line to the north-east. His own flagship, the *Crescent*, which was coaling at Swarbacks Minn, in the Shetlands, joined up with the squadron on the 29th.

At 1630 that afternoon a suspicious vessel was sighted and followed. But she outpaced the old *Edgars*, whose engines were becoming increasingly unreliable. De Chair hoisted the signal for general chase, but even with every ship doing her utmost they could only just keep the quarry in sight. Later that evening Jellicoe ordered out the First Light Cruiser Squadron to assist, and de Chair despatched them to the Norwegian coast to intercept the suspect.

Then soon after midnight the *Endymion*, which had been going flat out continuously, finally managed to overtake her. To every-one's disgust she turned out to be the Norwegian liner *Bergensfjord* returning home from a routine voyage to New York. She had on board the German Consul from Korea, but according to previous instructions issued by the Admiralty he was not to be molested.

The battleship *Audacious* sinking after having been mined in October, 1914

Nevertheless Jellicoe ordered the liner into Kirkwall for examination, and she was escorted into that port by the *Endymion* despite vigorous protests from a high official of the Norwegian Government who happened to be on board the ship as a passenger.

Nothing was seen of the minelayer, and the Tenth Cruiser Squadron returned to their normal beat. While they had been chasing after the *Bergensfjord* the *Berlin* had quietly slipped round the north of Iceland and headed eastward to try to attack merchant ships on the Archangel trade route. In this she was unsuccessful, and was by now suffering from boiler defects and a shortage of coal. Since her operational orders permitted her to intern herself in a neutral port if no other course was practicable, she put into Trondheim. Next day she was disarmed and interned by the Norwegians.

However, the *Edgars* were soon to disappear from the Northern Patrol, which was to be entirely re-constituted.

During the pursuit of the *Bergensfjord* several ships of the squadron had broken down, and it became clear that they could not carry on without being extensively refitted. A particularly severe gale in mid-November highlighted their lack of seaworthiness and unsuitability for the arduous work of the Patrol during the winter months. The *Crescent's* forebridge was wrecked by heavy seas, the admiral's sea cabin swept overboard, and the ventilating cowl of the foremost stokehold carried away, with the result that tons of seawater poured below and put out the fires. Deck planking had become so rotten that hawser reels and other metal fittings were wrenched away and washed overboard.

The *Endymion* was compelled to put into Scapa to make good immediate defects, and the *Theseus, Edgar* and *Gibraltar* forced to run for shelter at Busta Voe to carry out urgent repairs. The only units of the Patrol remaining at sea were two armed merchant cruisers stationed between Iceland and the Faeroes. But their coaling base was Liverpool, and its distance from the patrol area necessitated an absence from station of one or more of the vessels for about eleven days.

Admiral de Chair was summoned to Scapa and informed by Jellicoe that it had been decided to refit half the squadron at a time in the Clyde shipyards. Accordingly three of his ships, *Crescent, Royal Arthur* and *Grafton*, were to leave at once for Greenock. No merchant vessels had been sighted by the Patrol for some time, but there was probably nothing passing. The three *Edgars* at Busta Voe were ordered to take up a new patrol line, west-north-west of the Hebrides.

The Commander-in-Chief was again beset by doubts as to the utility of the Patrol. In a letter to the Admiralty he complained that of ships boarded since the beginning of October, twenty-five had been sent into Kirkwall and several into other northern ports. Only one of these had been permanently detained, and one other compelled to land part of her cargo. All the rest had been released, although they were bound for the Baltic and Dutch ports with cargoes such as copper, grain, petroleum, sulphur and coal, some of which were openly destined for Germany. He therefore felt that the squadron would be better employed on duties other than the risky and destructive work of boarding ships which were eventually released, and suggested that the practice of boarding ships should be discontinued.

In reply the Admiralty pointed out that there were considerable legal difficulties in dealing with neutral ships trading between neutral ports. Satisfactory guarantees had been obtained that most of the cargoes brought in were for neutral consumption and would not be re-exported. Such guarantees could not have been obtained had the ships not been brought in, while their arrest had had a valuable effect in restraining shipowners from embarking contraband and underwriters from insuring it. Many neutral countries were prohibiting the export of objectionable articles. All this pressure on German trade was the direct consequence of the delay, anxiety, and extreme inconvenience caused to neutrals by the British Navy's interference.

So important did the Admiralty consider the work of the Northern Patrol that when they became aware of the physical conditions which had to be endured by the ships, they decided to replace the *Edgars* by a large squadron of more suitable vessels. Jellicoe was accordingly informed that:

> The following arrangements are in hand and will be completed with the utmost despatch in order to put the Northern Patrol on a more satisfactory footing. The Patrol will consist of 24 large liners constituted as follows: three already on patrol; four now commissioning with full crews and armament; 17 further vessels now being taken up. Their speed will be 14 to 17 knots; tonnage 4,000 to 6,000, somewhat reduced armament. These vessels will be manned by the crews of the *Edgars* supplemented where possible by RNR firemen. The *Edgars* will be paid off as the liners become available. These 24 vessels will be under the command of Rear-Admiral de Chair and will be employed exclusively for patrol duty.

CHAPTER THREE

Armed Merchant Cruisers Take Over

On 20th November the Admiralty ordered the *Edgars* to return to their home ports and pay off, sufficient repair work being done on them to enable them to do this. Admiral de Chair hauled down his flag in the *Crescent* on 3rd December, and the work of the *Edgars* on the Northern Patrol came to an end.

Up to the date of their withdrawal these old cruisers had stopped and boarded more than 300 merchant vessels, while many other ships had been intercepted and interrogated on the numerous occasions when the weather was too bad for a boat to be lowered. In recognition of their services Jellicoe sent a letter to de Chair congratulating him and his crews on their successful work in spite of the age of their ships and the difficulties of keeping the machinery efficient.

During the period of their patrol the nature of contraband had been considerably modified. At the outbreak of war all British warships had been issued with a Naval Prize Manual dated January 1914, which was in general accord with the provisions of the Declaration of London 1909. Thus a ship carrying absolute contraband was to be detained if she was scheduled to call at an enemy port, was off course as shown by her papers, or in other suspicious circumstances. A ship carrying conditional contraband was not to be detained unless she intended to call at an enemy port or meet an enemy fleet. She could, however, be detained although she herself might not be proceeding to a hostile country if the goods were consigned to an enemy government or to a fortified base in hostile territory; or again, if she were off course. But a great many articles were excluded from the contraband list.

These regulations had been modified by Order-in-Council of 20th August 1914, when conditional contraband became liable to seizure even though consigned to a neutral port, if the consignee of the goods was an agent of an enemy state or a person under control of that state. This extended the principle of 'continuous voyage' to conditional contraband. That same day it was reported that the German Government had taken control of all foodstuffs, thus constituting them contraband if consigned to places in

Germany through neutral ports.

By Order-in-Council of 20th September copper, rubber and iron ore were transferred from the free to the conditional list, and ships carrying such cargoes were to be sent in, unless it was certain that the goods were not for the use of an enemy government. A further Order-in-Council, issued on 29th October and intended as a concession to the United States — the principal dealer in contraband — introduced additional modifications. It added copper, rubber, lead and other metals to the absolute list, and permitted neutral ports, if abused, to be treated as enemy bases. But its wording allowed any consignee in neutral territory to receive contraband although he might be a known enemy agent. In effect, conditional contraband could be seized in a vessel bound for a neutral port only if the goods were consigned 'to order' if the ship's papers did not show who was the consignee, or if he were in enemy territory.

In actual fact the German Government had not taken control of foodstuffs at that time, so food ships sent in had to be released. In addition, the October Order-in-Council set free many other vessels which had been detained in good faith, and it was through the operation of these orders that the arduous work of the Northern Patrol had produced comparatively meagre results in preventing the arrival of goods into Germany.

The employment of armed merchant cruisers to supplement regular cruiser squadrons on the principal ocean trade routes had long formed part of the Admiralty's initial War Plan. Thus on 1st August 1914 a number of fast liners were taken up for conversion. They included the *Aquitania* and *Caronia* of the Cunard Line; the P & O steamers *Macedonia* and *Marmora*; and next day the Union Castle's Line's *Armadale Castle*, the White Star's *Oceanic*, and the Cunarders *Lusitania* and *Mauretania*. Two days later when war became inevitable the *Carmania, Kinfauns Castle, Empress of Britain, Alsatian, Otranto, Mantua* and *Victorian* were added to the list.

But because they burned too much coal the *Mauretania* and *Lusitania* were soon returned, and, following a collision shortly after being taken up, the *Aquitania* was handed back to her owners. Of the remainder, the *Oceanic, Alsatian* and *Mantua* were assigned to the Northern Patrol. The *Lusitania* was fated to be sunk by U-boat on 7th May 1915 while voyaging from New York to Britain as an innocent passenger liner.

The *Alsatian*, a nearly new vessel with a top speed of 22 knots, joined the Patrol on 18th August, being followed by the *Mantua* on the 24th, and the *Oceanic* three days later. But the latter's career as an armed merchant cruiser was short-lived. On 8th September while returning from temporary detachment to the Faeroes, she ran aground on a reef near Foula Island and became a total wreck.

In the same month the 10,000-ton White Star liner *Teutonic* joined the Patrol. The first commercial vessel to have been specially designed to become an auxiliary cruiser in wartime, she was to have been fitted with as many as twelve 5-inch guns and an equal number of 3-pounders. When taken up in 1914, however, she was given an armament of eight 6-inch. Described as an 'armed merchantman', the *Teutonic* had been present at a naval review held at Spithead in August 1889 in honour of Kaiser Wilhelm II and had been inspected by him. Ironically enough, it was from what he learnt during his inspection of the *Teutonic* that the Emperor modelled his own scheme for an auxiliary cruiser fleet. Known as the 'Greyhound', she was not, however, a good sea boat, being apt to 'take it green' in a seaway, which reduced the efficiency of her foremost guns.

In response to Jellicoe's request for more armed merchant cruisers to reinforce the Northern Patrol, the Admiralty had taken up three more liners. They were the 12,000-ton *Otway* of the Orient Line; the 21,000-ton *Cedric* belonging to the White Star Line; and the 10,700-ton Allan Line's *Virginian*, the latter being intended as a replacement for the wrecked *Oceanic*. She and the *Victorian* were famous as the world's first turbine liners.

The additional 17 vessels which were now to bring the newly constituted Tenth Cruiser Squadron up to 24 were all requisitioned by mid-November, and arrangements made for them to be fitted out on the Clyde, at Liverpool, Avonmouth, London, Hull and on the Tyne. As will be seen they were a mixed bag, including several banana boats and a 26-year old former cruise ship. But only vessels which were actually in port were taken up because of the urgency with which they were required. Their names and details are given in the table on the facing page:

Name	Tonnage	Built	Speed	Owners
Patia	6100	1913	16kts	Elders & Fyffes
Patuca	6100	1913	16kts	Elders & Fyffes
Bayano	6000	1913	14kts	Elders & Fyffes
Motagua	6000	1912	14kts	Elders & Fyffes
Changuinola	6000	1912	14kts	Elders & Fyffes
Ambrose	4500	1903	14kts	Booth Line
Hilary	6200	1908	14kts	Booth Line
Hildebrand	7000	1911	14½kts	Booth Line
Caribbean(ex *Dunnotar Castle* of Boer War fame)	5800	1890	14kts	Royal Mail Lines
Oratava	6000	1899	14kts	Royal Mail Lines
Eskimo	3300	1910	14kts	Thos Wilson & Co. Hull
Calypso(renamed *Calyx*)	2800	1904	12kts	Thos Wilson & Co. Hull
Oropesa	5300	1895	13kts	Pacific S.N. Company
Digby	4000	1913	14½kts	Furness Withy
Columbia (renamed *Columbella*)	8200	1902	17kts	Anchor Line
Viking (renamed *Viknor*)	5300	1888	17kts	Viking Cruising Company
Clan McNaughton	5000	1911	11kts	Clan Line

Subsequently various changes had to be made. The *Cedric* was returned to her owners as being too big. The *Eskimo* was also returned to civilian ownership, later to be captured by a German raider while on a voyage to Norway. The *Viknor* was lost in 1915, and the *Clan McNaughton* disappeared during one of the worst gales experienced by the squadron; the *Calyx* was paid off as unsuitable.

Among later additions to the squadron were the Royal Mail Steam Packet Company's liners *Alcantara* (15,300 tons); *Arlanza* (15,044 tons); *Andes* (15,620 tons), and *Ebro* (8470 tons); the Pacific Steam Navigation Company's 11,500-ton *Orcoma*; the 7940-ton P & O liner *India*; also the 15,000-ton oil-burning *Avenger* which was being built for the Union Steamship Company of New Zealand when war broke out and was completed to Admiralty specification. All were capable of speeds of 15 to 16 knots and an endurance of 30 days at 15 knots without fuelling.

Conversion for naval service necessitated removing all passenger fittings and stiffening the decks with steel supports to enable guns to be mounted. At first the latter were obsolete 4.7-inch taken from broken-up cruisers built under the 1889 Naval Defence Act. But as they were found to be useless against German ships likely to be armed with 5.9-inch or 4.1-inch high velocity guns, they were replaced with six to eight 6-inch guns mounted so as to allow a broadside of four; two 12-pounder or 6-pounder anti-aircraft guns being added later.

The problem of fitting magazines which would comply with the stringent safety regulations in normal warships was solved by building large steel tanks in the fore and after holds, with appropriate ventilating and flooding arrangements. Some ships arranged for cofferdams to be built round these tanks as an additional precaution. This measure was fully justified as they thereby escaped magazine explosions.

Another difficulty was the provision of an adequate system of ammunition supply to the guns. But in the Northern Patrol all ships stacked plenty of ready-use projectiles in racks around the guns — which were kept loaded day and night — with due precautions against frost and ice, since they always had to be ready for instant emergency. Fire control was by voicepipe only, although there were telephones to the bridge. Most of the gunnery was entirely independent, however, and much depended on the efficiency and intelligence of individual gunlayers. Guns' crews were always kept closed up when the ships were on patrol, and it became necessary to erect special shelters near their weapons for the protection of the crews against the weather.

For gunnery training when on patrol and in harbour, the ships used tubes and dotter gear, and they all carried loading machines in order to exercise guns' crews. In fact the squadron became so efficient that later on they trained gunlayers for defensively armed merchant ships. In addition special drills were instituted for fighting submarines.

Because of their vulnerability in action against enemy warships and surface raiders, as shown by the action between the British armed merchant cruiser *Carmania* and the German *Cap Trafalgar* in September 1914, buoyancy was increased by stowing a large quantity of timber and empty metal drums below the waterline.

Accommodation for officers and men was more comfortable than in the normal warship. Peacetime public rooms were utilised as messes, lounges and smoking rooms. In converted passenger liners the first-class lounge and ballroom, stripped of decorations and furniture, was used as an assembly place for holding daily Divisions and Prayers in cold weather, for church on Sundays, and as a recreation space. The second-class lounge was turned into a smoking room for the crew where concerts, boxing matches and other sporting competitions could be held. The accommodation normally allotted in peacetime to stewards, cooks and firemen was turned into storerooms, their naval equivalents occupying passenger quarters with the rest of the ship's company.

Practically all the cargo space in the lower holds was filled with coal; the *Alsatian* carried as much as 5,600 tons in addition to her normal bunkers. The coal had to be trimmed into the bunkers as necessary in order to use it. Although a dirty job, the task did afford some relief from the monotony of patrol.

With their large fuel capacity the ships could remain at sea for periods of up to a month, unless consumption became abnormal through chasing suspects. Some 500 tons were always kept in the bunkers to aid stability. Normal speed on patrol was 10 to 13 knots, but all boilers had to be kept alight in case it was necessary to work up to full speed at short notice — which was often the case when a suspicious ship had to be chased.

All the vessels were manned on a similar basis. A regular naval officer of either captain's or commander's rank was appointed in command, most of the other officers being RNR, either permanent or temporary. Many of these had served in the same ships in peacetime and were thus thoroughly familiar with them. The Gunner and Boatswain were also Royal Navy, as were a proportion of the senior ratings. A marine detachment was included, usually comprising one sergeant and from twenty to forty marines. In addition each ship of the Northern Patrol carried a number of seamen belonging to the Newfoundland Naval Reserve. Fishermen in civil life, they were expert boat-handlers, and invariably crewed the boats which took boarding officers across to intercepted merchantmen.

The rest of the ships' companies were usually Reservists and former Merchant Navy ratings serving under special agreements. This system was, however, a serious handicap to smooth shipboard organisation, and caused a good deal of trouble from a disciplinary point of view. Another awkward arrangement affected wireless operators and engineers. In the Merchant Navy these held officer or quasi-officer status, but in the Royal Navy their work would have been performed by ratings. Thus volunteers were difficult to obtain unless officer rank was promised. Complements varied from 600 officers and men in the larger ships to about 240 in smaller vessels.

Internal organisation was arranged so that the executive officers were employed mainly in watchkeeping. They were divided into four watches, two in each watch being on duty at a time, one on the bridge and the other on general duties, supervising the guns' crews, etc. Certain officers were detailed for boarding work and the examination of papers and cargoes of vessels intercepted; others to take charge of armed guards. The navigating and gunnery officers did not keep regular watches as they had their own special duties, but they relieved the bridge in action and at odd times during the day.

Ships' companies, both seamen and engine room personnel, were divided into three watches designated 'Red', 'White', and 'Blue' which allowed of four hours on duty and eight off. During the day the off-duty hands were employed on ship cleaning, general duties and drills. Boarding boats' crews had to be ready to go away at any time of the day or night. One important duty in those days before the advent of radar was that of masthead lookout. Men told off for this did two hours aloft in the crow's nest and six off, except in severe weather when one hour aloft was as much as a man could stand. It was essential that he should not become tired or slack, as a sharp lookout was needed since the ships being watched for would alter course away at the first sign of smoke.

The daily routine was based on naval practice as far as possible, having regard to the varied composition of the crews, the service on which the ships were engaged, and the arduous nature of the patrol with everyone under strain. Thus while the mornings were spent in cleaning ship, drills, exercises and routine tasks, the men were not required again until 1600 when general quarters was held. This was followed by supper, after which the evening could be spent in recreation. As already stated, at least one of the vessel's former public rooms was set aside as a ship's company smoking room where the men could write letters, play games, and hold concerts on a stage rigged at one end. Most ships also contrived to rig up a miniature rifle range in one of the holds where keen competitions were held between officers and men, and between seamen, firemen, cooks and stewards and marines. So popular was this particular activity that the participants were even willing to pay for the ammunition out of their own pockets. Every possible effort was made to keep the men healthy and lighten the strain of thirty to forty days of dreary patrol.

As one man wrote of his service in the *Alsatian*, which was typical of all the others:

> Her crew was composed of Reserve and Volunteer Reserve men from many parts of the Empire, but mostly from Britain and Newfoundland. The greater number had never served in anything much bigger than a sailing ship or fishing vessel, so for a considerable time they were bewildered by the network of alleyways below decks which seemed to lead everywhere and nowhere. When a bugle call was sounded — and half the ship's company had never heard a bugle — they ran hither and thither, doubling on their tracks and generally ending in the wrong place. It wasn't long, however, before naval tuition, discipline and order took the place of chaos, and remained that way.

Usually there was plenty of excitement. Admiral Sir Reginald Tupper, who took over the Tenth Cruiser Squadron from Admiral de Chair in 1916 recorded:[1]

> As soon as any ship was sighted, course was altered towards at full speed to intercept. When close enough a flag signal — usually a large red pennant, of which previous notification had been sent to every maritime nation — was hoisted to stop her engines, and a blank charge or rocket fired to attract her attention. Rockets were used as often as possible as the real nature of the vessel intercepted was not known, and all guns were kept ready for immediate action. If the vessel did not obey, a shot was fired across her bows, and the action bells rung on board the armed merchant cruisers.
>
> Normally unless there were definite grounds for suspicion, only the watch on deck was closed up at night, which meant that about half the armament was manned. Every vessel intercepted had to be treated as an enemy until the boarding officer was satisfied that she was friendly or neutral. Although he had with him a book of instructions, he had to rely largely upon his own knowledge and experience. At times he also needed to be something of an acrobat, for there is nothing more difficult than trying to board a ship in a seaway from a small boat, especially when no one on board is prepared to lend a hand. All the ship's papers had to be carefully examined and checked as far as possible, and the crew and passengers inspected.
>
> When a ship was finally stopped, the armed merchant cruiser kept to windward of her, or ahead when there was no wind, in order to lower the boarding boat. In addition to the boarding officer, this carried two other officers armed with revolvers, and from six to eight armed sailors. Some ships' boats had an outboard engine, but most had to rely on oars and sail. While the boat was on its way the intercepting vessel was kept on the move, zigzagging to avoid submarine attack, until the boarding officer

[1] *Reminiscences*, Jarrolds 1929.

sent a prearranged signal which meant that the suspect was unarmed and could offer no resistance. This could generally be ascertained quite quickly, the first thing being to examine the lifeboats and hand steering gear to make sure that they were genuine. Sometimes a gun was discovered concealed beneath the woodwork of the hand steering gear.

The ship was then searched as thoroughly as possible, while the boarding officer inspected the crew to see if any enemy aliens were taking passage. The boarding officer usually separated the captain from his chief officer, examining papers with the former while one of the other British officers went round the ship with the latter. Meanwhile the armed guard would engage members of the crew in conversation to learn what they could.

We discovered all sorts of artful dodges on the part of the neutral ships carrying on trade with the enemy. Double bottoms, dummy decks and false bulkheads to conceal rifles and ammunition; hollow steel masts filled with rubber and copper; rubber made up to look like anything from onions to honeycombs; barrels of flour containing cotton for making munitions. Thus with all these tricks, manifests had to be carefully examined for falsification.

If the boarding officer considered anything to be suspect he reported to his captain, and the intercepted vessel was sent in to the nearest convenient port for a thorough search. In such a case a new armed guard was put on board, usually under one of the RNR officers who possessed a master's certificate, who was given orders where to take the ship and what to do if attacked by a U-boat. If this did happen the armed guard were to disguise themselves as members of the crew, or otherwise be taken prisoner.

Just such an event as this occured July 1915 when the large full-rigged American sailing ship *Pass of Balmaha*, which was voyaging to Archangel with a cargo of cotton, was stopped by the armed merchant cruiser *Victorian*. The latter put an armed guard on board to take her in either to Lerwick or Kirkwall according to how the wind served. While she was en route to her new destination *U-36* surfaced and came alongside to capture the ship. At the time the question whether armed guards were entitled to defend themselves was under consideration at the Admiralty. Pending a decision, the Commander-in-Chief, Grand Fleet had given instructions that an armed guard must not fight until the U-boat committed a hostile act.

The armed guard in the *Pass of Balmaha* therefore remained below out of sight, having changed into borrowed clothing. The U-boat captain put a petty officer on board with instructions to compel the vessel to sail to Cuxhaven. The British sailors made no attempt to recapture the ship because they had been told by the Americans that the vessel was actually being escorted by the U-boat, which was to be relieved by another off the Shetlands. Thus they did not discover the truth until the *Pass of Balmaha* arrived in Cuxhaven, and they shamefacedly had to give themselves up as prisoners. It is of interest that *U-36* was herself destroyed soon after intercepting the American vessel by one of the earliest British Q-ships.

We shall hear more about the *Pass of Balmaha*.

At the best of times the British armed guards had an unenviable job, for even friendly neutrals were annoyed at being held up and their voyages delayed. One British officer and at least two of his men had to remain on the bridge day and night to ensure that the ship kept to the course and speed ordered. The rest slept or passed the time as best they could, being constantly ready to assist their comrades. For food they had to cook what provisions they had brought with them, or subsist on iron rations, since they had no right to the ship's galley and were only allowed in there by courtesy of the master.

When a considerable number of merchantmen had to be sent in under armed guard, individual ships on patrol could become seriously short-handed. Recovery of their officers and men could only be effected by periodically detaching one ship of the squadron to go into Kirkwall especially to collect them. They were then transferred back to their own ships as these were met in the various patrol areas.

*

Although the work of converting the newly taken-up vessels was speeded up as much as possible, this inevitably took time. Even the *Alsatian*, in which Admiral de Chair hoisted his flag on 4th December 1914 had to be taken in hand for re-arming with 6-inch guns instead of the 4.7's originally mounted.

The Admiralty decided that the new squadron was to use Liverpool as a coaling and repair base, and a Base Office under a rear-admiral was set up in that port from which orders and communications could be distributed.

New patrol lines were allocated. Thus the squadron was to operate north and west of the Shetlands on base lines designated 'A', 'B', 'C' and 'D'. Line 'A' ran between Iceland and the Faeroes, the meridian of 5 degrees west longitude being its easternmost point. Line 'B' ran from north of the Shetlands along the meridian of 1 degree west longitude; Line 'C' south of the Faeroes with its easternmost point a line joining Sydero Island and Sule Skerry; and Line 'D' west of the Hebrides, the easternmost limit running slightly west of north from the island of St Kilda.

These base lines were constantly altered so that the actual position of the patrols did not become known to the enemy, and it was Jellicoe's intention to change the entire patrol areas after a time so as to minimise the chance of a successful raid on the armed merchant cruisers by enemy surface warships. It was intended that trawlers should patrol the Fair Isle passage, and cruiser squadrons of the Grand Fleet to work in conjunction with the new Tenth Cruiser Squadron. Traffic through the Pentland Firth would be dealt with chiefly by armed boarding steamers based on Scapa.

Originally eight of these vessels had been allocated by the Admiralty to work with the *Edgars*, thus obviating the necessity for the cruisers to stop and lower boats when intercepting merchantmen, which rendered them liable to submarine attack. They were small ships capable of speeds of up to 20 knots. But four proved unsuitable for the arduous weather conditions in northern waters and were transferred to the Downs patrol. The other four were sent to patrol east of the Pentland Firth as much to prevent enemy minelaying in an area frequently traversed by the Grand Fleet as to intercept neutral shipping.

At that time also the trawlers which had been allocated to Jellicoe were mostly concentrated around Scapa to protect the battlefleet from submarine attack, and the Grand Fleet cruiser squadrons were insufficiently strong to allow of regular blockade patrol.

In the interval between the departure of the *Edgars* and the arrival of the newly converted armed merchant cruisers the watch on the northern approaches had to be practically abandoned, except for occasional movements of the Grand Fleet. At the end of November 1914 only one armed merchant cruiser, the *Teutonic*, was on patrol cruising to the west of the Hebrides, being joined at the beginning of December by the *Otway*. Thus the northern entrance to the North Sea was virtually unguarded when the German collier *Rio Negro* passed on her way homewards with some highly important passengers on board. They were the survivors of the German cruiser *Karlsruhe* which, since the outbreak of war, had been raiding in the Atlantic and sunk more than 76,000 tons of British shipping.

One of the most modern German light cruisers, she had been lying up in an out-of-the-way anchorage in the Florida Strait when war broke out, and her first task had been to arrange for the con-

Admiral Sir John Jellicoe

Vessels of 10th Cruiser Squadron at anchor in Swarbacks Minn

version at sea of the liner *Kronprinz Wilhelm* into an auxiliary cruiser. Having narrowly escaped being caught by Admiral Cradock, whose squadron was later to be destroyed in the Battle of Coronel, she carried on her depredations until 4th November. Off the coast of Venezuela while on her way north to attack Barbados, she was suddenly rent in two by an internal explosion.

The fore part of the ship went down at once with her captain, but the after part floated long enough for the survivors to get aboard the two vessels which were in company. These were the captured British steamer *Indrani* and the *Rio Negro*. The senior surviving German officer, aware that British warships were hunting for the *Karlsruhe*, decided not to make for a neutral port, which would reveal the fact that she had been destroyed, but to try to reach home. The survivors were accordingly transferred to the *Rio Negro* and the *Indrani* was sunk. After a chilly passage round the north of Iceland the *Rio Negro* safely reached Aalesund, in Norway, and Kiel a few days later.

Thus not only were we deprived of the satisfaction of knowing that the *Karlsruhe* had been destroyed; the fruitless search for the enemy cruiser, which at times involved as many as twenty-six warships including a battleship, continued for several months afterwards.

A week or so after the *Rio Negro* incident two German merchantmen, the *Alma* and *Marie*, put into Thamshavn, near Trondheim, and began to load copper ore. This information was communicated by a secret agent to the Admiralty, who promptly telegraphed it to Jellicoe. Unfortunately the name of the port was read as Thorshavn, which is in the Faeroes. The *Teutonic*, at that time the only ship on the Northern Patrol, the *Otway* having had to return to Liverpool to coal, was accordingly despatched to watch that port. When the error came to light the Commander-in-Chief decided that it was too late to take action. But in fact the two German ships did not sail from Thamshavn until almost a week later.

As they left their fitting-out yards the armed merchant cruisers proceeded direct to their designated patrol lines. The *Alsatian* arrived on patrol on 26th December, the rest of the available ships of the squadron being disposed as follows: 'A' north of the Faeroes — *Teutonic, Cedric, Columbella, Mantua, Virginian.* 'C' south of Sydero — *Otway Oropesa, Hilary.* 'D' west of the Hebrides — *Hildebrand, Patuca, Calyx, Ambrose.* No ships were stationed on 'B' patrol line. Despite reports that large quantities of contraband were passing that way, few vessels had been intercepted north of the Faeroes. But because of the long winter darkness in those latitudes it was difficult to ascertain whether there was much traffic passing.

When the *Teutonic* became due for coaling, de Chair sent the *Cedric* to take over 'B' patrol line, and ordered the *Caribbean*, which was on her way up from the conversion yard, to join her. The *Clan McNaughton*, which arrived on the same day as the *Alsatian*, was allocated to 'D' patrol. Thus at the end of 1914 eleven armed merchant cruisers were actually on patrol; five were away coaling; two on their way to join the squadron; and four still being completed, their conversion having been delayed by labour troubles.

In those northern latitudes severe weather is almost continuous during the winter months, and the first Christmas of the war proved to be no exception. A south-westerly gale with driving snow and hail raged throughout 27th and 28th December, forcing many of the ships to ease down or lie to. Patrolling off the Hebrides, the *Clan McNaughton* rolled continuously 45 degrees each way and lost her wireless aerials, but did not leave her station. Two days later a second gale whipped up almost identical conditions. Merchantmen intercepted had to be escorted to a position under the lee of the nearest land before an armed guard could be put on board.

The question of a convenient base for the squadron had for some time been worrying the Admiralty and the Commander-in-Chief. In the early weeks of the war Admiral de Chair had used Swarbacks Minn, an inlet off St Magnus Bay in the Shetlands, as a 'flying base' for the *Edgars*. Jellicoe had asked the Admiralty for a submarine obstruction to be placed in position at the entrance to that haven, but no action had been taken.

In mid-November Admiralty Intelligence learned that the Germans were sending U-boats to carry out an operation round the Shetlands. Once again there were fears that the enemy was planning to seize the islands, which were poorly defended. There were only two 12-pounder guns in place on shore, and a local defence force of no more than 250 men to man 33 lookout posts and guard the temporary wireless station. A dozen armed trawlers patrolled the Voes to prevent their use by submarines. Accordingly Jellicoe ordered the base to be evacuated, and sent a division of destroyers to hunt for the U-boats.

In fact the purpose of the enemy operation was to search for the Grand Fleet. But the latter now sailed to carry out a sweep of the Heligoland Bight. Although three of the five enemy submarines involved in the operation tried to enter Scapa Flow, they were unsuccessful. One of them, *U-18*, was caught and rammed by a patrolling trawler in Hoxa Sound, which led to her subsequently being wrecked on the Pentland Skerries.

In December an Admiralty official was despatched to Swarbacks Minn to report on a method of defence for that harbour, but the Commander-in-Chief considered the place unsuitable for the armed merchant cruisers, and the project was not proceeded with. Loch Ewe however, which the Admiralty had intended should become a coaling base for the Grand Fleet, was to be provided with a boom instead. But since the latter would not be ready for some time, the Tenth Cruiser Squadron was ordered to use Liverpool. This was 600 miles from the Shetlands and involved a voyage of four days there and back, which meant that half the ships were generally away from patrol. In fact they frequently coaled at Busta Voe and Olna Firth, in the Shetlands, as well as Loch Ewe.

By early January 1915 all the newly taken-up vessels had joined the squadron except the *Motagua*, which was still fitting out at Avonmouth. Fourteen were on station, five coaling at Liverpool and two returning from that port to resume patrol when an incident occurred which resulted in the squadron's first casualty and highlighted some of the perils they had to face.

Orders had been received from the Admiralty that a special effort was to be made to intercept the Norwegian liner *Bergensfjord* homeward bound from America, which was suspected of carrying German reservists travelling on neutral passports. Although she was one of the vessels permitted to use the northabout route, it was known that her captain was averse to calling at Kirkwall if he could successfully evade our warships. It will be seen that in the opening months of the second world conflict the Norwegians were equally unco-operative.

Admiral de Chair therefore disposed his ships so as to spread the net as widely as possible to catch the *Bergensfjord*. In this he was helped by the Grand Fleet, which had put to sea in order to carry out exercises west of the Orkneys and Shetlands. Jellicoe detached two of his cruisers to patrol to the north-east of Sule Skerry, and four gunboats to cover the stretch of water between Cape Wrath and the Butt of Lewis. These dispositions were intended not only to intercept the *Bergensfjord* but also to catch the

Danish steamer *Mjolnar*, which had sailed from Kristiansund for a point west of Ireland with suspected ill-intent.

Early in the morning of 10th January faint wireless transmissions between the *Bergensfjord* and the port of Bergen were picked up by several of the ships on patrol. At that time there was no sophisticated wireless direction-finding apparatus available to pinpoint the position of a transmitting vessel, this being dependent on the strength of the signal. Nothing further was heard until twenty-four hours later when the *Viknor* reported that she had intercepted the Norwegian vessel some 90 miles north-west of the Shetlands, the latter having apparently passed undetected through de Chair's net.

Ordering the ships on 'B' and 'D' patrols to continue to watch out for the *Mjolnar*, de Chair in the *Alsatian*, with the *Patia* and *Teutonic* in company, headed at top speed for the point of interception of the *Bergensfjord*. On arrival he learnt that the *Viknor's* boarding officer had discovered a certain Baron von Wedel of the German secret service travelling in the Norwegian liner under a false name and with a neutral passport, also six stowaways. These, together with another suspect passenger, thought to be a German reservist, were transferred to the *Viknor*. Admiral de Chair ordered her to put an armed guard on board the liner, whose captain admitted that he had passed north of the Faeroes during the night in order to dodge our patrols, and escort her into Kirkwall.

This was done despite the liner captain's protests that he was carrying international mails and could not be sent into harbour. The *Viknor* escorted her as far as the Fair Isle Channel where she was turned over to a British destroyer to take her on to Kirkwall. The armed merchant cruiser then headed for Liverpool where she was due to coal, to land her prisoners. But that was the last anyone saw of her.

At 1600 on 13th January she reported her position, course and speed by wireless, which placed her somewhere north of Tory Island on the usual route for vessels proceeding to Liverpool. Nothing more was known of her until five days later when the Admiral Commanding, Queenstown reported that bodies and wreckage had been washed up at Portrush, which meant that she had gone down with all hands.

Her loss was attributed either to foundering or, more probably, striking a mine from the field which had been laid by the *Berlin*. A large number of mines had broken adrift due to heavy weather, and they lacked any safety device. Although the *Otway* took the same route next day and arrived safely at Liverpool, the Admiralty issued an order that all warships passing north of Ireland in daylight were to use a route which kept them well clear of the Irish coast. A fortnight later the *Mjolnar* was duly intercepted by the Shetlands patrol and taken in to Lerwick.

The next tragedy was not long in coming.

Towards the end of January a second U-boat sortie into the Northern Patrol area was expected, and the patrol lines were altered. Ships were ordered to steam twenty miles apart at 13 knots and to zigzag. Despite the addition to the existing conditions of bad light and foul weather of this fresh cause for worry, the squadron managed to intercept 122 merchantmen during the period from 24th December to 24th January, and in no case did they fail to send in any vessel specially designated by the Admiralty to be stopped.

Now came a threat to their base at Liverpool. Six ships of the squadron, including the *Alsatian*, had just completed coaling at that port when reports were received that three merchant vessels had been sunk by a U-boat off Liverpool Bar. For some days previously there had been reports of U-boat sightings in the Irish Sea which led the Admiralty to conclude that several submarines were operating in the area.

In fact there was only one, *U-21* commanded by Kapitänleutnant Hersing. Coolly surfacing off the North-West lightship, less than twenty miles from the shore, Hersing sank his three victims by placing explosive charges on board. When news of the sinkings reached the Admiralty, the armed merchant cruisers were ordered not to sail until the full moon had waned. Meanwhile other ships of the squadron due to refuel were to be sent to Loch Ewe and the Clyde, the latter becoming their temporary coaling base. When after a week the *Alsatian* and her consorts were able to leave Liverpool they had to dodge, not U-boats, but floating mines during their passage through the Hebrides.

Then, on 2nd February, the worst gale of the winter hit the north-west. HMS *Clan McNaughton*, which was then on patrol to the west of St Kilda, failed to reply to signals. Three of the squadron, the *Hildebrand, Patuca* and *Digby*, searched the area for a week, but except for some anonymous wreckage, found no trace of the missing vessel. The inference was that she had either been overwhelmed by a freak wave during the gale, or had fallen victim to drifting mines.

Her loss added weight to Admiral de Chair's report to the

Admiralty a few weeks later that some of the vessels taken up in the previous November, mostly older and slower ships, had proved to be unsuitable for various reasons. The vessels subsequently taken up to relieve them were all much bigger.

CHAPTER FOUR

Un-neutral Neutrals and the U-Boat Menace

Ever since the *Bergensfjord* incident it had become increasingly evident that the Scandinavian shipping lines which had been accorded permission for certain of their vessels trading to America to use the northabout route were not keeping to the agreement to call at Kirkwall. Admiral de Chair complained that on 11th February a steamer belonging to the Danish United Shipping Company had had to be chased and caught. When finally stopped her master said that he was unaware of the necessity for calling in when he was westbound.

Two days later another ship belonging to the same company tried to evade the British patrols by passing north of the Faeroes. Next day a third Danish vessel could only be stopped after a four-hour pursuit, and it was evident that her master had no intention of calling at Kirkwall. All three were sent in to that port in charge of armed guards. Many more ships than had been authorised were now using the northabout route, and few — if any — were likely to call at Kirkwall unless sent in with an armed guard.

Earlier, on 4th February, had come the enemy's delayed response to our closure of the North Sea in the previous November. The German Admiralty announced that the waters around Great Britain and Ireland, including the English Channel, were now considered a military area, and that from 18th February every hostile merchant ship found in these waters would be destroyed. Neutrals were warned not to enter the area, but to pass north of the Shetlands and cross over to within thirty miles of the Dutch coast where they would not be endangered.

Since we had ourselves announced that passage north of the Shetlands was dangerous, neutral nations had no choice but to disregard one or other of the belligerents. It was obvious, therefore, that the work of the Northern Patrol would greatly increase.

In consequence the patrol lines were rearranged. 'A' was now to operate north of the Faeroes from a base line established at 5 degrees 30 minutes west longitude; 'B' north of the Shetlands from 1 degree west longitude; 'C' south of the Faeroes from a base line drawn through Sydero Island to Sule Skerry; and 'D' west of the Hebrides from a point slightly north-west of St Kilda. Spaced twenty miles apart, the ships were to maintain a mean course at right angles to the base line, steering west during the day, and turning 16 points at nightfall.

The southernmost ship of patrol line 'A' was to be twenty miles north of the Faeroes; that of 'B' patrol 15 miles north of Muckle Flugga; 'C' 45 miles from Sule Skerry; and 'D' 15 miles from St Kilda. The only area remaining unwatched was the little-used Denmark Strait, north-west of Iceland. To obviate the necessity of detaching an armed merchant cruiser from her patrol line periodically to go into Kirkwall and collect the accumulation of armed guards, these officers and men were returned to their ships from time to time by one of the armed boarding vessels from Scapa.

But these patrol lines were still liable to be shifted, either in consequence of intelligence reports warning of a projected U-boat attack on the armed merchant cruisers; the presence of drifting mines — there was even one scare when some thirty-odd German trawlers said to be laden with mines were reported heading for the Northern Patrol area — or to intercept some particular vessel which was trying to evade the Patrol. In fact, every time a merchantman was stopped the patrol lines were thrown out of routine.

Then a new complication arose, to reveal the wiliness of our principal opponent and bedevil still further our already sensitive relations with certain neutral countries. Two German oil tankers, the *Kiowa* and *Prometheus*, formerly owned by the Deutsche-Amerikanische Petroleum Gesellschaft of Hamburg, changed their names to *Pioneer* and *Cushing* and their port of registry to New York. Laden with petrol, they then sailed under American colours bound for Denmark and Sweden.

Both were duly intercepted and sent in by the Northern Patrol. But although the change of names and registry had taken place after the outbreak of war, the transfer of flag was recognised by the British Government on the grounds that the former German owners were a subsidiary of the Standard Oil Company of New York, and both vessels were released.

Another case which hit the headlines was that of the Hamburg-Amerika steamship *Dacia*, whose transfer to American ownership had not been recognised by Britain. In order to 'test the water' she was sailed from Norfolk, Virginia, for Rotterdam on 11th February 1915 with a cargo of cotton. It was suspected that the ship would try to evade our patrols, and special dispositions were made to intercept and bring her in. But the *Dacia* made no secret of her movements, and was duly arrested by French patrols as she entered the English Channel and condemned by the French Prize Court.

During the special lookout which was being kept for her by the Northern Patrol an incident occurred which exemplifies the work of the ships of the Tenth Cruiser Squadron at this time.

In the early hours of 27th February the masthead lookout in the *Patuca* on 'D' Patrol sighted a vessel steering westward. The *Patuca* immediately gave chase and, on being spotted by the mystery ship, the latter promptly reversed course. She was overhauled and stopped, but the weather, which was very bad, was too rough for boarding. The ship was identified as the American *Navahoe*, originally German-owned, bound from Bremen to Norfolk, Virginia.

Commander France-Hayhurst, captain of the *Patuca*, ordered her to follow him into the lee of the land, but the *Navahoe's* master signalled that his condenser had broken down and would take three hours to repair. Accordingly the *Patuca* remained close by, and at the end of that time the American signalled that the repairs had been effected, but added: 'No contraband — refuse to follow you.'

France-Hayhurst was not to be put off by Yankee intransigence, however, and continued to circle at slow speed round the *Navahoe* until her master finally gave in and was escorted to St Kilda. Even there the weather was so violent that the *Patuca's* boarding boat was swamped while alongside the *Navahoe* and had to be cut adrift — fortunately after its occupants had boarded the merchantman.

However the gale was too strong to allow of the ship's hatches being opened for examination, and now the *Navahoe's* master complained that he was running short of water. France-Hayhurst informed Admiral de Chair by wireless of the situation, and was ordered to take the *Navahoe* to Stornoway for thorough examination. This was done, but nothing suspicious was found, and the American ship was released. During the entire episode the *Patuca* had either remained stopped or was zigzagging at slow speed and was thus wide open to attack by U-boat. Less than a fortnight later one of her consorts, the *Bayano*, was not so fortunate.

After coaling at the Clyde base, the *Bayano* left harbour after dark on 11th March and steamed down the Firth on her way back to patrol. Unknown to our intelligence, however, *U-27* commanded by Kapitänleutnant Wegener, who could claim among earlier victims the British submarine *E-3* of the Harwich Striking Force, and the seaplane carrier *Hermes*, had left Germany on 25th February with orders to proceed northabout and operate on the west coast of Scotland and in the Irish Sea north of the Isle of Man. She was the first U-boat to attempt the northabout passage since the announcement of the German blockade.

As part of our preparations to meet this threat, more than twenty areas around the British Isles were being hastily provided with anti-submarine indicator nets, watched over by special trawler patrols. One of these netted zones, designated the 'Larne area', covered the North Channel from the Mull of Galloway to Malin Head, and from thence as far up as 56 degrees 40 minutes north latitude. In order not to enter this area until daylight the *Bayano* reduced speed to about 8 knots.

Soon after five o'clock in the morning when she was off Corse-well Point, north of Stranraer, she loomed up in the periscope sights of *U-27*. Wegener promptly torpedoed her, and she sank so suddenly that there was no time to lower the boats — only to cut the falls in the hope that they would float clear. But in fact fewer than fifty of her company survived, being picked up by a passing steamer who transferred them to one of the Auxiliary Patrol vessels. Because there were so few the usual court of inquiry was waived.

Wegener might well have added to his bag, for after torpedoing the *Bayano* he went on to lie in wait in the Oversay Channel, between Rathlin Head, in Ireland, and the island of Islay, and there attacked the armed merchant cruiser *Ambrose* of the Tenth Cruiser Squadron which was on her way back from patrol to Liverpool.

But Commander Bruton's crew was very much on the alert. The first two torpedoes fired by *U-27* were successfully dodged, although the maximum speed of the *Ambrose* was only 14 knots. When Wegener made his third attack he brought his submarine so close to the surface that the armed merchant cruiser was able to drench her in a storm of gunfire, one of her 6-inch shells appearing to hit the U-boat's conning tower. Unfortunately there was no kill on this occasion. Only a short time before this, two other ships of the squadron, the *Caribbean* and *Columbella*, steaming north-wards from the Clyde, had passed through the Oversay Channel and seen nothing.

As soon as the presence of a U-boat in the North Channel was reported, orders were given that four other ships of the Tenth Cruiser Squadron which were in the Clyde, the *Changuinola*,

Hildebrand, Digby and *Patia*, were to remain in port until the danger was thought to be over. Even then when the *Digby* was on her way northwards she was chased by a U-boat — probably Wegener's — south of Skerryvore and had to take refuge in Tobermory until the destroyers which had been sent by the Commander-in-Chief, Grand Fleet to scour the Larne area arrived to escort her out of the danger zone. At Jellicoe's suggestion the route to be followed by ships of the Tenth Cruiser Squadron rejoining their patrol was altered to pass south of Rathlin Island where minesweepers were regularly operating.

The Tenth Cruiser Squadron had now lost three ships, and two others which were regarded as unsuitable were ordered to be paid off. This left only 18 vessels to maintain the Northern Patrol. Not only that, the increasing number of merchantmen sent in with armed guards had heavily depleted their ships' companies. Admiral de Chair now asked for an increase in ratings of all categories for this most unpopular duty, and more ships to bring the squadron up to the original 24. These demands were made all the more necessary because of the passing of a new Order-in-Council dated 11th March, 1915.

Aimed at bringing about the complete isolation of Germany through naval blockade, the Order directed that no ship would be allowed to proceed to any German port; that vessels sailing from German ports would have to hand over to the Allies all goods embarked in those ports; and that goods either belonging to the enemy, or destined for an enemy port, would have to be discharged in a British or Allied port. Any vessel which called at an enemy port after being allowed to proceed ostensibly for a neutral destination would be liable to condemnation if captured on a subsequent voyage.

The effectiveness of the new order depended on the alertness and efficiency of our blockading ships, and obviously increased their work enormously. Every intercepted ship now had to be searched. Most of them were sent in to an examination port in charge of an armed guard, where Customs officials scrutinised their papers and analysed their cargoes, sometimes using X-rays for this purpose. The information thus obtained was passed to London for action to be decided by one or other of two committees.

Intercepted eastbound ships were dealt with by the Contraband Committee. Composed of representatives of the Foreign Office, Admiralty, Board of Trade and the Treasury Solicitor's Department, this committee decided whether a vessel should be released or not, and whether the whole or part of her cargo should be put in the Prize Court. A second body, set up as a result of the Order of 11th March and known as the Enemy Exports Committee, dealt with westbound ships sent in for examination. Both committees were aided in their work by the War Trade Intelligence Department, a specialist organisation which collected and sifted every scrap of information about the enemy's trade activities and collated it on a comprehensive card index. By this means information could be supplied about every firm likely to be mentioned in ships' papers.

That the Order was proving effective was shown by the fact that by July 1915 practically no neutral shipping line would knowingly accept German cargoes. Even so, certain vessels carrying meat, grain, wool, etc., sent in for examination were often released for fear of offending neutral opinion, much to the disgust of Admiral Jellicoe who, along with other senior naval officers, continued to be bitterly critical of the pusillanimity of the Government's blockade policy.

As the spring of 1915 merged into early summer, bringing shorter nights and opening up the passage round the north of Iceland, the patrol lines of the Tenth Cruiser Squadron were rearranged by the Commander-in-Chief. 'A' Patrol was now to operate from a base line extending due north from a position in latitude 62 degrees 55 minutes north, longitude 5 degrees west — that is, from the northern tip of the Faeroes to the latitude of Seydisfjord, in Iceland. Spaced at intervals of 25 miles, they were to cross this line at 0800 daily and steer roughly south-west. Six ships were to comprise the patrol, but only five were available.

'C' Patrol south of the Faeroes was extended to include the North Minch and the Butt of Lewis. Seven ships comprised this patrol spaced at 25-mile intervals. 'B' and 'D' Patrols were withdrawn and three new patrol lines instituted. These were 'E' north of Iceland, to consist of six ships when available; 'F' south of Iceland, of four ships when available; and 'G' off the Norwegian coast on the meridian of 3 degrees east between latitudes 62 and 63½ degrees north, in the neighbourhood of Stadlandet. Three ships when available were to operate this patrol with the addition of a cruiser from the Grand Fleet.

This rearrangement needed more ships than Admiral de Chair could muster, but six additional and larger vessels had been requisitioned by the Admiralty and were in the process of conversion. As stated earlier, they were the Royal Mail Line's *Alcantara*, *Andes* and *Arlanza*; the Pacific Steam Navigation Company's *Ebro* and *Orcoma*; and the P & O's *India*.

The persistently un-neutral behaviour of the Norwegian liner *Bergensfjord* has already been mentioned. It now came to the notice of Admiral Jellicoe that although this ship on an inward bound trip from New York had been boarded on 29th March by the *Otway* and sent in to Kirkwall with an armed guard, a German reserve officer and sixteen other Germans of military age travelling under false (Norwegian) passports had nevertheless safely managed to reach Christiana (Oslo). Oddly enough, although Kirkwall was most frequently used by the Tenth Cruiser Squadron for the reception of intercepted ships, there were only three examination officers stationed at that port. Admiral de Chair had been under the impression that they examined not only cargoes but also passengers. The *Bergensfjord* had been sent in twice previously, each time having tried to evade our patrols. In June she was again intercepted and this time found to have ten Germans, including naval officers and women, among her passengers. Most of her cargo was also suspect.

She was not the only neutral vessel to run enemy nationals back to the Fatherland. Soon after the latest *Bergensfjord* incident an American ship, which had also been intercepted earlier in the year and sent in to Kirkwall, was released although she was full of contraband cargo. On her arrival in Bremen fourteen Germans who had been travelling as passengers stepped jubilantly ashore, while the vessel's chief engineer, who happened to be British, was arrested and interned. It was no wonder that Jellicoe waxed indignant over our blockade policy, largely imposed by the Foreign Office, which went to such lengths to avoid offending neutral susceptibilities.

*

Despite earlier suggestions by Admiral de Chair regarding the suitability of Swarbacks Minn, in the Shetlands, a permanent coaling base for his squadron had still to be decided. While on 'C' Patrol in his flagship the *Alsatian* the admiral looked in at West Loch Roag, in the island of Lewis, to assess its possibilities. His visit convinced him that Swarbacks Minn with its neighbouring, almost landlocked, inlets of Busta Voe and Olna Firth, was greatly superior. The place was easier to enter, there was a greater depth of water and it was far more secure. There was plenty of room for as many as seven of his armed merchant cruisers to lie at single anchor, and good supplies of fresh drinking water and boiler feed water were available.

Only four days would be needed for coaling, etc., as against the ten necessary for a visit to the Clyde or Liverpool. It was also a much more central position from which the squadron could operate.

A senior naval officer in charge was eventually appointed to Swarbacks Minn in the person of Rear-Admiral Fawckner, and the old cruiser *Gibraltar*, one of the original Tenth Cruiser Squadron's ships, moved up to become a depot and repair ship, together with a coal hulk and four colliers, the latter always to be available since the squadron consumed some 1,600 tons of coal daily. An anti-submarine boom was placed in position at the entrance commanded by the guns of the *Gibraltar*, with Auxiliary Patrol vessels and minesweeping trawlers to keep the channel open in case of enemy minelaying. It was a wise move since the waters around the Hebrides were soon to become infested with U-boats, necessitating 'C' Patrol being moved some miles westward.

In order to check the activities of German submarines in the English Channel a net and mine barrage had been placed in position across the Dover Strait early in 1915. In April *U-32*, on her way to the Western Approaches to attack troop transports, became entangled in a section of the net, which she dragged along for several hours pursued by British destroyers. Having finally managed to free his vessel, her captain, badly shaken by the experience, elected to return to base northabout round the Orkneys. In consequence of this and of the mysterious loss of another U-boat, the German Admiralty ordered all High Sea Fleet submarines to use the northern route, bringing an unwelcome increase in U-boat traffic in that part of the world. Instances now began to occur of enemy submarines stopping neutral vessels which were being sent in under British armed guard.

Jellicoe had issued revised rules for the guidance of officers in charge of armed guards. These directed (a) that the neutral ship should first try to escape; (b) it should not attack unless actually attacked; and (c) the armed guard must not fight on deck unless the U-boat had committed a hostile act, when they could fight to the last. But these rules had been referred for confirmation to the Admiralty, and were still being discussed with the Foreign Office and the Law Officers of the Crown. Information was then received that the German Naval Attaché in Stockholm had announced that the Germans considered they had the right to torpedo any neutral ship which had an armed guard on board. Jellicoe was furious, and wanted the guards to be issued with lance bombs so that they could attack any U-boat coming alongside without waiting for her to take action.

Meanwhile some German submarine captains adopted their own ruthless method of dealing with the presence of British armed guards on board neutral ships stopped by them. For example, *U-36*, Kapitänleutnant Ernst Graeff, operating in the Shetlands-Faeroes-Hebrides area, surfaced and stopped the Norwegian steamer *Fimreite*. The latter already had an armed guard placed on board by a vessel of the Tenth Cruiser Squadron to compel her to call at Kirkwall.

When Graeff learnt of this from her master, whom he summoned to the submarine for interrogation, he shouted, 'Don't let them go into the boats — let them sink!' But the guard had already removed their uniforms and were in the boats along with the rest of the crew. Thus when Graeff sank her there was no one on board the *Fimreite*. Soon afterwards *U-36* was herself destroyed by one of our Q-ships, Graeff and fourteen members of his crew being saved.

Thus the position of British armed guards on board neutral vessels sent in for examination became even more unenviable. If they did not fight — as in the case of the *Pass of Balmaha* — they could become prisoners of war. If they did, it was necessary for them to initiate action in order to gain any advantage, and they thus committed an act of war under a neutral flag. It was eventually ruled that an armed guard had the same right of resistance as a prize crew, and Jellicoe issued instructions that if a U-boat ordered a neutral to abandon ship, the armed guard was justified in taking steps in their own defence.

Although 'G' Patrol of the Tenth Cruiser Squadron extended as far as the Norwegian coast, it was known that German ships were using the Inner Leads to voyage to and from ports in northern Norway. In June 1915 the *Teutonic* on patrol sighted the German merchantman *Konsul Schultze* between Stadlandet and Trondheim. She at once gave chase, but the enemy vessel escaped into Trondheim. Reporting the incident to Jellicoe, Admiral de Chair added that he considered if a British submarine had been available she could have sunk the *Konsul Schultze*. The Commander-in-Chief agreed and arranged with the Admiralty for a submarine to cruise in the vicinity of Stadlandet for seven days. An E-class boat was sent, but she ran into bad weather, developed machinery defects and saw nothing.

The armed trawler *Tenby Castle* commanded by Temporary Lieutenant John Randell, RNR was now sent to the area. Soon after arriving on patrol he sighted the German steamer *Pallas* just outside Norwegian territorial waters. When he challenged her she refused to stop until he put a shot across her bows. Even then the German continued stealthily to edge towards the shore. Randell put two of his men on board as armed guard, but they were unable to prevent the German captain from gradually closing the coast. Then the *Victorian* arrived, having been apprised of the situation by Randell by wireless. She went after the *Pallas*, which by then had reached territorial waters and a Norwegian patrol boat had come up. When the latter demanded the German ship's release, the *Victorian*'s captain had no option but to comply.

A week later Randell intercepted the German steamer *Friedrich Asp* and ordered her to steer to the south-west. Her captain ignored the order and made for the shore. Randell fired a shot into her stern and ordered her to steer as directed, warning that otherwise she would be sunk. Again her captain refused, and Randell accordingly sank her, rescuing her crew and pilot. She had been on her way from Narvik to Stettin with a valuable cargo of iron ore. The day before, Randell had intercepted a Swedish ship carrying 7,000 tons of ore for Germany, and handed her over to the Tenth Cruiser Squadron. These incidents struck a severe blow at the trade and led to strong protests from Norway, who claimed a 4-mile limit to her territorial waters.

Randell's success led to the institution of a regular trawler patrol of that area, backed up by vessels of the Tenth Cruiser Squadron, at least one of which was ordered to be within 100 miles. But the Germans soon got wind of our plans to interfere with their iron ore traffic, and when an enemy agent reported that a British armed merchant cruiser was operating in the Vestfjord, a U-boat was sent up to deal with her. *U-22* commanded by Kapitänleutnant Hoppé duly arrived and torpedoed the *India*, the latter sinking in five minutes with considerable loss of life. Because of the continuing U-boat threat her survivors had to be interned in Norway.

At the Admiralty it was thought that the submarine which sank the *India* had been sent down from a base in the White Sea. Earlier a report had been received from Russia that the Germans intended to use Bear Island as a base for submarines working on the route to Archangel. Accordingly Jellicoe was asked to send an expedition to reconnoitre the supposed base. Designated Operation 'M', the expedition consisted of the armed merchant cruiser *Columbella* (Captain Arthur Bromley, RN) of the Tenth Cruiser Squadron, a sloop and two armed trawlers. But nothing was found, Captain Bromley considering Spitzbergen an impossible base, and was doubtful if any German submarine had ever been in the White Sea. In fact no U-boat had at that time rounded the North Cape.

However, the ships of the Tenth Cruiser Squadron were not always the hunted. In mid-June the *Motagua*, patrolling off the Flannan Islands, sighted a sinking steamer with a U-boat lying surfaced nearby. The latter was *U-33* which had been cruising west of the Hebrides where the squadron was known by the Germans to be operating.

The U-boat had already sunk the Russian steamer *Dama*, and was firing on the Norwegian *Davanger* when the *Motagua* appeared. Captain Webster, the latter's commander, did not hesitate. His well-drilled guns's crews opened fire and shells soon began to fall perilously close to the submarine. Earlier in the year the latter, too, had run foul of the Dover net barrage, and it was her captain's report that had added weight to the decision of the German Admiralty to prohibit High Sea Fleet submarines from using the Straits. Now she not only found herself under attack by an armed merchant cruiser, but British patrol boats attracted by the sound of gunfire were racing to the scene. Hurriedly she submerged.

Next day, however, she surfaced again north of the Butt of Lewis with the intention of stopping a Danish steamer. But again she was nearly caught out. The armed merchant cruiser *Orotava* hove in sight, and as soon as the latter's lookout spotted the U-boat her guns' crews went into action. Once more the submarine was forced to seek safety in the ocean depths. Soon afterwards she was ordered to the Mediterranean.

In August a new worry arose. Information reached the Admiralty that Iceland was becoming a source of supply to the Germans. Since 1814 Iceland had come under the rule of Denmark, and that country was neutral. Accordingly the armed merchant cruiser *Digby* was ordered to pay a visit to Reykjavik. There she discovered a number of merchant ships whose masters and crews were boasting of their success in evading our blockade. They had brought cargoes intended for Germany via Denmark. In fact a new shipping line had been formed to handle this traffic. Soon after the *Digby*'s visit the *Orcoma* intercepted a vessel belonging to the new line and sent her in under armed guard. In addition to her cargo of wood, oil and fish, she was carrying twenty-five passengers.

Pressure was then put on the Icelandic authorities by the Foreign Office to instruct all vessels to call at a United Kingdom port for examination, yet de Chair was told that he need not as a rule send in ships belonging to the three companies which owned the new line trading between Iceland and Denmark. Nevertheless there was still need to do this, for one of their vessels subsequently intercepted was found to be carrying a German among her fifteen passengers.

At that time much of Iceland's exports of herrings were carried in small sailing vessels, and these were frequently sent in under armed guard, thus adding to the latter's tribulations. For not only did they have to contend with almost continuous bad weather, they had to help man the pumps and trim the sails, and were thus more or less wet through the whole time. Food frequently ran out and they were forced to exist on salt herrings from the cargo.

Another hazard of those radar-less days was the risk of collision in the frequent dense fogs which came down to shroud the patrol areas, particularly as the armed merchant cruisers were completely darkened at night. Early in September the *Patia* collided off the west coast of Scotland with the *Oropesa*. While the latter got off comparatively lightly, the *Patia*'s bows were so badly damaged that she could only steam safely stern first.

She was ordered into the Clyde, as also was the *Oropesa* which was found to be leaking. The *Ebro* was sent out to escort the *Patia*, but the latter was able to steam so slowly that the Commander-in-Chief ordered out tugs to take the crippled vessel into Loch Long for emergency repairs. Then a U-boat appeared which the *Ebro* tried to ram, but the submarine escaped by crash diving.

By now Captain Vivian in the *Patia* had succeeded in shoring up his damaged bows sufficiently to be able to turn the ship round and head cautiously for the Clyde. Speed was gradually increased until she was making 13 knots. Then, around midnight, a U-boat — presumably the earlier one which had been shadowing the little flotilla — fired a torpedo at the *Patia*. Fortunately it missed, and she eventually arrived safely in port.

The area in which these events took place had become particularly hazardous for the vessels of the Tenth Cruiser Squadron, but now the Kaiser himself unwittingly came to their aid. Impressed by the strongly worded protests of the United States over the sinking of the liners *Lusitania* and *Arabic* with the loss of American lives, he forbade further U-boat activities on the west coast of Britain and in the Channel. Admiral von Tirpitz, Secretary of State for the Navy, demurred, as also did Admiral Bachmann the naval chief of staff, but both were severely snubbed for their pains.

German submarines, ordered the All-Highest, were not to sink passenger vessels in the prohibited zone, even of enemy nationality, without first warning them and making arrangements to save the passengers. The order in fact brought to a standstill the destruction of British merchant ships. Thus the Liverpool and Clyde bases were safe — for the time being at least.

With the approach of winter, which always brought increased hours of darkness, changes were again made in the patrols, and ships were ordered to steam in line abreast instead of line ahead. The centre line of 'A' Patrol was now to be 315 degrees from a position at latitude 62 degrees 30 minutes north, 5 degrees east, the ships keeping 40 miles apart, crossing the centre line at noon daily and steering to make good 280 degrees, or slightly north of due west. They were to turn in time to cross the line at midnight, steering a reciprocal course of 100 degrees until it was time to turn again.

The centre line of 'C' Patrol, north of St Kilda, was to be the meridian of 11 degrees west, the southernmost point being latitude 58 degrees 6 minutes north. The ships were to maintain position 25 miles apart, crossing the centre line at 1100 steering to make good 280 degrees, and turning in time to cross it again at 0100, steering 100 degrees. The southernmost vessels were not to approach within 40 miles of St Kilda or the Flannan Islands. 'F' Patrol was to operate to the east of Iceland, keeping outside the 100-fathom line in thick weather.

'A' Patrol comprised the *Motagua, Ebro, Oropesa* and *Alsatian*; 'C' Patrol the *Otway, Victorian, Hildebrand, Hilary, Almanzora* and *Teutonic*; and 'F' Patrol the *Andes*. 'G' Patrol off the Norwegian coast consisted of the *Alcantara* and *Orcoma*, with an armed trawler. Eleven ships were therefore covering a 430-mile stretch of ocean between the northernmost tip of Scotland and the southernmost point of Iceland. But there were no patrols north of that island to watch the exit from the Denmark Strait.

Of the remainder of the armed merchant cruisers, the *Changuinola* and *Columbella* were coaling at Swarbacks Minn, and the *Cedric* was on her way there for the same purpose. The *Virginian* was coaling at Liverpool, and the *Mantua, Patuca, Digby* and *Patia* either coaling or under repair in the Clyde. The *Arlanza* had taken a British military mission to Archangel, but on her return voyage she struck a mine and had been towed into the Kola inlet to await repairs. The *Orotava* was on her way to the White Sea to contact her.

Now a change was to be made in the composition of the squadron. In order to impress on the United States and other neutral nations that our policy regarding trade was shared by other Allied Powers, the French were asked to take part in our blockade operations. At first they proposed to send only an auxiliary cruiser, but she was too small and unsuitable for the work. Accordingly we handed over the *Digby*, which was duly commissioned at Brest with a French crew and renamed *Artois*. When the French asked for a second ship of the same type, the *Oropesa* was transferred. She, too, was commissioned under the Tricolour and renamed *Champagne*. She did not, however, immediately return to the squadron, but was employed for a time in making regular trips between France and Archangel.

CHAPTER FIVE

Raiders Break Out

At the end of 1915 Admiral de Chair's report on the year's work of the squadron revealed that his ships had patrolled an area some 200,000 square miles in extent in all weathers and in circumstances rendered especially difficult by the presence of enemy submarines. 3,098 merchantmen had been intercepted and carefully examined. 743 found to be carrying contraband or other suspicious cargoes had been sent into port for further examination. Of an aggregate of 3,900 ships passing through the patrol area, only eight whose interception was considered important had managed to slip through the net.

Two ships of the squadron had been sunk by U-boats; one had foundered in heavy weather; one had been mined and was awaiting repair; and one lost with all hands from an unknown cause. Casualties amounted to 863 officers and men out of an estimated total of 9,000.

During the year the *Alsatian* had spent 262 days at sea, had steamed a distance of 71,000 miles and consumed nearly 41,000 tons of coal, these figures being considered typical of the whole squadron. Of British armed guards, one had been taken prisoner; one carried to Norway where the ship had been retained but the guard allowed to return to this country; and two had had their prizes sunk under them by U-boats. In conclusion the admiral drew attention to 'the cheerful willingness of these young officers and men who take this constant risk without the satisfaction of being allowed to strike a blow in defence of their own safety'. One point not stressed in his report was that before his armed merchant cruisers left harbour after coaling or refit, they always had to be thoroughly searched for 'infernal machines' among the coal and stores, this form of sabotage having been tried on more than one occasion.

Now the Admiralty issued new orders for armed guards. It was considered that any attempt by them to attack an enemy submarine was unlikely to be effective, and was thought to be inadvisable for political reasons. Jellicoe was accordingly requested to issue orders that resistance should not be offered by armed guards to submarines or other enemy vessels. Not surprisingly, this decision was not too popular with the 'Muckle Flugga Hussars'.

The year 1916 began with a succession of gales which caused considerable damage to the base at Swarbacks Minn, wreaked havoc elsewhere, and hampered patrolling and minesweeping. Sailing vessels sent in for examination were blown so far off course that they frequently ended up in Norway, although subsequently permitted to return to British ports together with their armed guards. The French crew of the newly joined *Artois* underwent a brusque induction to the squadron when they had to struggle for four days to tow to safety a dismasted Danish vessel they had stopped for examination.

Thus far the weather had formed one of the three principal hazards to which the squadron was exposed, the others being mines and U-boats. Now a fourth made its appearance.

In August 1915 an armed boarding vessel working with the Grand Fleet was surprised and sunk by a German decoy ship which was also laying mines. Jellicoe thereupon warned the squadron to exercise the greatest care when closing vessels for boarding or examination, emphasising that their armament should be kept ready for instant action. In the following February the squadron had its first taste of the new threat.

On the 28th of that month Jellicoe was informed by the Admiralty that a German merchant auxiliary with a submarine escort had been sighted off the Skaw heading westward. Accordingly he ordered out a number of light cruisers and destroyers to patrol likely lines of approach by the enemy vessels. The *Columbella*, about to quit 'G' Patrol to coal at Swarbacks Minn, and the *Patia* en route to relieve her, were ordered to remain and patrol farther north. Two other vessels of the squadron in the neighbourhood, the *Andes* (Captain G.B. Young RN) and the *Alcantara* (Captain T.E. Wardle RN), the latter being due to leave for Liverpool, were also ordered by de Chair not to leave the area.

These two ships had been due to rendezvous with each other at a position north-east of the Shetlands in the evening of the 29th to transfer secret papers. Wardle was approaching this position in the morning of that day when he received de Chair's instruction not to depart until further orders, the message adding, 'Armed disguised merchant auxiliary from the south may pass patrol line today.' The *Andes* also received this signal.

Wardle immediately went to action stations, and soon afterwards sighted smoke away to port. From the *Andes*, to the north of him but not yet visible, he received the signal, 'Enemy in sight steering north-east 15 knots,' followed by another message stating that the enemy ship had two funnels. A third signal from Young reported: 'Vessel steering north when sighted, then altered to north-east. Painted black, black funnel, two masts. Speed about 15 knots.'

Increasing to full speed, Wardle turned north-west, a course which took him between the *Andes* and the smoke of the stranger. By this time the latter was fully in sight and seen to be a one-funnelled vessel flying the Norwegian flag with the same national colours painted on her sides and the name *Rena* on her counter. Shortly afterwards the *Andes* was sighted apparently steaming at full speed in a north-easterly direction. Wardle decided that before going to help his consort he should investigate the *Rena*, which had already been stopped and had hoisted an unidentifiable signal.

As his boarding boat was being lowered he asked the *Andes* by visual signal, 'Is the enemy still in sight? This ship is the *Rena*, armed guard being put on board.'

To his surprise Captain Young replied, 'This is the suspect ship!'

But the warning came too late. The '*Rena*' suddenly dropped her ensign staff overboard, flaps collapsed revealing hidden guns, and she opened fire on the *Alcantara* which had closed to a thousand yards. The first enemy shells wrecked the latter's boarding boat, and cut all electrical leads of the armed merchant cruiser's telemotor steering gear, while her bridge was swept by machine-gun fire. A messenger sent by Wardle to order the after steering gear connected having been killed, it was some time before his ship could be brought under control, during which she took considerable punishment. But his own guns' crews had already opened fire to good effect, although the training gear of some of their weapons was so bad they had to be pushed bodily round by hand.

Soon, however, she had wreaked such execution that her opponent was enveloped in smoke, her guns had fallen silent, and boats were being hastily got away. Unhappily the *Alcantara* had herself been mortally hit, probably by a torpedo from the German ship, and she was listing ominously. Wardle decided that she would have to be abandoned, and she sank soon afterwards, two officers and 67 men being lost.

When not masked by her consort the *Andes* had also been firing at the enemy, although standing well off to avoid torpedoes. Then, shortly after the *Alcantara* had sunk, one of the Grand Fleet light cruisers which had been on lookout for the raider, and her attend-

RMS *Virginian* before conversion to AMC

SS *Hildebrand* before conversion

ant destroyer, came racing up and joined in shelling the blazing
wreck of the enemy since the German ensign was still flying. An
hour or so later she, too, went to the bottom.

From her survivors it was learnt that their vessel had been the
Greif, formerly the merchantman *Guben* of 4963 tons. Built in
1914, she had been secretly converted to her new role, armed with
four 5.9-inch guns and two broadside torpedo tubes. With a crew
of 360 she had left the Elbe in the evening of the 27th, preceded
by a U-boat and disguised as the Norwegian *Rena*, with orders to
attack commerce in the South Atlantic, particularly grain-carrying
vessels from the River Plate.

The rumour that a raider might be coming out had also spread
alarm farther south, since it was known that a surface vessel could
safely pass over the Dover net barrage. In fact two unknown ships
had passed the Folkestone gate at high speed after dark on the
29th. Anxious for the safety of troop transports, the Admiralty
ordered all sailings in the Channel to be held up, and additional
destroyers were sent out from Portsmouth and Plymouth.

When they first informed Jellicoe of the movements of the
German raider, the Admiralty had also mentioned that intercepts
of certain German wireless transmissions placed the transmitting
ship near Ekersund, in Norway, and suggested that she might be
the German raider *Möwe* returning to port.

The latter, a 5,000-ton former banana-carrier, armed with four
5.9-inch and one 4.1-inch guns, two torpedo tubes, carrying 500
mines, and disguised as a Swedish merchantman, had left the Elbe
on 29th December, 1915, preceded by a U-boat to escort her out
of the North Sea. She laid half her complement of mines west of
the Orkneys on 2nd January and the remainder off the Gironde a
week later. She then proceeded to carry out a successful raiding
foray in the Atlantic, capturing 57,000 tons of Allied shipping.
Her victims also included a battleship of the Grand Fleet, for on
6th January HMS *King Edward VII*, a unit of the Third Battle
Squadron, sank after striking one of the mines she had laid off the
Orkneys.

Commanded by Korvettenkapitän Graf Nickelaus zu Dohna-
Scholdien, the *Möwe* slipped back into the North Sea in her
Swedish disguise, passing 100 miles south of Iceland, and reached
home safely on 6th March. Although she sighted a number of
British warships south-west of Norway, they were not stopping
neutral vessels. If they had been, said her captain, discovery would
have been inevitable.

The Germans were so delighted at the raider's safe return that they actually struck a commemorative medal deriding de Chair and the British Navy. The medal depicted a seagull (*Möwe*) with a fish in its beak flying over a chain guarded by two somnolent lions. Beneath was the mocking inscription, '*Wie die Möwe Seelowen spottet,*' and on the reverse '*Dem Britischen Vice-Admiral Dudley de Chair Gewidmet.*' They also announced that the admiral had been killed. De Chair himself later came into possession of one of these medals. In the following November, as we shall see, the *Möwe* again eluded our patrols and carried out a second and more devastating sortie in the Atlantic.

The Tenth Cruiser Squadron was now to undergo a change of command. While the action between the *Alcantara* and the *Greif* had been taking place, Admiral de Chair was on his way to Liverpool to take up a new post. A Minister of Blockade had been appointed to co-ordinate the work of the contraband committees, and the government asked for a naval adviser of flag rank to give his expert advice and assistance. De Chair was selected, and Rear-Admiral (later Vice-Admiral Sir) Reginald Tupper, formerly Senior Naval Officer, Stornoway, took over command of the squadron. The blockade, which had become the subject of considerable criticism — not because of any fault of the squadron — was about to be tightened up.

Supplies were reaching Germany through the agency of neutral shipping and from neutral countries on her borders. The Navy's principal task was to intercept neutral shipping bound for Dutch and Scandinavian ports. The routes by which they had to pass were through the Dover Strait and round the north of Scotland. In the Downs all shipping was stopped and examined, and none was known to have evaded this checkpoint. Unhappily the same could not be said for the northern route, which stretched for more than 600 miles between Scotland and Greenland. Once past that area neutral ships could make for Norway. Yet, despite appalling weather conditions, the Tenth Cruiser Squadron continued to intercept scores of ships each week.

Tightening the blockade was effected by rationing the imports of those neutral countries in contact with Germany, and by the introduction of purchasing schemes under which Britain took a proportion of exported foodstuffs. The neutral nations concerned, especially the United States, bitterly protested at our interference with their trade and the practice of sending vessels in for search, although Britain frequently bought their cargoes to prevent them reaching the enemy. Even so, delays and losses were caused to shippers. A Black List of neutral companies known to trade with the Germans was also kept, and such firms were debarred from trade with Britain and refused bunkering coal.

Considering the insults and injuries continually offered by the Germans to the Norwegians by sinking their ships and misusing their flag, it might have been expected that the latter would have been more sympathetic to the Allies. Instead their ships continued to be a thorn in the flesh of the Tenth Cruiser Squadron, and did all they could to evade our patrols by steaming at high speed and without lights. Admiral de Chair had asked for strong measures to be taken against them, and that their ships should be seized. An agreement regarding the supply of bunkering coal had some effect, however, which increased the percentage of vessels voluntarily calling in for examination, and lowered that of ships trying to evade our patrols.

Jellicoe suggested that Norway's territorial rights should be infringed when necessary to prevent raiders escaping and to interfere with the contraband traffic. While the Admiralty agreed with the naval considerations, they held that Allied dependence on the goodwill of neutral nations was more important. The War Cabinet concurred in this view, and indicated that if the Germans attacked Norway, Britain would go to her assistance.

However, the effect of the blockade on the Germans was steadily increasing, although enemy civilians suffered more than the armed forces. There were shortages of leather and wool for shoes and clothing, and of milk and meat because of dwindling supplies of forage. Because of the lack of imported fertilisers, harvests were poor, and there was not enough food to honour ration cards. German service chiefs were worried, as were the troops themselves, about the effect of the 'hunger blockade' on wives and families. Yet Jellicoe and Beatty remained convinced that this was not being enforced sufficiently rigorously, and continued to be critical of the politicians who were reluctant to upset neutral opinion.

In May 1916 came the long awaited clash between the British and German fleets at the Battle of Jutland. But the indecisiveness of the action left the nation dissatisfied, and added to the chorus of criticism in the press and elsewhere of the way in which the war was being handled. Then a few days after the battle came the stunning news that Field Marshal Lord Kitchener, Secretary of State for War and the idol of the masses, had been drowned while on a voyage to Russia in a cruiser of the Grand Fleet.

Increased minelaying by the Germans and rumours of enemy raiders trying to break out into the Atlantic necessitated reinforcement of the Tenth Cruiser Squadron as well as frequent shifts of their patrol areas. At one stage the route west of St Kilda and between the Faeroes and Iceland was patrolled by 14 cruisers and 18 destroyers from the Grand Fleet. In March the second U-boat campaign was started on the pretext that defensively armed British merchant ships had fired on German submarines, and this brought about the temporary abandonment of the patrol between the Shetlands and Norway. But in April the campaign was called off because of threats by President Wilson to sever diplomatic relations with Germany.

In September, however, the U-boat campaign was resumed and intensified. During the early part of that month the Germans sent out a commercial submarine called the *Bremen*, which was intended to voyage to America and bring back a special cargo. Designed to break the British blockade, this was a unique venture of its kind. But it was to end in disaster, brought about in all probability — if unwittingly — by a ship of the Tenth Cruiser Squadron.

On 3rd September the British transport *Huntspill* reported sighting a submarine some 300 miles south of Iceland steering south-west. This was probably the *Bremen* on her way out to the Atlantic. On patrol west of Rockall and thus in the area was the armed merchant cruiser *Mantua*, whose crew were keeping a special lookout for the submarine merchantman. But, due to rendezvous with *U-53*, whose commander had undertaken an extended cruise to Newfoundland, as she was nearing the end of her transatlantic voyage, the *Bremen* was never seen or heard of again.

Some time later when the *Mantua* was taken into dry dock in the Clyde, unmistakable signs were found on her bottom that she had been in contact with a heavy yielding object. The surface of her underwater plating was rubbed smooth, there were long striations and scars, and her bilge keel was bent for several feet. Although no one on board had felt a bump or shock, it was considered that she had unknowingly collided with the merchant U-boat and that the latter had sunk. Curiously enough, Admiral Tupper in the *Alsatian*, who had been informed that the *Bremen* was leaving Wilhelmshaven for New York, claimed that the *Alsatian* hit an underwater object while returning to patrol from Swarbacks Minn.

The Germans actually converted to merchant submarines two of a special class of U-boat. Named *Bremen* and *Deutschland*, the second of these successfully completed two voyages to America. Whilst a notable achievement in its own right, they made not the smallest dent in our blockade. So optimistic were the Germans that their new venture would succeed that on 22nd December it was announced from Berlin that ordinary mail from Germany to the United States could soon be forwarded by commercial submarine. But they did not continue with the idea, and in 1917 the *Deutschland* was re-converted into the cruiser-type submarine *U-155* armed with four guns in addition to torpedoes.

In mid-October, while patrolling north of St Kilda in a heavy gale, the *Otway* sighted the British steamship *Older* flying Norwegian colours. When challenged the latter claimed that she was en route from Halifax to Leith. But Lloyd's Weekly Index reported the *Older* to be at Le Havre. In spite of the heavy sea running Captain Booty of the *Otway* decided to board. To the astonishment of the boarding officer, a young midshipman who had with him only two armed sailors, he found that the ship was in the hands of a prize crew of nine Germans who had been put on board by the U-boat which had stopped the *Older* in the Bay of Biscay to take her and her valuable cargo of coal back to Germany. In addition she was carrying the survivors of an Italian steamer and the crew of a British trawler sunk by the U-boat.

For a time the situation remained tense, for the Germans claimed to have planted bombs in position to sink the ship, and in fact some did explode. But Captain Booty closed the vessel and successfully transferred all hands to his own ship. They totalled 64 British, Germans and Italians. The vessel did not sink however and next day was brought safely into Stornoway. The Germans said that it had been intended to convert the *Older* into a raider. They also stated that their U-boat had unsuccessfully hunted the *Alsatian*, the squadron flagship, for thirty days on end.

*

Towards the end of the year there was an increasing spate of rumours of enemy raiders being sent out to break the blockade. As early as September Jellicoe had formulated special plans to foil such attempts. The first of these, code-named Operation 'XX' was designed to be put into effect when information was received from the Admiralty in time for patrol forces to be sailed before the raider was likely to reach latitude 59 degrees north, or roughly a line drawn between the Orkneys and Stavanger, in Norway.

A Grand Fleet cruiser squadron would be sent to patrol between the Shetlands and Norway; Grand Fleet cruisers and destroyers would patrol the passage between the Shetland and Faeroe Islands north of Muckle Flugga, also the Fair Isle Channel between the Orkneys and Shetlands. In case the raider got through either north or south of the Shetlands, the Tenth Cruiser Squadron was to form a second patrol line, with the centre ship stationed between the Butt of Lewis and the south-east corner of Iceland. If ice conditions permitted, two ships would patrol north of Iceland.

Operation 'YY', to be put into effect when the raider was likely to have passed latitude 59 degrees north before information became available, involved similar dispositions of patrolling ships, the intercepting line being stationed further west. Operation 'ZZ' placed the patrolling Grand Fleet cruisers farther north and east; brought the Tenth Cruiser Squadron (6 to 7 ships) forward to patrol to the north-east from the Faeroe Islands; and stationed three ships of the squadron to cover the Denmark Strait, two to the north-west and one to the south-east of Iceland. The efficacy of these plans, however, depended entirely upon receipt of prior warning from the Admiralty of enemy sailings.

With the onset of winter, once again bringing longer hours of darkness and consequently greater opportunities for raiders to break out, the Commander-in-Chief reinforced the Tenth Cruiser Squadron by the Second Cruiser Squadron, consisting of five ships of the *Duke of Edinburgh* class armed with 7.5-inch guns, together with some armed boarding steamers. Based on Swarbacks Minn, they were to patrol north of the Faeroes. Unfortunately their presence at Swarbacks Minn increased the risk of U-boats being sent to lie in wait in the approaches to that port, and the sowing of special enemy minefields in that area.

As will be seen, when it came to the crunch these efforts proved unavailing.

The first hint of something untoward in the wind came soon after midnight on 2nd December, when the *Teutonic* on 'C' Patrol north-west of St Kilda, intercepted a vessel claiming to be the Dutch ss *Gamma* voyaging from Amsterdam to New York. The night was very dark and squally with half a gale blowing. Commodore Luard of the *Teutonic* noticed that she was not flying the flag of the day, which was an alphabetical letter issued at Kirkwall to enable merchant vessels to pass through the patrols. His suspicions were not aroused, however, because instructions had earlier been issued that outward bound Dutch ships taking the northabout route need not call in at Kirkwall but could proceed direct to Falmouth. The *Gamma* was therefore allowed to proceed. One important point that went unnoticed in the *Teutonic* was that the vessel was 150 miles west of the route she should be taking.

Half an hour later the *Gamma* was sighted by the *Avenger*, one of the *Teutonic's* sister ships on patrol, which was engaged in examining another vessel. The *Gamma* passed with her navigation lights burning, and in due course was chased and stopped by the *Avenger*. But the weather conditions made boarding impracticable. Once again she claimed to be the Dutch ss *Gamma* en route from Holland to Falmouth and thence to New York. Commander Ashby of the *Avenger* also noticed that she was not flying the flag of the day but he, too, did not ask for it. It was observed that she had a black funnel. Ashby reported the interception to Admiral Tupper in the *Alsatian*, and in due course was instructed to allow the ship to proceed.

But in the forenoon of the 2nd the real *Gamma* had arrived in Kirkwall, together with two other Dutch ships. Her funnel was yellow with a black top and a red, white and blue band. All three ships were cleared and proceeded.

On board the Tenth Cruiser Squadron flagship a special chart was maintained which showed the position of every warship on patrol, every merchantman being chased or under suspicion, and those being sent in to examination ports. In addition to these particulars Tupper received a daily list from the Flag Officer Commanding, Orkneys and Shetlands, of ships cleared at examination ports in his area.

As soon as this list was received in the *Alsatian* in the evening of 3rd December it was noticed that the *Gamma* had already passed the patrol, and further details were sought from the *Avenger*. When Tupper asked Longhope if there was more than one ship named *Gamma* he was informed that there were two, with a noticeable difference in tonnage. On the 5th the Commander-in-Chief asked urgently for a description of the vessel stopped by the *Avenger*, and instructed Tupper to warn his patrols.

But it was too late. While this had been going on, and unknown to the Admiralty, the Commander-in-Chief and the Tenth Cruiser Squadron, the *Möwe* had passed through the patrol area outward bound and was again at large in the Atlantic.

Under the command of her former successful captain, she had

sailed from Kiel in complete secrecy on 22nd November. Hugging the Norwegian coast as far as Skudesnaes, she left territorial waters on the 24th and passed well north of the Shetlands and Faeroes. Seventy miles north of the latter by noon on the 26th, she was making for 'A' Patrol line, where the *Ebro, Artois* and *Moldavia* were on station. She intercepted and was able partly to decipher a helpful signal from Admiral Tupper which established a rendezvous between the southernmost *Ebro* and the *Virginian* on 'F' Patrol in latitude 62 degrees north, 11 degrees west at 0800 on the 27th, where the *Alsatian* was to meet with her consorts. The true position for the rendezvous was in fact further to the south-west.

At midnight on the 25/26th the *Möwe* passed to the north of the *Virginian*, and at nightfall on the 26th was steaming safely through the widening gap between the *Ebro* and the *Artois*. By noon on the 27th she was well clear to westward of the patrol.

There were no further alarms until 7th December when the Belgian relief ship *Samland* arrived in Falmouth from the United States. Her master reported that his ship had been stopped three days earlier west of Ireland by a heavily armed German auxiliary cruiser. After destroying the *Samland's* wireless installation the raider allowed her to proceed.

Now ensued something like panic, for obviously the *Möwe* had slipped through the Navy's net again. The light cruiser *Weymouth* was despatched in pursuit, and four of Tupper's armed merchant cruisers, the *Almanzora, Orcoma, Arlanza* and *Gloucestershire*, ordered out. The French sent three warships to help watch off Newfoundland. Troopships in various locations were ordered to remain in port. Eventually no fewer than 24 warships were hunting for the elusive raider. The Tenth Cruiser Squadron vessels were not ready to sail until the 14th, and although they swept as far south as Sierra Leone they found no trace of the *Möwe*, which was in fact operating in the middle of the South Atlantic. It was then that Admiral Jellicoe suggested the formation of convoys, but the notion was turned down largely because there were insufficient escorts.

In the event the *Möwe* succeeded in remaining at large for four months, during which time she destroyed 124,713 tons of Allied shipping — more than any other raider — and returned safely to Germany for the second time in March 1917.

So far the mystery of the *Gamma* remained unsolved. She might have been sent out as a supply ship, or as a decoy to divert the attention of our patrolling warships and enable the *Möwe* to pass undetected. At any rate, she did not turn up again until June 1917 when she ran herself ashore near the Naze while being pursued by Grand Fleet cruisers and destroyers, and was destroyed. Although unarmed, she was found to be carrying excessive stores and crew.

Soon after the *Möwe* affair, which became the subject of an official inquiry, another red herring turned up at a critical moment to divert the attention of the Grand Fleet. While they were thus occupied an even more powerful German raider escaped into the broad oceans.

On 9th December information was received at the Admiralty from the British Consul at Haugesund, in Norway, that a large German vessel was preparing for sea. This was thought to be the *Prinz Friedrich Wilhelm*, which since 1914 had been lying at Tromso. Plan 'XX' was immediately activated and preparations made to intercept. The Tenth Cruiser Squadron patrol line was, however, shifted still further west as the Commander-in-Chief had been informed that a submarine attack on Tupper's ships was probable. The *Prinz Friedrich Wilhelm* was reported to be quitting the coast at Udsire where shoal water would compel her temporarily to leave Norwegian territorial waters.

The enemy liner duly sailed, but was reported to be accompanied by a Norwegian destroyer. Thus escorted she made her way down the Norwegian coast successfully, but subsequently went aground near the island of Samso in the Kattegat. Once again the exasperated Commander-in-Chief demanded that pressure be brought upon Norway to debar the use of her territorial waters to enemy merchantmen, but to no avail. The goodwill of neutrals was still considered to be paramount.

Meanwhile, however, the German raider *Wolf*, formerly the Hansa liner *Wachtfels* of 5,809 tons, sailed from Kiel on 30th November. Commanded by Fregattenkapitän Karl Nerger, she was armed with seven 5.9-inch guns, four torpedo tubes, and carried 465 mines and a small seaplane. Escorted by three U-boats and towing a fourth, she made her way cautiously up the Norwegian coast before leaving territorial waters. Then on 9th December, having slipped the towed submarine, she passed undetected round the north of Iceland despite the presence of a vast icefield, and out into the Atlantic.

On 'E' Patrol at the time should have been the *Changuinola* and *Gloucestershire*, but the latter had been ordered out after the *Möwe*, and the *Otway*, which was to relieve her was still en route to the patrol area. The weather was as usual at its worst.

Nerger's orders were to mine the approaches to the most important ports in British India and South Africa, raid the interconnecting trade routes, and in particular attack the grain trade from Australia to Europe. He duly laid his mines in eight different areas, from Capetown to New Zealand, which resulted in the sinking or damaging of 18 merchantmen, and destroyed more than 38,000 tons of Allied shipping. The position of some of the mines she had laid, however, was given away by a prisoner on board who threw bottle messages over the side. The *Wolf* reached home safely in mid-February 1917.

Unknown to the Admiralty, yet a third enemy raider was waiting to set out. She was the former *Pass of Balmaha* which we met earlier on. Cleverly converted into a schoolboy's dream of a modern pirate ship, she was fitted with a 1,000 hp auxiliary motor and stocked with sufficient fuel for a lengthy cruise, and provisions for two years. Armed with two 4.1-inch guns hidden beneath a 'cargo' of timber, she had sliding panels, hollow masts, secret doors and hatches for men and weapons, extra bunks, and a special cabin for important prisoners. Bombs were strategically placed throughout the vessel to scuttle her if her disguise should be penetrated. In command was Korvettenkapitän Graf Felix von Luckner, a former High Sea Fleet gunnery officer who as a young man had been trained in sail.

Luckner intended that the *Pass of Balmaha*, which he rechristened *Seeadler* (Sea Eagle), should assume Norwegian identity, and went to considerable lengths to bolster the deception. Officially she became the Norwegian sailing vessel *Hero*.

After being delayed to await the return of the merchant submarine *Deutschland* from her second transatlantic cruise, Luckner sailed from Heligoland on 21st December and passed up the North Sea without challenge. Unfortunately it was now that the Admiralty, while enjoining Beatty* to take all possible steps to prevent the escape of further German raiders, added that they could not depend upon receiving prior information of possible sailings.

On the morning of Christmas Day the *Seeadler* was well to the north of the Faeroe Islands when she was stopped by the *Patia* of 'A' Patrol. The latter's boarding officer examined her papers and told Luckner they were in order, but said that he would have to wait until clearance was received from the senior officer of

*Beatty had taken over command of the Grand Fleet from Jellicoe in November 1916 on the latter's translation to the post of First Sea Lord.

patrol. This nearly proved fatal to the *Seeadler*, for the remark was overheard by a crew member who passed it on to another. Thinking that all was lost the man lit the scuttling fuses, but Luckner managed to have these extinguished while he anxiously awaited the next signal from the *Patia*. Clearance was eventually received and passed to the *Seeadler* with an added wish for a pleasant voyage. Luckner signalled a courteous acknowledgment, sheeted home his sails and hastened to part company with the warship.

Why in the light of previous occurrences no one in the boarding party noticed the auxiliary motor, or tested the linguistic ability of the *Seeadler's* 'Norwegian' master, who could in fact speak only about a dozen words of that language, is almost beyond belief. Yet the only other sailing vessel intercepted that day, a Danish ship, was sent in under armed guard.

During the next eight months Luckner sank eleven ships totalling 26,000 tons, and might well have gone on destroying Allied merchantmen had the *Seeadler* not been wrecked on a South Sea island. Luckner was captured soon afterwards and ended the war in a prison camp in New Zealand. A gallant and chivalrous individual, Luckner took the greatest care to see that not a single life was lost during his raiding activities.

Although the raider scare died down soon after the beginning of the year 1917, the Germans made one more effort in this direction, the story of which may conveniently be related at this point.

In the previous December the British steamship *Yarrowdale*, 4652 tons, which had been captured by the *Möwe* west of the Azores and sent home in charge of a prize crew, safely reached Germany. It was unfortunate that at the time she passed through the Tenth Cruiser Squadron's patrol lines Admiral Tupper had only six of his 23 armed merchant cruisers available, a situation due partly to delays in refitting at Liverpool caused by a strike of boilermakers. Labour troubles at this port had more than once bedevilled the work of the squadron, on one occasion armed marines being brought in to recall the strikers to a proper sense of duty.

Converted for raiding, the *Yarrowdale* was armed with five 5.9-inch guns, four 3.4-inch and two torpedo tubes, and renamed *Leopard*. Under the command of Korvettenkapitän Hans von Lassert, she sailed during the second week in March. Since at this time the Tenth Cruiser Squadron was still reduced in numbers, the Commander-in-Chief, Grand Fleet had again detached the Second Cruiser Squadron to take over part of their patrol area. These cruisers, together with some armed boarding steamers, were disposed in a line north of the Shetlands.

On the 16th when the *Leopard*, flying Norwegian colours and calling herself *Rena*, was about 140 miles north of Muckle Flugga, she was chased and stopped by the cruiser *Achilles* which had the armed boarding steamer *Dundee* in company. While the *Achilles* lay off some three miles distant, the *Dundee* sent a boarding boat over to examine the stranger. After the boat had been lying alongside her for some fifty minutes, the *Leopard* suddenly disclosed her identity by dropping her gun screens with a crash.

Commander Day R N R of the *Dundee,* who had been suspicious of the vessel from the start and had kept his guns' crews at action stations, promptly opened fire and raked the *Leopard* at almost point blank range, and she was soon enveloped in a cloud of smoke and steam. He then cleared the range and the *Achilles* came in to pound her with 9.2-inch and 7.5-inch shells into a blazing wreck, although the Germans continued to fight back with their one remaining gun. The raider sank soon afterwards, but the suspected presence of a U-boat in the vicinity precluded any possibility of picking up survivors.

That was the end of the enemy raider scare, although three of the most dangerous were still at large on the high seas.

CHAPTER SIX

Stranglehold Released

By now, it could be said that the days of the Tenth Cruiser Squadron were numbered, for the war, which was going badly for the Entente because of the new U-boat campaign — ship losses being higher than anything hitherto recorded — was about to enter a new stage. America was soon to join the Allies.

In the previous November President Wilson had been re-elected for a second term of office. Thus the cautious, if unattractive, course he had steered since the beginning of the war was vindicated. For although a large majority of his countrymen were in sympathy with the Allied cause, they ardently wished to keep clear of actual hostilities. Now, however, despite Wilson's efforts to bring about peace, Germany's decision to wage unrestricted war against commerce in February 1917 with the object of bringing Britain to her knees within six months, followed by the sinking of American ships with considerable loss of life, finally impelled him to declare war on the Central Powers.

Also in November the Emperor Francis Joseph of Austria died and was succeeded by his grand-nephew Karl, who would have liked to take his country out of the war to save his crumbling heritage. Earlier Rumania had declared war on the Dual Monarchy, but her army was first defeated by the Bulgarians, and finally smashed by the Germans. This catastrophe contributed to the fall of the Asquith ministry in this country and brought the advent to power as Prime Minister in December of Lloyd George. A new government was formed a few days later, and for the first time a War Cabinet which, under Lloyd George's dynamic leadership, was to prove a most effective instrument for waging war.

This was in fact our darkest hour, and not least for the Tenth Cruiser Squadron. Within the first six months of the year four of its ships were to fall victim to U-boats in the new phase of unrestricted submarine warfare.

First to go was the *Hilary* (Captain Frederic Dean RN). Early in the morning of the 25th May while she was heading back to Swarbacks Minn from 'C' Patrol, she temporarily reduced speed in order to stream her paravanes. [Developed by two naval officers as an anti-mine device, the paravane consisted of a torpedo-shaped welded steel body 12 feet long with a small steel plane for stability, two rudders actuated by a hydrostatic valve to control the depth at which the paravane was required to run, and horizontal and vertical fins. At the fore end was fitted an eye for a towing cable and a fixed cutter for severing a mine mooring. Paravanes were towed in pairs, one at either side of a ship's stem, streaming out at an angle of 50 degrees, thus forming a wedge to deflect the mine away from the vessel before cutting it adrift from its mooring wire.]

The evolution was completed in about twelve minutes, and Captain Dean had just ordered speed to be increased again when a torpedo struck the ship on the port side abreast the boiler room. At once the sea rushed in and put out the fires. Although the wireless set had been severely damaged by the explosion, the operator managed to get a message through to the depot ship *Gibraltar* at Swarbacks Minn. Then a second torpedo struck the crippled ship, followed half an hour later by a third which finally sealed her fate. All hands got away safely in the boats, and by dint of rowing and sailing reached the nearest land 40 miles away. Casualties were light, only five men having lost their lives.

The next victim was the *Avenger* (Commander Arthur Ashby RN). On 14th June she was returning from patrol to refuel at Scapa Flow, and had been ordered to rendezvous with two escort destroyers at a point a few miles west of the Shetlands. She was steaming at 16 knots and zigzagging when, at 0200, a torpedo was seen approaching. Although so early in the morning, it was almost broad daylight in those northern latitudes. There was a light breeze, a slight sea and an overcast sky with fairly good visibility.

It was impossible to dodge the torpedo, which struck the ship on the port beam, bursting the auxiliary steampipe. The helm had been put hard to port, but as the boiler pressure fell, the ship rapidly came to a full stop. Since all the pumps had been put out of action, there seemed little that could be done to save the vessel. Ashby ordered her to be abandoned, but remained on board himself with a handful of officers and men. About half an hour later the crew of the motorboat, which was lying alongside, reported a periscope coming up astern. But after surfacing and firing half a dozen rounds of 3-pounder at them, the submarine disappeared. She was *U-69* commanded by Kapitänleutnant Ernst Wilhelm, fated to be sunk herself a month later.

Within two hours the escort destroyers arrived and picked up the survivors. By this time the wind had strengthened, and the ship's list increasing as the water in her holds continued to rise. At 0830 Ashby decided that there was no hope for the doomed vessel, and he and his helpers were taken off. The *Avenger* sank four hours afterwards. Her loss was speedily avenged, for off the Frisian Islands that same day a Zeppelin was shot down by a patrolling British flying boat.

The third ship of the squadron to be lost was the 12,000-ton *Otway* (Commodore Philip Colomb RN). While on 'D' Patrol she was torpedoed on 22nd July by the High Sea Fleet minelaying submarine *UC-49*. In a brief cruise lasting just over a fortnight during which he laid three separate fields of mines around the Orkneys, her commander, Kapitänleutnant Karl Petre, thus added a worthwhile victim to his bag of a solitary British collier which foundered after striking one of his mines. Fortunately casualties in the *Otway* were negligible, all twelve of her boats containing the survivors being picked up soon afterwards by a vessel of the Stornoway Auxiliary Patrol.

The fourth unit of the Tenth Cruiser Squadron to fall victim to a U-boat was the French-manned *Champagne*, which had returned to the squadron in 1916. She was torpedoed and sunk in the North Atlantic in October 1917 with the loss of five officers and sixty ratings.

The reason for the deathroll being much lower in British-manned ships of the squadron was the special attention paid in the latter to boat and abandon-ship drill. These evolutions were practised at every opportunity when ships were in harbour. Boats were always kept swung out, watered and provisioned, and in practising abandon ship they were manned by all hands and pulled away from the vessel. So long as the holds of the armed merchant cruisers were kept well packed with timber and empty oil drums to give maximum buoyancy, sufficient time was usually available after being mined or torpedoed for the crew to take to the boats in orderly fashion and without confusion.

Despite the protection afforded by paravanes, mines remained an ever-present menace to ships of the squadron, for enemy submarine minelayers were continually sowing their deadly 'eggs' in the approaches to focal points at which the ships had to call for coal and provisions. Thus on 7th March, *U-80*, a large minelaying submarine, laid a field off the entrance to Swarbacks Minn. Five days later trawlers found three of the mines, and all ships were warned of the danger. When on the 14th a heavy explosion was

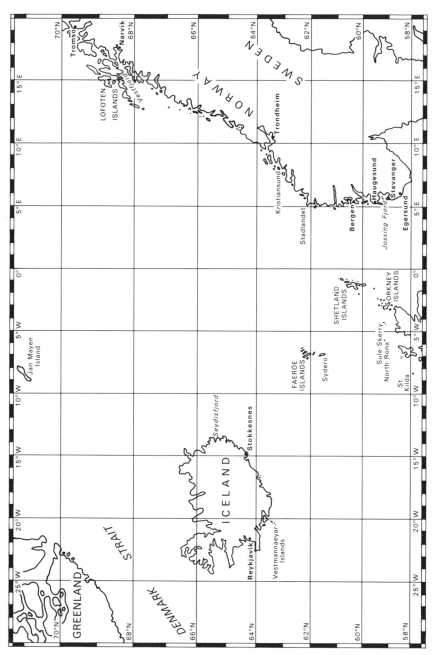

Area patrolled by the Blockaders in both World Wars

heard, Admiral Fawckner gave orders that no ships were to attempt to enter harbour until the approach channel had been thoroughly swept.

At that time the *Changuinola* and *Motagua* were on their way back from patrol, and Fawckner instructed them to stand off during the night. Early next morning when the entrance was considered clear, the *Changuinola* led the way in. She passed inside the boom without incident, but while the *Motagua* had still some six miles to go, a mine exploded under her starboard bow. The resultant damage was severe, her rudders being disabled and compass put out of action, but she could still steam. After three hours of tense manoeuvring she, too, was safely got inside the harbour.

On one occasion Admiral Tupper's flagship was herself saved from destruction only by her paravanes. With these streamed, she was steaming up the Minches on her way out to patrol from Liverpool when she actually passed through a minefield which had just been sown by an enemy submarine minelayer. The first indication of her peril came when two mines bobbed to the surface on her port bow, followed by a third on the starboard side. All three, however, were well clear of the ship.

The torpedoing of the *Avenger* now drew attention to the Tenth Cruiser Squadron. The advent of unrestricted submarine warfare had led to the organisation of examination services overseas, and with the entry of the United States into the war the *raison d'être* of the blockade had begun to lapse, for the stoppage of goods was being enforced on the quays before they got as far as shipment.

On 27th June, therefore, a conference was held at Scapa on the work of the Tenth Cruiser Squadron, as a result of which the Admiralty decided to withdraw eight of the armed merchant cruisers for convoy work. The first Atlantic convoy had in fact crossed from America to Britain in the previous month. At that time, before the loss of the *Otway* and *Champagne*, there were 23 of these vessels in the squadron. Their reduced number was now made up by the addition of armed trawlers.

But in fact this was really the beginning of the end. America had been the chief source of contraband, and when she declared war on Germany our blockade policy was greatly simplified. Since few ships were coming in to Kirkwall, there was virtually no need for a blockade fleet to intercept and examine suspect cargoes.

At the end of November therefore, the Tenth Cruiser Squadron was finally abolished, its armed merchant cruisers transferred for employment on convoy work, and the trawlers for anti-submarine operations. During the period of its existence, the squadron had intercepted and boarded 12,979 vessels at sea, and a further 2,039 ships had voluntarily reported to British examination ports. 1,816 had been sent in under armed guard, and 642 vessels had successfully eluded interception. Seven armed merchant cruisers had been sunk by U-boats, one in action with a raider, and two foundered in heavy weather. 103 officers and 1,063 ratings had been lost. Torpedo tracks had been spotted 53 times, some being only narrowly missed. 16 merchant ships with armed guards on board had been sunk, and others fired on. Wrote one historian of the economic blockade: 'So came to no inglorious end the Tenth Cruiser Squadron. With its crews of merchant seamen, it earned the gratitude of the nation.'

A more eloquent tribute was paid in a speech by the First Lord of the Admiralty. 'With a silent, irresistible and grim force, his Majesty's Navy has thrust the life out of enemy countries and secured for all time the freedom of the world. The blockade is what crushed the life out of the Central Empires. The blockade was exercised by a little-advertised power, the Tenth Cruiser Squadron. That squadron held the 800-mile stretch of grey seas from the Orkneys to Greenland. In those waters they intercepted ten thousand ships taking succour to our enemies, and they did it under Arctic conditions and mainly in the teeth of storm and blizzard. Out of these ten thousand ships they missed just four per cent, a most remarkable achievement under the conditions. In every individual case when an armistice was signed by our enemies . . . the one cry that went up was 'release the blockade'. If anything more strikingly demonstrating the value of sea power can be given, I do not know of it.'

In his *Reminiscences*, Admiral Tupper himself wrote:

Here we were, a weakly armed squadron of excessively vulnerable liners maintaining a strangling blockade of Germany month in and month out and making all the difference to the balance of the war. Yet if one properly built and commissioned German cruiser had contrived to get among us for 24 hours she might have wiped out the whole squadron.[1]

---

[1] Jarrolds, 1929.

In assessing the importance of the blockade and the tremendous contribution made by the Tenth Cruiser Squadron, it should be remembered that the Germans later strenuously maintained that their eventual defeat came from within and not on the battle-field. 'We were', they claimed, 'stabbed in the back.' But it was not only war weariness and a weakening of morale among the civilian population of Germany that sparked off the revolution which overthrew the Kaiser and his generals, but chiefly privations and the shortage of food, clothing and fuel.

> The rigour of the blockade made food more and more difficult to obtain and less palatable, deprived the young of milk and fats and enormously increased the deaths of infants and tuberculous persons. The whole country was growing out-at-elbows. Almost every article that could be bought was a dingy or repellent substitute for the original.[1]

Small wonder that blockade remained an essential part of future British economic war strategy. But in the second world conflict that strategy was to be blunted by entirely new methods of warfare.

[1] Cruttwell, *A History of the Great War*, OUP 1934.

CHAPTER SEVEN

The Second World War

In the late summer of 1939 history repeated itself. For, only a week or so prior to the outbreak of the First World War, the British Fleet had been inspected by his Majesty King George V at Spithead. In a test mobilisation no less than 22 miles of warships, from battleships to submarines, which included the Home and Reserve Fleets, steamed in line ahead past the royal yacht. Twenty-five years later, on 9th August a British fleet paraded in Weymouth Bay before the reigning monarch, King George VI. But the assembly of warships which he inspected, accompanied by Admiral Jean Darlan, then the Commander-in-Chief of the French Navy, was but a pale reflection of that earlier display of Britain's naval might.

This time there were only some 130 warships present, ranging from a couple of obsolescent battleships to a handful of motor anti-submarine boats. Commanded by Vice-Admiral Max Horton flying his flag in the 9550-ton cruiser *Effingham*, they represented the Navy's Reserve Fleet. Specially activated for service, the ships were manned chiefly by Royal Fleet Reserve and Royal Naval Reserve personnel called up under the Reserves and Auxiliary Forces Act which had been passed earlier in the year.

For once again war clouds were piling up over Europe. In March Nazi Germany had invaded Czechoslovakia, and soon afterwards the 'free city' of Danzig fell to Hitler. Now Poland was threatened by the German dictator. From June onwards 15,000 naval reservists were called up in Britain, 12,000 of them for the Reserve Fleet as its ships were brought forward and put into commission. By 9th August the latter were fully manned.

Almost all of them, however, were aging vessels. Thirteen of the seventeen cruisers present were of the 'C' and 'D' classes, vessels of between 4,000 and 5,000 tons built under the Emergency World War I programmes, the oldest having been launched as far back as 1916. They were armed with from five to six 6-inch guns, two 3-inch, four 3-pounders, and eight 21-inch above-water torpedo tubes; and their top speed was 29 knots. They had been designed to work with the Grand Fleet in the North Sea, but, like the *Edgars* of the first World War, they were soon to find themselves

facing far tougher seagoing conditions. By yet another coincidence, six of them were employed as boys' training ships. For a
time they were to form the backbone of an important naval force
in a second world conflict which was less than a month away.

Their names were *Capetown, Calypso, Colombo, Ceres,
Diomede, Delhi, Dunedin* and *Dragon*. In addition to Horton's
flagship, *Effingham,* they were to be briefly reinforced by two
'E' class cruisers, *Enterprise* and *Emerald*. Displacing between
7,000 and 8,000 tons, the latter had been built in 1919 and 1920
respectively, and were distinctive for having the third of their
three funnels sited abaft the mainmast. Their armament comprised
seven 6-inch guns, three 4-inch HA, two 2-pounders, and four sets
of quadruple above-water 21-inch torpedo tubes. They could also
carry a spotter aircraft, and they had a top speed of 33 knots. The
Effingham herself had been built in 1919, and was armed with
nine 6-inch guns, eight 4-inch HA, eight 2-pounder AA, eight .5-
inch and four 21-inch torpedo tubes. Her top speed was slightly in
excess of 30 knots.

After the royal inspection Admiral Horton took his ships to sea
for drills and exercises, and by the end of the month they had
reached a reasonable standard of efficiency, and were dispersed to
their war stations. That such a standard had not been easy of
attainment is attested to by a former RNVR rating, who recalls
of the ship to which he found himself drafted:

HMS *Delhi* may have been considered the last word in light cruisers when
she was built, but she presented a sorry, and to my wondering 'green' eyes,
horrifying sight to behold on that bright summer day when her exhumation
and resurrection began. I do not know how long the old girl had been
interred in that scrap heap under the far from tender and loving husbandry
of a small care and maintenance party, but nothing could have looked
more remotely removed from Everyman's idea of a ship of the Royal
Navy, or from the description 'ship-shape and Bristol fashion' than she did
on the day of recommissioning. Nevertheless a miracle of transformation
and resuscitation was performed on this cadaver in one week flat by
everyone on board putting about 72 hours' work into each 24.

Apart from our RN officers and a handful of regular petty officers and
ratings, the ship's company was made up almost entirely of men who had
served their 12 or 22 years and were then RFRs and RNRs, together with
a petty officer and about a dozen ABs and Ordinary Seamen from the
RNVR; there were also a few Boy ratings aboard. The 'Rockies', or 'Week-
end sailors', as we RNVRs were called by the others, certainly came
in for some stick in the early days, but those two- and three-badge Petty
Officers, 'Killicks' (Leading Seamen) and ABs were very good teachers,
and of themselves would have made a stout backbone for any ship's

Admiral Sir Max Horton

company. Real seamen, one and all, they had learned their profession in a
hard school, and learnt it well. It was to stand us in good stead.

By the end of August the Home Fleet was at its war station in
Scapa Flow. Under the command of Admiral Sir Charles Forbes, it
comprised the battleships *Nelson, Rodney, Royal Oak, Royal
Sovereign* and *Ramillies*; the battle cruisers *Hood* and *Repulse*, and
the aircraft carrier *Ark Royal*. Smaller units included the 18th
Cruiser Squadron, consisting of the *Aurora, Sheffield, Edinburgh*
and *Belfast* — the last three modern 6-inch gun cruisers of the
Southampton class; the 12th Cruiser Squadron, consisting of the
Effingham, Emerald, Cardiff and *Dunedin*; and the 7th Cruiser
Squadron, comprising the *Diomede, Dragon, Calypso* and *Caledon*;
also 17 destroyers. The *Enterprise* and *Delhi* joined up a few days'
later.

Based on the Humber to guard against enemy hit-and-run
attacks were the cruisers *Southampton* and *Glasgow* and nine
destroyers; and at Portland the battleships *Resolution* and *Revenge*;
the aircraft carriers *Courageous* and *Hermes*; the cruisers *Ceres,
Caradoc* and *Cairo*, and nine destroyers. Temporarily under
the command of the Flag Officer, North Atlantic at Gibraltar,
were the cruisers *Colombo* and *Capetown*.

The Home Fleet was thus a meagre force compared with the
massive armada commanded by Admiral Jellicoe in 1914. But then
the German Navy was also comparatively small, having embarked
on a long-term building programme since Hitler had assured his
naval chiefs that there would be no war before 1944. Nevertheless
the ships it did possess were the most modern examples of their
classes. Besides two powerful battle cruisers, six cruisers and a
score of destroyers and torpedo boats, they included three
'pocket' battleships, the *Admiral Scheer, Admiral Graf Spee* and
Deutschland. Armed with six 11-inch, eight 5.9-inch, and six 4.1-
inch guns, and capable of a top speed in excess of 30 knots, these
vessels were ideal for commerce-raiding. Grand-Admiral Raeder,
head of the German Navy, intended to use them for that purpose
from the outset of hostilities.

Indeed, unknown to us, the *Graf Spee* sailed from Germany on
21st August and passed between the Faeroes and Iceland to the
Atlantic. Three days later she was followed by the *Deutschland*.
Both vessels were accompanied by supply ships. In addition,
Raeder planned to convert 26 merchantmen into armed surface
raiders.

Building in German shipyards were two giant battleships, an aircraft carrier and five heavy cruisers. There was no comparable version of our own Fleet Air Arm, but any deficiency in this respect was more than made up for by the swarming Luftwaffe.

On 23rd August a series of coded telegrams went out from the Admiralty directing certain Flag- and Naval-Officers-in-Charge designate to take up their dormant appointments at various seaports in the United Kingdom. 17 U-boats sailed from Kiel for the Atlantic, and a smaller group took up position in the North Sea, there to remain submerged while awaiting orders. On 29th August, as Hitler continued to rant that his patience with Poland was almost exhausted, general mobilisation was ordered in Britain, and the remainder of the naval reserves were called up.

Three days later, without any declaration of war, Nazi legions swarmed over the Polish border, and Warsaw erupted in the smoke and flame of Luftwaffe bombs. In the morning of 3rd September Britain, and a few hours later, France, declared war on Germany. In the evening of that day the Anchor-Donaldson liner *Athenia* was torpedoed and sunk off the west coast of Ireland, and U-boats laid mines in the Thames estuary and off the Tyne and Humber. It was obvious that hostilities at sea were to be conducted ruthlessly from the outset.

As in the first world conflict, British plans for combating the enemy included the establishment of a special squadron of warships to guard the northern exits from the North Sea and enforce the economic blockade of Germany. Cruisers would be used to patrol between the Faeroe Islands and Iceland and in the Denmark Strait, while armed boarding vessels patrolled the shallower waters of those regions. The warships detailed for the task were to be relieved in due course by liners converted into armed merchant cruisers. Some fifty of these had been earmarked for requisitioning by the Admiralty, half to be allocated to the Northern Patrol.

The latter was started on 6th September, and it had been intended by the Commander-in-Chief, Home Fleet to cover the passages between North Rona and the Faeroe Islands, between the Faeroes and Iceland, and the Denmark Strait. But as the 7th and 12th Cruiser Squadrons were all he could spare, it was possible only to keep an average of two cruisers on patrol south of the Faeroes, three between the Faeroes and Iceland, and none at all in the Denmark Strait.

The English Channel was closed by a mine barrage laid across the Straits of Dover within the first three weeks of hostilities. It was effective against U-boats, but merchant ships held up for examination in the Downs were liable to attack by enemy submarines and aircraft.

Admiral Horton, formerly in command of the Reserve Fleet, had earlier been offered the post of First Naval Member of the Australian Navy Board. At that time this appointment, along with several other key posts in this Dominion Navy, such as Flag Officer Commanding, HM Australian Squadron, could be held by seconded Royal Navy officers. But Horton, a distinguished ex-submariner of the First World War, who felt certain all along that war with Germany was coming and was anxious to be employed nearer the centre of things, declined the offer. On 18th September he was appointed Vice-Admiral, Northern Patrol (VANP), continuing to fly his flag in the *Effingham*.

It had been decided before the outbreak of war that the conduct of all aspects of economic warfare should be controlled by a single independent Ministry, counterpart of the earlier Ministry of Blockade, but with wider functions. Accordingly, the Ministry of Economic Warfare was set up on 3rd September. The French Government created an analogous organisation called the *Ministère du Blocus*, representatives of which were attached to the Ministry in London.

Contraband control bases were set up in Weymouth, in the Downs (later shifted to Falmouth to obviate congestion), at Kirkwall, Gibraltar, Malta, Aden and Haifa, at which all shipping bound for the enemy, or for neutral ports with access to enemy territory, had to submit to examination. The evidence collected at these bases was sent to the Ministry in London for assessment by the Contraband Committee, which included representatives of the Admiralty, the Board of Trade, Ministry of Supply, the Procurator-General, *Ministère du Blocus*, Foreign Office and Colonial Office. The Procurator-General's department became responsible for the disposal of all goods seized.

To avoid delays at the control bases, the 'Navicert' system, which had been devised in the First World War, was soon re-instituted. Thus shipping companies were encouraged to forward advance copies of their vessels' manifests, giving details of all cargo carried, and the names of the shippers and consignees. British Missions in foreign countries could then issue a navicert (certificate of destination for specified cargoes) to speed these goods through contraband control.

HMS *Cardiff*

MV *Circassia* before conversion

The activities of the Ministry of Economic Warfare were first directed at Germany's most vulnerable flank — commodities in which she was most deficient: petroleum, rubber, iron, copper, tin, aluminium, phosphates, oils and fats, dairy produce, coffee, cacao and tobacco. To deprive her of badly needed imports, exports, and securing of foreign currencies.[1]

As in the First World War, one of the principal difficulties of the Ministry was to prevent contraband goods consigned to neutral countries being resold to Germany, and to aid in this respect, agents abroad reported as to the ultimate destination of contraband shipped to neutrals. Just as had happened in the first world conflict, Britain herself, through the agency of a specially set up purchasing organisation, bought certain goods to prevent them from reaching the enemy.

In the case of some neutral countries it was possible to negotiate a War Trade agreement by which they undertook to limit the sale of specified goods to Germany in exchange for an undertaking by Britain to facilitate their imports. In other cases, to prevent re-export to Germany by neutral countries, their imports were subjected to compulsory rationing schemes introduced at the same time as other stricter controls. Needless to say, the imposition of our blockade measures led to pressures arising from allegations of deprivation of the inhabitants of enemy-occupied countries.

In connection with the British blockade of Germany in the Second World War, it is of interest to note that in November 1939 President Roosevelt declared a certain area around the British Isles closed to American shipping. This zone extended from the southern arm of the Bay of Biscay outwards to 20 degrees west longitude, northward along this degree, and eastwards along a line passing between the Faeroe and Shetland Islands, and ending at a point in southern Norway. This veto helped considerably to obviate the difficulties experienced with the ships of this important neutral in World War I. Nevertheless American vessels intercepted along this northern route and sent in for examination at Kirkwall had perforce to enter the closed zone. When the United States protested, regulations were relaxed as regards American ships.

When enemy exports were embargoed from January 1940 after the Germans had breached International Law by illegal mine-laying, an Enemy Exports Committee was set up. The Ministry's Intelligence Division received interpreted, and collated economically important information, and supplied evidence about firms and

[1] *Inside SOE*, E.H. Cookridge.

individuals suspected of having dealings with the enemy to a Black List Committee. Special sections of the Ministry were brought into being to deal with other aspects of the blockade, but complaints from neutral countries about the application of economic controls and their extent were chiefly the concern of the Foreign Office. As in 1914, however, the physical exertion of the blockade itself was the responsibility of the Northern Patrol.

With the aid of captured German naval archives we can now look over his shoulder at the enemy's plans for coping with the blockade. In mid-August 1939 the Reich Ministry of Transportation warned all German merchantmen abroad to maintain a large fuel supply. On the 25th of that month, as the deadline for Hitler's planned attack on Poland drew near, all German merchant ships were instructed to return home if possible, otherwise to seek the shelter of friendly harbours. To do this they should leave their customary routes and avoid the English Channel.

Two days' later they were ordered to try to reach German or friendly neutral harbours within the next four days, but first to attempt the passage home, and on 3rd September Nazi agents in Norway reported that a number of German merchantmen from the Atlantic were arriving in Norwegian ports. On the 6th, with the Second World War in its opening stages, a secret message from Berlin instructed the masters of all German ships abroad to scuttle their vessels if in danger of sudden seizure on the high seas.

In a general survey of the merchant shipping situation specially prepared for the German High Command, the Reich Ministry of Transportation reported that 493 vessels were in home waters; 337 in neutral harbours, and 9 at sea. The whereabouts of five were unknown, and eight had been reported lost. 11 had been recalled from Spain, South America and East Africa.

Little or nothing of these details were, however, known to us at the time, since the Admiralty's Operational Intelligence Centre, which had been mobilised in August 1939 was 'not over successful in providing the intelligence for which it had been created, owing to the inadequacy of all sources of its information. Only tentative studies of the pattern of German wireless traffic were available; D/F organisation was far from complete; and agents' reports were scanty.'[1]

Unfortunately, through the agency of their Radio Intelligence Service, known as the *Beobachter Dienst* (or B-Dienst), the Germans were able for many months to decypher a great deal of

[1] *Very Special Intelligence*, Patrick Beesley, Hamish Hamilton 1977.

British naval signal traffic intercepted in home waters, and they had penetrated our British and Allied Merchant Ship Code. Thus while our Naval Intelligence Division's sources were poor, the German Navy knew a great deal about British merchant shipping and naval movements. But when early warning was needed by us of sorties by enemy warships and surface raiders, this was not forthcoming.

Although efficient in European waters and the Atlantic during the 'phoney war', the blockade leaked like a sieve.

> In the first eight months of hostilities Germany was able to import everything she was able to pay for, only a small percentage being seized by Allied contraband control. The main leaks were (a) shipments through Vladivostock; (b) blockade-running through Norwegian territorial waters; (c) evasion through the intermediary of neutral firms lending their names to German transactions; (d) the resale of essential materials by neutrals under German pressure; (e) exemptions from the blockade through diplomatic concessions; and (f) the fear of upsetting Russia, Japan and the United States.[1]

*

In the evening of 31st August the Home Fleet sailed from Scapa Flow to patrol between the Shetland Islands and Norway. Next day Hitler invaded Poland, and 48 hours later, at 1149 in the morning of 3rd September, the following coded signal from the Admiralty was received in all ships of the Fleet:

GYU v GYB3 NR 010H-NR283HD-NRH803-0-U-XILTUSZKAP-ACAAP-SZBFC-SXUYZ. Translated in respective wireless offices, the message ran: 'Commence hostilities at once with Germany.'

A number of cruisers from the 7th and 12th Cruiser Squadrons, among them the *Effingham, Emerald, Calypso* and *Dunedin*, were immediately detached from the main fleet, which continued at sea, with orders to return to Scapa to fuel and proceed to establish the Northern Patrol. In a diary he had already begun to keep, Charles Griffiths, a sergeant of the Royal Marines who was serving on board the *Emerald*, gives a vivid impression of those early weeks of patrol. All cruisers carried a Royal Marine detachment who, as is customary in the Navy, carried out similar duties to the seamen and manned a proportion of the ship's armament.

[1] *Economic Warfare 1939/40*, Paul Einzig, Macmillan, 1941.

11 September. At sea. I awoke with a start from a poor night's sleep at 0350. It was my watch (Red Watch) for the morning watch. I hurriedly dressed, an operation which did not take more than two minutes as I always sleep with my trousers and cardigan on while we are on patrol. I was wide awake by the time I reached the upper deck. The morning was intensely cold. Groped my way in the dark past the torpedo tubes and up the ladder to take over my gun. There was no one to be seen when I reached No 6 gun, and I wondered what had happened until I heard voices at No 5 gun. The Royals (Marines) had changed over during the night. The gun had also been loaded with armour-piercing shell. Red Watch take over, Blue Watch fall out. The middle watchmen don't need telling twice; they scurry away to catch up with a few minutes' sleep before action stations are sounded off.

The first streaks of dawn make an eerie picture of the upper deck and funnels when the bugler sounds off 'Action Stations'. The men hurriedly don overcoats or oilskins and gas masks and off they go to their stations: to the guns, shellrooms and magazines; fire and repair parties, stretcher-bearers and first-aid people — not one man in the whole ship is asleep now. The heaving bows seem to lift the sun bodily up from the sea; flaming golden bars laid on the ocean dazzle the keen-eyed submarine lookouts. Slowly the range of vision becomes greater; every man is at his post and alert, ready for instant action — for these are the danger hours.

It is now day: not a ship or submarine to be seen on the ocean. The mountainous Faeroes look like gaunt sentinels of the North Atlantic. The notes of the bugle ring out over the waters; action stations are over. The ship reverts to the third degree of readiness: Red Watch to cruising stations.

The sea is much calmer now, and the brilliant sun shining from a cloudless sky soon dries up the decks. I am glad when it is 0800 and I can go below for breakfast — the messman had a mackerel he caught just before the ship left Scapa.

About 1700 we stopped ship and hailed a Grimsby trawler. The skipper told us he passed a Norwegian tanker three days' ago going in a south-westerly direction. The crew of the trawler waved a friendly goodnight as we gathered speed and left them far astern.

12 September. 0900 and the glass is falling. Visibility becomes worse, and at 1000 one cannot see more than 300 yards in any direction. There are so many different kinds of alarm in operation; day and night alarm, with director sighting target in one case, and a member of the gun's crew another; sighting aircraft, day, and submarine at night, and starshell. Each target requires a different system of control or initial method to get the gun on to the target, and in most cases a different shell or fuse. All this requires careful pre-arrangement; but on the alarm being given, perfect understanding between the gun's crew and control must be maintained and guns brought to the ready with all speed.

Noon and tot time — I always enjoy my tot of rum these days; it is the one daily diversion from the routine of war. 1230. Take over the gun for the afternoon watch. There is a very strong sea running, and as we steer a zigzag course during the day, the ship has plenty of motion. 1500. Waves are getting higher and higher. Hundreds of tons of water crash down on the forecastle, and as she rises to the swell the ship shakes and vibrates in an effort to rid herself of the extra burden. 1600. Change over the watch. It takes some time to get for'ard as it is difficult to keep one's feet. Many of the compartments below decks are flooded.

2000. Take over the first watch. Sight a small Norwegian tramp. She is signalled to heave to. She is rolling gunwales under. Train guns on her. As we draw alongside the captain hails her from the bridge. After acquiring the necessary information, we quickly gather speed and lose her far astern. Dusk and action stations. I shall not be sorry when it is midnight and I can get a few hours' sleep. I have had one full night's sleep in the last 14 days: that was last time in Scapa and was from 2230 to 0530. On patrol we assume what is termed in the Navy a 'watchkeeper's trance'. When one reaches this condition one can drop down at any time in almost any place and in any rig and go to sleep instantly.

16 September. We are going to carry out a 6-inch reduced charge throw-off shoot today with the *Effingham*, but visibility became so bad we had to cancel it. Hands went to action stations at 1030. Royal Marines' and seamen's 4-inch high-angle gun crews to drill p.m., 15 rounds. At 1800 while in company with the *Effingham* we sighted a suspicious looking vessel off the port bow. Keeping at a respectable distance, we circled round her twice as she had been ordered to stop. She proved to be a Norwegian vessel of about 3,000 tons, and from all outward appearances she was down to the Plimsoll mark with a cargo of timber. The first boarding party went across in the whaler. This party consists of one officer and a wireless rating. It is their duty to examine ships' papers and find out what cargo she carries, from whence she came, and where bound.

Shortly after the inspecting officer went on board, I was ordered to stand by to take over the Royal Marine armed guard. This party consists of myself and six marines in drill order, with rifle and side-arms and 20 rounds of .303-inch per man. But it was eventually decided to leave the inspecting officer on board plus four ratings. They were two able seamen, a wireless operator and one stoker. My boarding party and I were very disappointed, but as we were only one day out from Kirkwall (where all contraband-carrying vessels are taken to be disposed of), and we finish our patrol tomorrow, we soon got over it.

The vessel herself appeared, even from close quarters, to be carrying a cargo of timber, but it was only a very smart piece of camouflage. Huge wooden hoardings all round the upper deck, with odd planks sticking up over the top made it look like a proper deck cargo of timber. Behind the innocent looking hoardings, however, she carried a cargo of iron ore to Germany!

17 September. Last day of patrol. Up at 0350. Very dark morning; sea flat calm. Report suspicious looking craft bearing Red 135. But it was only the *Effingham*. When the Red Watch had closed up again at cruising stations, we had the pleasure of seeing the most beautiful dawn imaginable. The sun came up in a blaze of glory, slowly changing the wisps of white cloud to a flaming red. Truly a sailor's warning. Just before the sun came into view it seemed as if the very heavens were pouring down their wrath of fire on a war-stricken earth. As our two ships nosed their way between the narrow entrances into Scapa, passing the guard vessels on watch at the boom defence, the news went round the ship of the loss of the *Courageous*. This spread a mantle of mourning over the *Emerald*.

What had happened was that on the evening of 17th September, the aircraft carrier *Courageous* was cruising in the Western Approaches to the Channel screened by only two of her four-destroyer escort, the others having gone to the assistance of a merchantman which was being attacked by a U-boat, when she was sighted by *U-29*. After stalking the carrier for two hours, the U-boat captain put three torpedoes into her while she was flying on her aircraft, and she sank in fifteen minutes with the loss of her captain and more than 500 of her crew.

Three days earlier, unknown to the crew of the *Emerald*, the carrier *Ark Royal*, while temporarily detached from the Home Fleet and cruising west of the Hebrides, had herself been attacked by a U-boat whose torpedoes narrowly missed her. In this case, however, the enemy submarine was sunk by the screening destroyers and its crew captured. This was the first U-boat loss of the war.

After a brief stay in Scapa, the *Emerald* returned to patrol, and Sergeant Griffith's diary continued:

20 September. Leave for the patrol area in company with the *Effingham* at 0600. Do a 4-inch high-angle shoot at a sleeve target. 1000. Action stations, and a 6-inch throw-off shoot. 21 September. Just a day of war routine. Had the middle watch and saw the Northern Lights — a wonderful sight.

22 September. Shortly before 0400 sighted a merchantman, but did not make contact with her until daylight, when we sent the examination officer on board. She proved OK and shortly afterwards was permitted to proceed.

23 September. Stopped two merchantmen today, both of them Norwegian and one a large tanker. The latter was sighted about 0930, and although we signalled her to heave to, she did not. We then fired a 3-pounder blank, but had to fire two before she eventually did stop. We then circled round her, keeping at a range of about 5,000 yards, which is our usual routine before sending over the examination officer. No sooner had he got on board than a thick belt of fog came down and we lost sight of each other. All necessary signalling was then carried out in morse by means of the syren and foghorn. Later she was allowed to proceed.

25 September. Stopped Belgian ship of about 200 tons. 26/27 September.

War routine. Put boarding party on board Norwegian merchantman.

28 September. Arrived Scapa 0600. Beautiful sun over the islands. *Nelson* and *Rodney* in the Flow doing gunnery exercises.

29 September. Plenty of work today — oil and provision ship. P.M., Make and mend (half holiday). Went ashore in Kirkwall. At the other side of the island from where we landed saw all the contraband-carriers that the Northern Patrol has brought in. There were so many I could not count them; they ranged from liners to small sailing vessels.

Although the *Emerald* and her sister ships returned again to patrol on 1st October, it was only for a brief period, for they were soon to be detached from Horton's command. As the war was about to enter on its second month, the Admiralty received intelligence that a powerful enemy raider was at large in the South Atlantic, and a number of hunting groups were hastily formed to seek out and destroy her. The three 'E' class cruisers were ordered to Halifax, Nova Scotia, to strengthen our Atlantic convoy escorts. But first they were to participate in one of the best kept secret operations of the war.

When they sailed from Plymouth on 7th October for Halifax in company with the battleships *Revenge* and *Resolution*, each vessel carried in her magazines £2 million in gold from the Bank of England. This operation was the continuation of a movement of bullion from the United Kingdom to Canada to pay for our purchase of war materials from the United States, which had begun when the two cruisers which escorted the liner conveying King George VI and Queen Elizabeth on a state visit to Canada in the previous May each took with them £15 million worth of gold. From now on, therefore, these three cruisers disappear from the story of the Northern Patrol.

Admiral Horton had earlier struck his flag in the *Effingham* and re-hoisted it ashore in Kirkwall, having soon found it impracticable to co-ordinate the work of his widely spread cruisers from a flag-ship at sea. He also wished to be in close touch with the Admiralty, and RAF Coastal Command which was co-operating with the Northern Patrol with aircraft working from bases in Scotland, Northern Ireland and Iceland, and provided an important extension of our maritime blockade.

On 8th September he wrote from the hotel in Kirkwall in which he had established his headquarters:

I have decided to move out of the flagship to this my shore base as soon as possible, since all the ships are being continually ordered in every direction (my flagship included) and it is impossible to do my proper duty in a ship at sea with wireless silence naturally always imposed ... I feel miserable at leaving the ship. Of course, I am no use aboard a single ship working on its own. All the fun has gone out of the war anyway ... my business is the dullest of the lot — blockade — the sure weapon after ages and ages, but stopping neutrals and arguing about contraband is not the sort of job I like.[1]

Although he continued to pay periodical visits to the ships on patrol, Horton later blamed himself for having gone ashore and living in comfort. He wrote of his ships: 'They work very much alone and away from all little craft that could come and help them if they cop one — so at the back of their minds is a bit of the dread of the submarines.'

Bona fide neutral ships when intercepted by a cruiser were usually diverted to Kirkwall or Lerwick for examination. But those suspected of carrying contraband had either to be escorted there or boarded in mid-ocean. All enemy merchant ships had to be boarded to prevent them from scuttling themselves, and an armed guard or prize crew placed on board to take the ship to a British port. We shall see later how this worked.

Early in September Horton recorded:

The first booty of my party came in today with a very young Sub absolutely overwhelmed with joy at having got her safely in. After all, it was a big responsibility for him to take charge of a big ship carrying over 10,000 tons of oil and a foreign crew, and command them to do this and that with his armed guard, and then leave her safely anchored where ordered.

And, a little later on: 'The young Sub I wrote about walked in again yesterday, having brought in another ship with 14,000 tons of good petroleum, which I expect we shall use and not the Hun.'

During those first three weeks of patrol, 109 merchantmen, all but one of them neutrals, were intercepted. The solitary German vessel encountered promptly scuttled herself when challenged. Since it was impossible to save her, she was hastened on her way to the bottom by a number of 6-inch salvoes fired by the intercepting cruiser after her crew had abandoned ship; which, although she lost a possible prize, afforded some useful gunnery practice. 62 of the neutral ships were eastbound, and 28 of these had to be sent into Kirkwall for examination.

[1] Quoted in *Max Horton and the Western Approaches* by Rear-Admiral W.S. Chalmers.

A lower deck view of what this work involved is given by a former member of the crew of the cruiser *Delhi*, who recalls:

> It will give a fair indication of the number of merchant vessels of all types stopped and boarded by the *Delhi* when I say that at the end of our patrol period we returned to our base with our personnel so depleted by the absence of boarding parties taking ships to the contraband control base at Kirkwall that we were only able to man about half the armament.
>
> Our boarding cutter's crew was continually being called away day and night (under oars, incidentally) in conditions which I am sure would have blanched the cheeks of the crew of a modern powered lifeboat. Many were the times, against all the odds, that the cutter was successfully launched without damage or disaster when most of us never expected to recover boat or crew again.
>
> It must also have taken a great deal of courage on the part of our captain to order the boat away at times, not only in mountainous seas and razor-edged hurricane force winds, but in pitch black darkness and without lights of any kind — darken ship being strictly maintained. Once the boat was launched we increased engine revolutions and steamed round our quarry at a safe distance in case of submarine attack, or the possibility that the innocent-looking merchantman might turn out to be a disguised raider.
>
> After allowing a reasonable length of time for the cutter to struggle the half mile or so to the intercepted vessel, board it, make a cursory examination, and head back with or without the boarding party, we made discreet signals with a shaded lamp to guide it back. Then the work of recovery began, often with the aid of many drums of oil being poured over the ship's side to make a slick. If we were not already at action stations, every launching meant that the watch not closed up were called out for lowering the boat, while for hoisting it on its return, everyone was required to man the falls; the nett result of all this being that hardly anyone got any rest.

But 'rest' was purely a relative word. Real rest was all but impossible in the old 'C' and 'D' class cruisers on the Northern Patrol — which were half the size of the *Edgars* of World War I — and comfort non-existent for ratings. At sea the men were seldom dry, never warm, often hungry, and at times wearied beyond belief from sheer physical exhaustion and lack of sleep. 'Without any hard physical labour, it would have been tiring enough simply coping with the watchkeeping in the intense cold and the insidious wearing-down process imposed by the ceaseless rolling, pitching and tossing of the ship.'

CHAPTER EIGHT

'Admiralty-Made Coffins'

In his first 14-day report to the Admiralty on the activities of the Northern Patrol, covering the period 29th September to 12th October 1939, Admiral Horton too, laid stress on the outstanding foulness of the weather, which was to figure prominently in subsequent reports. Gales had blown solidly for a whole week, making conditions very bad for the cruisers. Leaks had developed in their hatches and ventilators, and even in the decks themselves, so that the men had to sleep with their oilskins spread over their hammocks.

Visibility was often down to zero, and heavy seas prevented ships from covering the full extent of their patrol lines. Some had to leave their stations and escort merchant ships to Kirkwall when it was too rough to board. It was known that German ships were returning home via the Denmark Strait, but the low endurance of the older cruisers made it impossible to establish this patrol until the Commander-in-Chief, Home Fleet was able to detach one of his larger cruisers to cover this gap. U-boats were also active in the area, and on 22nd September the *Calypso* was narrowly missed by a torpedo. As we have seen, the *Ark Royal* had also been attacked, and on 19th September a second U-boat was sunk off the Butt of Lewis.

Just as had happened during the first world conflict, the ships of neutral nations showed themselves most unwilling to cooperate in any way with the Patrol. Although their attitude was understandable, it constituted an additional source of worry and irritation. The master of one Swedish vessel sent in to Kirkwall heatedly declared that on his next voyage he would go via the Denmark Strait in order to avoid our ships, and that his owners would order their slow ships to call in at Kirkwall but their fast ones to dodge the Patrol.

Yet the flags of neutrals were being flagrantly misused and their vessels callously sunk by the Germans. In a letter to a contemporary Admiral Horton wrote:

One of my trawlers did a fine bit of rescue work on Saturday in the middle of a gale far out at sea, taking off eight men from a torpedoed Swedish tanker that had been sunk without warning in the dark. She hadn't come from England and was on her way to America. I cannot understand why the Huns are doing such brutal and senseless things against neutrals, except to terrify them.

The objections given by the masters of neutral ships against calling at Kirkwall were, however, considered by Horton to be natural and sound. Navigation in the area was difficult; few ships carried adequate charts of the Orkneys and there were no shore lights. Tidal races and currents between the islands constituted added dangers — by mid-October two ships had gone aground on Sanday Island, north of Kirkwall, one becoming a total loss. There were no qualified pilots available locally, only fishermen to lead vessels in. Ships were subjected to what their masters and owners regarded as intolerable delays, even when they came in voluntarily, although orders had been given that they were not to be allowed to remain for longer time than necessary for their examination.

No facilities were provided for the convenience or well-being of the crews of vessels kept in detention, but local resources were limited. No communication was permitted with the shore, and ships were ordered to be anchored as far away from Kirkwall as possible. The master of one neutral merchantman angrily asked the boarding officer why, if there was an aerodrome in the Orkneys a German aircraft was allowed to sink the *Iron Duke*; and how was it that a U-boat entered Scapa Flow and sank the *Royal Oak*? Was Kirkwall any better protected? Thus there was a good deal to be said for the unhappy neutral.

In his first report Admiral Horton also asked for a seagoing rescue tug to be attached to the Patrol in order that German merchant ships whose crews scuttled and abandoned them on being intercepted might be salved and towed into port; otherwise they had to be sunk by shellfire. Two possible prizes, the 4165-ton Norddeutscher-Lloyd *Minden* and the 4564-ton *Gonzenheim* of Bremen registry — the latter carrying more than 8,000 tons of wheat — had thus been lost. The Germans themselves learnt of the fate of these two ships in due course, which they regarded as 'regrettable'. They assumed that the interception had taken place in the Denmark Strait 'where constant patrol by British auxiliary cruisers and destroyers has been observed'.

(It is probable that neither Horton nor anyone else in the Northern Patrol at that time remembered that every successful capture made of an enemy ship would add to the amount of prize money they could look forward to at the end of the war. In 1919, after the conclusion of the first world conflict, no less than £14 million in prize money — a relic of remote naval history once used as a recruiting lure — had been available for distribution to the officers and men of the Royal Navy who had served at sea).

However, the German Naval Staff regarded the continuation of the return passages of German merchantmen quite possible, and still worth attempting in spite of losses which might occur. Ships were instructed to pass dangerous areas after dark or in poor visibility. Meanwhile, on 22nd September, the Reich Ministry of Transportation recalled 11 merchantmen from Spain, South America and East Africa, and three days later received information that 12 more were homeward bound in the Atlantic. On the 27th a further 52 German vessels sheltering in neutral harbours were ordered to return home.

Since the outbreak of war the Germans had lost three vessels seized by the British and four scuttled, totalling some 40,889 gross tons. The British Prime Minister announced that by the end of September 300,000 tons of goods destined for Germany had been seized in prize, against a loss to ourselves of 140,000 tons by enemy action at sea. German ships totalling nearly 790,000 tons were immobilised in foreign ports. The German naval attaché in Madrid now reported to Berlin that the crews of German ships in Spain were deserting rather than run the gauntlet of the British blockade.

On 9th October the cruiser *Belfast*, temporarily attached to the Patrol from the Home Fleet, made an important capture. After completing full calibre gunnery firings in the Pentland Firth, she took up position to the south-east of Iceland on the 2nd. While she was en route to her station a southerly gale sprang up which reduced her speed to 12½ knots.

In the morning of the 5th she stopped a Norwegian whaling factory ship which was accompanied by six whalers. The gale was still blowing, resulting in a high swell and a confused and ugly sea. Nevertheless the factory ship was boarded, her bona fides established, and she was allowed to proceed with her flock. Weather conditions were now such that a speed of 15 knots could not be exceeded without damage to the cruiser.

In the afternoon of the 7th the *Belfast* intercepted the 5492-ton Swedish *Liljevalch* bound from Narvik to Baltimore with a cargo of iron ore. The bad weather was persisting and the mountainous seas would have made boarding extremely hazardous as the *Liljevalch* was rolling heavily. Had she been inward bound, Captain Scott of the *Belfast* would have tried boarding; as it was, he allowed her to proceed.

Two days later, while on the eastward leg of her patrol, the *Belfast* intercepted the Norwegian *Tai Yin* inward bound from Baltimore to Oslo. Special instructions had been received from the Admiralty that this particular vessel was to be sent in for examination if intercepted, so an armed guard was put on board and she was ordered to make for Kirkwall. Hardly had the cruiser's boarding cutter been hoisted than another merchantman hove in sight, and she promptly closed to investigate.

The newcomer was a cargo/passenger liner flying the Swedish flag and had the name *Ancona* painted on her bows. This alone gave rise to suspicion since it was quickly established that there was no Swedish ship of that name. Careful scrutiny revealed that another name had been painted out, the job having been done so badly that the original name could still be discerned. This was *Cap Norte* which, according to Lloyd's Register, was a 13,000-ton vessel built in 1922 and belonged to the Hamburg-Sud Amerika Line.

The weather was still very rough with a strong south-easterly wind whipping up heavy seas. As the boarding officer was to discover, however, it was these very conditions which had deterred the German captain from scuttling his ship. In the event there was no attempt at concealment, the latter himself meeting the boarding officer and admitting that his vessel was indeed the *Cap Norte*, eighteen days out from Pernambuco for Germany with a general cargo. Although he said that he carried no passengers, he had a total complement of 164 men and 7 women, the latter being the wives of members of the crew. In fact among the men were a number of naval reservists.

An armed guard of 21 ratings and one warrant officer under a lieutenant-commander was put on board. The *Cap Norte* was then given a course to steer and ordered to proceed at maximum speed. The *Belfast* herself escorted her almost as far as the Shetlands where she was turned over to the cruiser *Delhi*. The German captain was told that if his ship was not darkened and maximum speed maintained, the armed guard would be taken off and the ship sunk. She duly arrived safely at Kirkwall, and was subsequently taken into British service as a transport under the new name of *Empire Trooper*.

Because a large number of German merchantmen were believed

to be making their way back to their own country via the Denmark Strait or just south of Iceland, a powerful squadron from the Home Fleet, consisting of the battleships *Nelson* and *Rodney*, the aircraft carrier *Furious*, cruisers *Aurora* and *Belfast* and nine destroyers, put to sea on 15th October to assist the Northern Patrol to intercept. But although the squadron remained at sea for a week until the 22nd, no merchant vessels were captured by any of its units.

Now occurred two events, already briefly touched on, which profoundly affected the Northern Patrol. The first was the sinking by a U-boat of the battleship *Royal Oak* while at anchor in Scapa Flow during the early hours of 14th October; and the second a German air attack on the Flow four days later which resulted in the base ship, the old battleship *Iron Duke*, being severely damaged.

Although accounts of the sinking of the *Royal Oak* give the impression that, except for the ill-fated battleship and the old seaplane tender *Pegasus*, the Flow was empty, this was not so. Scapa had been the base for the Northern Patrol since the beginning of the war. It was also used by various newly commissioned ships due to join the Fleet in which to carry out their working-up exercises, among them the first batch of the armed merchant cruisers which had been taken up by the Admiralty at the outbreak of hostilities. Nine of these newly converted vessels were present when Lieutenant Günther Prien in *U-47* successfully made his stealthy entry through the partially blocked Kirk Sound. Only three of them had completed working-up and were due to proceed on patrol on the same day. The remaining six were in various stages of completeness, besides being short of warm clothing.

Following the *Royal Oak* sinking the few units of the Home Fleet remaining there were sent to Loch Ewe, and the Northern Patrol cruisers ordered to use Sullom Voe, in the Shetlands, as their temporary base, although that harbour was only lightly protected. The armed merchant cruisers were to be sent to the Clyde between patrols, their base being established at Greenock.

> This passage is not without danger [wrote Admiral Horton] and brought to light the fact that the complexity of modern Fleet communications is such that retired officers and untrained or out of date communications ratings find themselves initially at a grave disadvantage. Two armed merchant cruisers failed to receive a signal and in consequence crossed cruiser patrol lines at night. They had almost exhausted the patience of the cruisers which sighted them before they replied to challenges.[1]

[1] *Max Horton and the Western Approaches* by Rear-Admiral Chalmers.

Among the liners taken up by the Admiralty to assume the prefix 'HMS' and hoist the White Ensign were some of the finest ships in our merchant fleet. The names and details of those allocated to the Northern Patrol were:

Ship	Tonnage	Built	Speed	Owners
Andania	13,950	1922	15 kts	Cunard Line
Asturias	22,048	1925	17 kts +	Royal Mail Lines
Aurania	13,985	1924	15½ kts	Cunard Line
California	16,792	1923	16 kts	Anchor Line
Carinthia	20,277	1925	17½ kts	Cunard Line
Chitral	15,346	1925		P & O Company
Cilicia	11,136	1938		Anchor Line
Circassia	11,136	1937		Anchor Line
Corfu	14,170	1931		P & O Company
Derbyshire	11,660	1935		Bibby Line
Laurentic	18,724	1927	16½ kts	White Star Line
Letitia	13,595	1927	15½ kts	Anchor Line
Maloja	20,914	1923	17 kts +	P & O Company
Montclare	16,314	1922	17 kts	C.P.R. Line
Montrose (renamed *Forfar*)	16,402	1922	17 kts	C.P.R. Line
Patroclus	11,314	1923	15½ kts (Coal)	Alfred Holt
Salopian (originally *Shropshire*	10,549	1926	15½ kts	Bibby Line
Scotstoun (originally *Caledonia*)	17,046	1925	16½ kts	Anchor Line
Transylvania	16,923	1925	16½ kts	Anchor Line
Montcalm (renamed *Wolfe*)	16,418	1921	16½ kts	C.P.R. Line
Worcestershire	11,402	1931		Bibby Line
Rawalpindi	16,697	1925		P & O Company

Several more joined up as the war progressed.

The list included a number of interesting vessels. In 1938 the *Asturias* had been re-engined and had ten feet added to her bows, which increased her speed to more than 19 knots. The *Carinthia*, which had been used for cruising, boasted a swimming pool, gymnasium and squash courts, constituting in all a 5,000-square feet sports arena. The *Circassia* was the first of the Anchor Line's new motor ships, and had only completed her maiden voyage in 1937. One of her most publicised amenities was a special ventilating system whereby the air in her public rooms was changed a dozen times every hour.

The motor vessel *Derbyshire* was the largest and finest ship in the Bibby Line fleet. Employed on regular runs between the

6-inch gun practice

Cutter about to leave AMC with boarding party

United Kingdom and Burma, she, too, boasted a swimming pool on her sun deck, and every cabin had a porthole. The predecessor of the 18,000-ton *Laurentic* had also served as an armed merchant cruiser in World War I. While conveying gold bullion to the value of £3 million from Britain to Canada in 1917 she had been mined and sunk off Lough Swilly, but all the gold was recovered by divers after the war.

The *Maloja* was the first ship of the P & O fleet to exceed 20,000 tons, and was equipped to carry more than 700 passengers and cargo. The *Transylvania* was unusual in having three funnels — a hangover from the days when the number of funnels a ship carried was supposed to represent speed and reliability — but two of them were dummies. She had been commanded for many years by Captain David Bone, author of *The Brassbounder* and other sea stories. Her sister ship *Caledonia* was renamed *Scotstoun*. The *Montrose* and *Montcalm* were also renamed to avoid confusion in signals, as was the *Shropshire* since the Navy already possessed a 'Town' class cruiser of the same name.

On conversion they were armed with from six to nine 6-inch guns — some had 5.5-inch — two to four 3-inch or 4-inch high-angle guns, several smaller weapons, and a small outfit of roll-off depth charges. Unfortunately the main armament guns and mountings were old, and their maximum range only 14,000 yards at 20 degrees of elevation. Ammunition supply had to be largely manhandled. Fire control arrangements were no less primitive although they included directors, and they had virtually no protection.

Under various naval treaties to which we were signatory, auxiliary warships were not permitted to be armed with anything heavier than 6-inch guns. It had originally been intended to arm the armed merchant cruisers with 6-inch guns taken from the 'C' and 'D' class cruisers, but this proved impossible since the latter vessels were themselves required for service. It will thus be seen that those who blame the Admiralty for only lightly arming the armed merchant cruisers with obsolescent guns are not in possession of the full facts.

The ships were commanded by Royal Navy captains or commanders, most of them from the Retired List. Their first lieutenants, and sometimes the navigating and gunnery officers, were also RN, the rest of the officers being RNR — some of them the original ships' officers — RNVR and T.124. As had been the practice in the First World War, a retired Skipper Class officer was also carried to assist in detecting neutral and enemy trawlers met with in the Northern Patrol area, since the Patrol could not stop and examine them all. The Skipper Class officers were also useful in obtaining supplies of fresh fish from trawlers met with during a patrol. The latter, whose skippers were often personal friends or former colleagues, would pass over to the warship as much as 100 cwt of fish in return for half a dozen bottles of whisky! The ratings were a mixture of RN, RFR, RNR, RNVR, Hostilities Only and ex-Merchant Navy ratings on special agreements.

Accommodation was far superior to that in the 'C' and 'D' class cruisers, although all peacetime luxury fittings in the armed merchant cruisers had to be disposed of to minimise the danger of fire. The former first-class lounge became the wardroom, and there was also a gunroom for junior officers. Some of the former passengers' cabins were occupied by chief and petty officers, while others had been ripped out to make broadside messes for lower ratings. This made sense, since if the men had been distributed round the ship in individual cabins, a call to action stations, for example, would have taken too long to be effective.

Holds and certain 'tween deck compartments below the waterline were filled with thousands of barrels or sealed empty 40-gallon oil drums, officially designated buoyancy ballast but dubbed by the crews 'ping-pong balls', to help keep the ship afloat in the event of her being torpedoed or mined. Yet even when fully equipped with guns, ammunition, fuel and stores, however, the vessels were still below their normal peacetime gross registered tonnage, and needed to carry a certain amount of heavy ballast in the form of road metal or iron in order to maintain stability and reduce their freeboard.

Wrote a keen young midshipman of his first appointment to one of these vessels:

> There was a spice of romance, of adventure in the name 'armed merchant cruiser', suggesting the privateer of Elizabethan days. In fact it descends in direct line from the sixteenth century privateers equipped with their Letters of Marque, who swelled so considerably the squadrons of the Queen's ships against the Great Armada, and with Drake and Effingham helped to drum Medina Sidonia out of the Channel in 1588. Reality in the shape of an incredibly filthy passenger vessel, patchily assuming the war paint of the 'Grey Funnel Line', and swarming with dockyard mateys did nothing to quench my ardour.

But as the first fine flush of enthusiasm wore off:

Month followed month on Northern Patrol. We grew familiar with the
grim and frozen contours of Iceland and Greenland; we negotiated the
growlers of the Denmark Strait; and we shivered in those icy gales which
lash the North Atlantic into a constantly renewed fury, when the waves
run mountains high and the spray freezes on the deck beneath your feet.
The Northern Lights — the famous Aurora Borealis — soon lost their novel-
ty, though their beauty was unvarying. Occasionally the Faeroes would
loom up like Egyptian pyramids rising starkly from the sea. Every landfall
was an event, and when we put in to fuel and store, Glasgow for all its rain
seemed like heaven.

Admiral Horton was not over-enthusiastic about the newcomers
at first. They were, he said, ill-equipped for war, and many of the
officers and men bewildered at finding themselves part of a naval
squadron. He boarded each vessel on its arrival, taking with him
his technical staff officers to help the ships' officers to adapt to
the ways of the Royal Navy. He became anxious about their safety, and asked Coastal Command for more long distance reconnaissance aircraft to supplement their patrols.

Three days after the sinking of the *Royal Oak* the first seven of
the armed merchant cruisers, hereinafter referred to as 'AMCs',
joined the Patrol. They were the *Asturias, Aurania, California,
Chitral, Rawalpindi, Scotstoun* and *Transylvania.* On 2nd November
the *Laurentic* joined up, followed on the 19th by the *Montclare*,
the *Andania* and *Worcestershire* on the 25th, and subsequently the
Corfu and *Forfar.* By the end of November eleven AMCs were on
station. Before that, however, disaster had struck, and the first of
their numerous losses sustained. Not for nothing had the sailors
who manned them sardonically interpreted these initial letters to
mean 'Admiralty-Made Coffins!'

*

What happened was the realisation of one of the most feared of
the many hazards faced by the Northern Patrol AMCs — attack by
enemy surface warships, one of which in 1918 Admiral Tupper
considered could have wiped out his whole squadron.

In the afternoon of 21st November the German battle cruisers
Scharnhorst and *Gneisenau* under the command of Vice-Admiral
Marschall, Commanding Admiral West, sailed from Wilhelmshaven
to carry out a sweep into the Iceland-Faeroes area in search of our
blockade line. At that time the 250-mile stretch of water between
Iceland and the Faeroes was being covered by five warships. Patrolling along individual lines, some 40 miles apart, they were from

north to south the cruiser *Newcastle*, the AMC *Rawalpindi*, and the cruisers *Delhi, Calypso* and *Ceres*. South of the Faeroes were the cruisers *Cardiff, Colombo* and *Caledon*. Patrolling the Denmark Strait were the AMCs *Transylvania, California* and *Aurania*, backed up by two 8-inch gun cruisers from the Home Fleet, *Norfolk* and *Suffolk*.

The first hint of trouble came when at 1556 in the afternoon of the 23rd November the following startling enemy report was received in the Home Fleet flagship from the *Rawalpindi*: 'One battle cruiser, 280 degrees, 4 miles, course 135 degrees. Position 63.41 North, 11.29 West.'

This was soon followed by another signal from the *Rawalpindi* which added that the enemy was the *Deutschland*. While it was known that the latter had been at large in the Atlantic, the Admiralty was unaware that she had in fact already passed safely through the Denmark Strait on her homeward voyage on 8th November. In bad weather she had actually crossed our patrol lines undetected. On the 15th of that month she had been renamed *Lützow*.

The Home Fleet immediately raised steam for full speed, and the *Newcastle* and *Delhi* were ordered to close the *Rawalpindi*'s position and shadow the *Deutschland*. The *Cardiff, Colombo* and *Caledon*, together with two more Northern Patrol cruisers, *Diomede* and *Dunedin*, then at Loch Ewe or on passage, were ordered to concentrate off North Rona, west of the Orkneys, and patrol a line to cover the approaches to the Fair Isle Channel from the north-west. All AMCs were ordered to withdraw to the Clyde.

Meanwhile the *Newcastle*, which had received the *Rawalpindi*'s first enemy report several minutes earlier than Admiral Forbes, had already altered course to the east and increased to full speed. At 1715 she received a signal from Horton instructing her, subject to the orders of the Commander-in-Chief, to shadow the *Deutschland*. Horton also ordered the *Calypso* and *Ceres* to rendezvous with the *Newcastle* to act as a striking force for a night attack on the enemy pocket battleship.

At 1735 the *Newcastle* saw the beam of a searchlight on the horizon and altered course to close, then a few minutes later spotted gun flashes. Course was altered again to shadow from the north-west, there being a full moon to the south-east. Visibility was good, but periodically reduced by heavy rainstorms. Soon afterwards the cruiser reduced speed to 20 knots in order to render her bow wave and wake less conspicuous. At 1815 she sighted a darkened ship at approximately 13,000 yards distance, then a second. Both were to the north-west of the *Rawalpindi*, which was on fire and burning furiously.

When one of the enemy ships, which was thought to be the *Deutschland*, appeared to be heading towards the *Newcastle*, the cruiser turned away, and eventually lost sight of the enemy. Soon after 2000 the Commander-in-Chief, Home Fleet, signalled to the *Newcastle*: 'Consider *Deutschland* homeward bound. Make every endeavour to regain touch.' In the frequent rain and sleet squalls, however, there was little hope of success, but the *Newcastle* persisted in her search.

Meanwhile the *Delhi*, the cruiser immediately to the southward of the ill-fated *Rawalpindi*, was also speeding to the scene. Two of her then ship's company, the first a wireless operator, tell their own dramatic stories.

On the afternoon of the 23rd November between 3.30 and 4 pm I was in the mess for tea. Shortly after 4 pm one of the afternoon watch operators who had come from the office said that the *Rawalpindi* had sighted the *Deutschland*. No one in the mess believed him until one of the signalmen confirmed that a signal from the *Rawalpindi* had been passed to the captain from the W/T office. Within a few minutes the alarm rattlers sounded for surface action.

I was able to record the sequence of messages from the *Rawalpindi* as follows:

1. To VANP from *Rawalpindi*. Have sighted enemy battle cruiser. Time of origin 1545.
2. To VANP, C-in-C HF from *Rawalpindi*. Enemy firing four miles away. Time of origin 1550.
3. To VANP, C-in-C HF from *Rawalpindi*. A message in code at the end of which in plain language was added the word *Deutschland*. Time of origin 1559.
4. To *Delhi, Newcastle* from VANP. Shadow enemy. (No time of origin recorded.)
5. To *Rawalpindi* from *Delhi*. Am coming to your assistance. (No time of origin.)
6. To *Newcastle, Delhi*, from C-in-C HF. Consider enemy homeward bound. Make every effort to regain contact. (No time of origin recorded.)
7. The last signal from the *Rawalpindi* reads: On fire, abandoning ship. (No time of origin recorded.)

The *Delhi* was then about 50 miles away from the *Rawalpindi*, whose course seems to have been given as south-east. The *Newcastle* sighted gunfire and the two ships in the darkness. She challenged them and when no reply was received, assumed they were enemies. She soon lost contact with them and made a signal to this effect.

The *Delhi* remained closed up at action stations all night. I was sent down to the third, or auxiliary, wireless office. Outside the office was an open 6-inch shell hoist, and below the office an oil fuel bunker. The motion of the ship travelling at 29 knots (about the fastest ever done by the *Delhi*) caused the falling level of oil fuel to slap from one side of the tank to the other more and more viciously as the night wore on. This situation, with one operator in the office with me, and relatively isolated on or below the waterline, made me think about the consequences of a naval action for the first time. It is truly best not to have an imagination in wartime!

The other member of the *Delhi*'s ship's company, a seaman, wrote:

We were on patrol somewhere between Iceland and the Faeroes in company with a Town class cruiser and the armed merchant cruiser *Rawalpindi*. *Delhi* had sighted and pursued a distant merchant vessel, which was eventually stopped and boarded. This had placed us behind station in the northward sweep which the cruisers were making, and we were just picking up speed again to rejoin them when the rattlers sounded and we went to action stations. When closed up and cleared away, we were informed that the *Rawalpindi*, who had been next in line to us, had got off an ominously brief signal that she had been engaged by, or had engaged, an enemy pocket battleship. We had been specially on the alert because of information that the *Deutschland* was making her way home from an Atlantic sortie, and it was assumed, wrongly, that this was our quarry. A formidable opponent for our ancient 6-inch guns! And my own thoughts were: 'This is it!' This is what I joined for. I hope I don't let anyone down when the crunch comes.'

The old *Delhi*'s engines were revving so that she shuddered from stem to stern and from truck to keel as she battered her way north-easterly to what I expected to be her ultimate destiny as the gathering darkness descended over a very bleak sea. Unfortunately — or perhaps fortunately for us — we were not then equipped with radar (neither *Newcastle* nor *Delhi* had radar), so as the night and the weather closed in we failed to make contact with what we believed to be the *Deutschland*. I heard later from those whose action stations were on the bridge that the Skipper (Captain — later Admiral Sir — Louis Hamilton) had calmly announced that, 'If I miss with my torpedoes, I intend to ram. Lewis gunners stand by to sweep the *Deutschland*'s bridge.' Luckily, as my own action station was then sightsetter on No 1 6-inch gun on the forecastle — not the best place to be when ramming a battleship — I was blissfully unaware of the plan.

(This was in fact the gunnery station of Boy First Class Jack Cornwell of HMS *Chester*, who was posthumously awarded the VC at the Battle of Jutland.)

When next day the Commander-in-Chief, Home Fleet made his dispositions for a sweep and search for the enemy in the North

Sea, they did not include the *Delhi*. She was compelled to return to Scapa at a much reduced speed to refuel.

What had happened was that towards dusk on 23rd November the *Rawalpindi* (Captain E.C. Kennedy RN) was sighted by the *Scharnhorst*, which closed her rapidly. After being challenged, the German battle-cruiser opened fire at 8,000 yards, and although the AMC fought back, scoring one hit on her massive opponent, she was overwhelmed in 14 minutes, and sank with the loss of more than 270 of her company, including Kennedy.

The German Naval War Diary recorded:

23rd November. The reconnaissance planned of the Iceland-Faeroes area was cancelled because the Condor plane was damaged in take-off. As no reports have been received, it is presumed that the patrol of Iceland-Faeroes is proceeding according to plan, so the Commanding Admiral has been authorised to prolong the operation by 24 hours at discretion. Soon after sending this, a radio monitored from an unknown vessel south of Iceland in 63.40 North at 1649 that the ship was being chased by a battle cruiser. *1700*: Guard ship at Scapa reported this was assumed to be an auxiliary cruiser, adding the word *Deutschland* on the end. Shortly afterwards Commander-in-Chief, Home Fleet sent out the key word 'Yellow' to send out fleet. *26th*: British Admiralty reported sinking of *Rawalpindi*, only 17 survivors. No reports from the German battle squadron. *27th*: They arrived Wilhelmshaven towards noon. *Rawalpindi* sunk after short engagement; one officer and 25 ratings taken prisoner. Jubilation that the British cannot control their own waters. Germans think highly of the operation.

Horton wrote sadly: 'The *Rawalpindi* was one of my best AMCs. Kennedy, the captain, the proper old-type naval officer. Aged about 61, but fit and hardy and full of ginger.'

An odd sidelight on the loss of the *Rawalpindi* is that she was not originally intended for the Northern Patrol; the designated ship was the *Jervis Bay*. But while working up at Scapa Flow the latter suffered damage which affected her seaworthiness and was sent down to the Clyde for repairs. As will be seen, the *Jervis Bay* was also destined to come to grief.

Despite this disaster the work of the Northern Patrol continued normally. During the period up to the time of the destruction of the *Rawalpindi*, 171 merchant ships had been sent in for examination, and 17 German ships intercepted.

The 6369-ton motor tanker *Biscaya*, built in 1927 and of Hamburg registry, was captured by the AMC *Scotstoun* on 19th October. She was apparently taken by surprise, and although her chief engineer asked permission to scuttle the ship, the master refused as he feared that if he did the warship would open fire on her. The *Scotstoun*'s prize crew took her to Leith, the German engine room staff working the engines although at first they had refused to do so.

On the same day the *Rawalpindi* had intercepted the *Gonzenheim*, already mentioned, which scuttled herself. Although all German merchantmen had been ordered by their own authorities to radio their position when stopped, the *Gonzenheim*'s radio signals were not picked up by the enemy. Two days later the 5,000-ton Hamburg-registered *Bianca* was captured by the *Transylvania*. A prize crew was put on board, but her own German crew agreed to take her to Leith. While she was passing near to the north of the Shetlands, the officer in charge of the prize crew noticed that the German captain and his officers had suddenly become unusually cheerful. Adroit questioning elicited the reason; they were expecting to meet a U-boat in the area. The chief officer even suggested to the guard officer that he should allow the German officers at least to get away in one of the ship's boats!

Another enemy vessel carrying a cargo of wheat was taken by the cruiser *Sheffield*, and given a prize crew of one sub-lieutenant and ten ratings to take her to Kirkwall. En route a small fire broke out in one of the holds, but this was soon extinguished. There was no evidence that it had been started by the Germans, but the latter were doing their best to sabotage the grain cargo by burning wheat with the coal. During the last night before the ship arrived at Kirkwall three German seamen cut the falls of a lifeboat and got safely away unobserved in spite of a northerly gale. Next day they were sighted by the Fair Isle mailboat, who asked if they wanted assistance. This they declined and continued to sail south-east. But their desperate efforts came to nothing, for a week later they were picked up by a British armed trawler and landed at Methil.

On 21st October the German merchantman *Poseidon* was intercepted by the *Scotstoun* in bad weather in the Denmark Strait, and at first gave her name as the *Virginia*. After the AMC had escorted her for 29 hours to a point under the lee of the Icelandic coast, the German crew abandoned ship, and a prize crew was put on board. While she was being taken towards Iceland the *Poseidon* had managed to get off a wireless message reporting her interception, adding that as a British prize crew was coming on board she should be considered lost. The German naval authorities thereupon ordered her in plain language to scuttle herself. This message was picked up by the *Scotstoun*, whose captain threatened to open fire on her if she did.

According to the German Naval War Diary, however, she was simply told by the captain of the *Scotstoun*: 'You will be shot.' German shipping was therefore to be told that they were not to be intimidated by such threats!

The crew of the *Poseidon*, however, refused to work the ship, and she had to remain at anchor for several hours while the British prize crew tried to raise steam. After some difficulty they finally succeeded, and early next morning she was able to weigh anchor and proceed. But during a heavy snowstorm the *Scotstoun* lost touch with her charge, and for the best part of two days anxiously back-tracked along her course without regaining touch with the merchantman. Eventually the AMC reported the loss of her prize to Admiral Horton, who ordered her to return to the Clyde.

In the morning of 25th October, however, the *Poseidon* was found by the *Transylvania*. Her engines had broken down, and Lieutenant-Commander Armstrong, RNR in charge of the harassed prize crew reported that they were unable to raise steam. Accordingly the *Transylvania* took her in tow. But to bedevil matters further, a southerly gale now sprang up. Soon the *Poseidon*'s cable proved unequal to the strain, and the tow parted. Weather conditions had now become such that the captain of the *Transylvania* had no hesitation in abandoning any further efforts to get this troublesome prize into port. With considerable difficulty in heavy seas whipped up by the gale-force wind, he took off the prize crew and sank the vessel by gunfire.

It was in clear weather, however, that the 5050-ton *Rheingold*, another Hamburg-registered enemy merchantman, was sighted by the *Delhi*, who approached her quarry down sun. A round fired across her bows quickly stopped the vessel, and a prize crew was sent over by the cruiser. When they got on board they found the German sailors wearing their lifebelts and in a very jittery state. Search of the ship revealed that most of the condenser door bolts had been removed, and the door shored up but fitted with lanyards for quick removal. Asked why he had not given the order to scuttle, the master replied that it wasn't worth it as he would get his ship back in six or nine months when the Germans had won the war! In the charge of her prize crew the *Rheingold* was brought safely into Kirkwall, and taken into service under the name of *Empire Mariner*.

The affair of the *Poseidon* had an interesting repercussion, which revealed the enemy's touching faith in British chivalry, for

Cutter en route to board a neutral merchantman

Neutral sailing vessel being challenged

a few days after her capture the following message was sent to all German merchantmen by the Naval Staff:

> A British warship threatened to shoot the crew of a German steamer in case the ship was scuttled. Do not let yourselves be stopped by threats from doing your duty. Any British commander will shrink from carrying out a crime violating International Law.

Since we were aware that all German ships had been ordered to scuttle themselves if caught, it frequently became a race between the enemy and the intercepting vessel to try to prevent this. Then the British War Cabinet devised a counter-measure. Instructions were given that the intercepting warship was to order the German ship to lower her boats and cast them adrift, and inform her master that if she was scuttled the crew would be left to their fate. In fact, if this warning was disregarded, the crew would of course have been picked up.

Admiral Horton, however, was of the opinion that nothing whatever could be done to prevent a brave and determined man from sinking his ship. On the other hand, the promiscuous firing of guns, ordering boats to be cut adrift, and almost any other form of surprise action might possibly save a vessel commanded by a less strong-minded master. Yet every cargo denied to the enemy, whether a ship was captured or not, was a blow to the German economy, particularly as regards essential imports needed for her war industries.

During the next fortnightly period 112 merchantmen were sighted by the Patrol, 53 of which were sent in for examination. Their nationalities included British, Norwegian, Swedish, German, Icelandic, Finnish, Danish, Latvian, Argentinian, Estonian, Italian, Dutch and Panamanian. In the succeeding period, to 9th November, of 43 ships intercepted, 26 came into Kirkwall voluntarily, proof that the moral pressure of the Patrol was beginning to have its effect, since several of the vessels which came in voluntarily were not on our list of suspects. Unfortunately not all were prepared to co-operate.

A number of inward bound neutral vessels were caught trying to avoid the Patrol, almost all of them going north of the Faeroes and relying on D/F for navigational fixes. Their intention was then to try to make the Norwegian coast in the vicinity of Bergen, and continue on to their destination inside Norwegian territorial waters. Some of the masters gave as their excuse that the insurance on their ships lapsed, or the premiums greatly increased, if they went south of the Shetlands.

Before the Germans invaded their country Norwegian ships, as has already been said, caused the Patrol most concern. Certain vessels belonging to the Norske Amerika Line were the worst offenders, since they were fast ships and often suspect. As will be seen, we were to have further trouble with them.

On 29th October the small Norwegian steamer *Tare Jarl* was stopped and boarded by the cruiser *Cardiff* north-west of the Orkneys because she was suspected of giving warning the day before to a U-boat which was being attacked by a British aircraft. Her master, however, declared that he had been stopped by a German submarine which demanded medical assistance. His boat was on its way over to the submarine when the aircraft appeared and came in to attack, and the U-boat dived. This explanation was accepted, and the Norwegian allowed to proceed.

Unfortunately a number of suspect ships sighted by patrolling British aircraft managed to get through the Northern Patrol area without being stopped because there were no surface vessels available to the east of the air patrols, or, alternatively, because there were no air patrols west of the surface patrol lines. Thus the fast Norwegian liner *Oslofjord* evaded our surface patrols, and was only reported by an aircraft when it was too late to intercept. Horton always hoped there would be a fast cruiser available which could be sent out when it was known that a fast liner was due.

One British ship was reported suspect by a patrolling aircraft because she showed no flag and had her name painted out. When she was first sighted, the aircraft circled her signalling: 'What ship?' and ordering her to stop. The pilot repeated these signals, but they were neither answered nor complied with, so he dropped a bomb ahead of her, which produced the desired result. When a surface warship summoned by the aircraft appeared to take the vessel into Kirkwall, her master waxed indignant at the action of the aircraft, and had to be curtly informed that it was his own fault for not answering signals.

The 5,000-ton Norwegian ship *Mim*, sent in by the cruiser *Colombo* in charge of an armed guard, ran ashore on Reef Dyke Skerry, south of North Ronaldshay, at night in bad weather and began to break up. Early next morning the 1,000-ton Norwegian *Hansi*, which was voluntarily calling in at Kirkwall, went aground in the same spot and was abandoned, subsequently becoming a total loss. Fortunately no lives were lost in either incident.

While another Norwegian vessel, the *Carmelfjell*, was on her way to Kirkwall in charge of an armed guard from the cruiser *Cardiff*, she was intercepted by a U-boat in the Fair Isle Channel. The submarine came close alongside and kept company with the *Carmelfjell* for some twenty minutes while asking the name of the ship, where bound, etc. The Norwegian master did not give away the fact that he was bound for Kirkwall under armed guard, and fortunately for all concerned the U-boat did not stop the merchantman or board her. Had the *Carmelfjell* been one of our Q-ships in appropriate disguise, the enemy submarine would have been a sitting duck. At that date, however, none had yet been commissioned.

The submarine was the *U-59* which was operating in the Orkneys area, to which one of the smaller units of the Northern Patrol had already fallen victim. At the time a number of trawlers requisitioned from the fishing fleet and specially armed and equipped were attached to the Patrol to operate as boarding vessels in the inshore waters south of the Fair Isle Channel and around the Faeroes, Shetlands and Orkneys. The lack of small, fast armed boarding craft had on several occasions seriously hampered the work of the Patrol. One AMC, for example, found that with two prize crews out of the ship, she was seriously shorthanded.

U-59's victim was probably the *Northern Rover*, a 650-ton turbine-driven trawler built in Bremen in 1936 for Northern Trawlers Ltd. While on the Fair Isle Patrol on 30th October she intercepted and brought a Norwegian vessel into Kirkwall. Having escorted her charge as far as the boom gate, she immediately left again to resume her patrol. That was the last that was seen of her, and, despite an extensive search, no trace was ever found.

For the ships on patrol in the Denmark Strait the onset of winter was to make conditions even more hazardous. Although it was considered unlikely that any neutral would tackle this unpleasant passage until the winter was over, there were high hopes of capturing home-going German vessels, who had in fact been instructed to pass west or east of Iceland and to use the Denmark Strait at discretion where there was often fog near the ice limit.

On 15th November the *Scotstoun* reported that while on patrol some fifty miles south-east of the Greenland coast she struck ice and sustained damage which caused a leak into her forepeak and the bilge of one of her holds which took an hour to pump out twice a day. During this patrol, which lasted for three weeks, she encountered frequent gales, growlers and field ice, and experienced temperatures down to 16 degrees Fahrenheit. Her foremost guns, being entirely unprotected by gun shields, became a mass of frozen spray and unworkable if left uncovered. When on a course which took her into a wind and head sea they were kept shielded with canvas covers, and the after guns only manned while at cruising stations.

The ship also found herself to be something like seventy miles out of her correct position, due to the fact that no reliable observations had been possible for ten days of continuous bad weather. Constant zigzagging had helped to contribute to the accumulated navigational error. Although equipped with a gyro compass, echo sounding gear and D/F apparatus, the Scotstoun had been unable to use the latter as the set had not been calibrated. In fact it was not possible to take D/F bearings of radio stations in Greenland, Iceland, the Faeroes or Norway, except at Bergen and Tromso; and even these opportunities were limited as those stations were often silent for long periods.

Nevertheless in the late afternoon of the 15th when the AMC sighted a vessel hull down, she immediately closed to investigate. An hour's steaming brought her within signalling distance, and by searchlight she ordered the vessel to stop. The signal was ignored, so the Scotstoun fired a round of 6-inch across her bows at 10,000 yards. The suspect then hove to and gave her name as the Isa, Swedish-owned, bound from Murmansk to Boston. She had one funnel painted black with a white band and blue circle, and carried a deck cargo of timber.

According to Lloyd's Register, however, the Isa was the former Trellborg of Sweden, but the suspect vessel was at least a thousand tons larger, and from his scrutiny of her Captain Smyth of the Scotstoun was fairly sure that she was in fact the Eilbeck of Hamburg, built in 1936 and specially strengthened for ice. As the weather had become very bad, causing both ships to pitch and roll heavily, Smyth ordered her to steer to the south-east and keep her lights burning, intending to board her in the morning.

When daylight came the two vessels again hove to, but the weather was still too rough for boarding. That afternoon the Scotstoun tried again, and this time managed to put an armed guard of four officers and 11 ratings on board. They reported that the ship was indeed the German Eilbeck, that the master was willing to work the vessel into port, and that she had sufficient coal for three days. Accordingly Smyth sent her into Glasgow, having arranged for her to be met and escorted into the Clyde by a destroyer.

CHAPTER NINE

Weather – the Relentless Enemy

Much of Admiral Horton's next fortnightly report dealt in detail with the troubles besetting the smaller cruisers of his hard-worked squadron, brought about by the appalling weather conditions which prevailed during that first winter of the war. As one writer cogently put it, 'The winter of 1939/40 was of such extraordinary severity that the Second World War was nearly frozen stiff.' But there was nothing static about the war at sea, and men and ships suffered accordingly.

Gales blew on nine days out of the fourteen, the *Sheffield*, patrolling in the Denmark Strait, reporting hurricane-force winds in that area. Conditions in the 'C' and 'D' class cruisers were reflected in the tales of damage reported.

'Although the time spent at sea by the small cruisers between refuelling is comparatively short [wrote Horton] the hardships endured by their crews in the winter gales are as great as in the old days of close blockade. The 'wooden walls' could keep reasonably dry inboard, but these cruisers with their low freeboard are constantly washed down by heavy seas. It is often impossible for the men to dry their clothes or get a square meal.'

Nevertheless, while Horton emphasised that the morale of officers and men remained excellent and the engine room efficiency of ships was still high, he added that it was quite evident that the damage they were sustaining to their hulls and equipment was assuming serious proportions. In spite of the care and attention paid to watertightness while they were in the Fleet Reserve, material could not be expected to stand up to the strain of 25 years' service and two world wars.

Among reports from individual ships was that of Commodore E. B. C. Dicken commanding the *Diomede*. Of a gale experienced on the 15th of the month, he wrote:

It was impossible to control the ship at a speed of less than 8 knots on the engines, and we had to steam into the wind's eye. Considerable bumping was experienced, and seas were coming green over the bows. Two Carley floats were lost, guard rail stanchions bent, depth charges worked in the chutes and scourings, and one was lost overboard.

Writing about the same gale, Captain Lambe of the *Dunedin* recorded that when the first gusts hit the cruiser she was immediately brought round to head into it and speed reduced to 7 knots. But it was too late. The motor boat and its crutches, the accommodation ladder and the cutter's griping spar were smashed, while the tail of the port paravane was snapped off like a carrot.

Commodore Scott commanding the *Colombo* wrote:

> During this period the whole of the upper deck below the level of the fore and aft bridge became unsafe. The marine butcher was swept overboard by one wave, but brought back by the next and safely recovered. The chief cook was swept off his feet in the waist, but fortunately did not go overboard. The beef screen, bakery and officers' galley had to be vacated, while the movement of the ship prohibited the use of the ship's galley for cooking purposes.

Of another gale three days later Captain Clarke of the *Caledon* reported:

> I was hove to from 1300 for 24 hours, and even then it was dangerous for men on the upper deck as the seas were coming over green. The cutter was forced upward at the davits and its disengaging gear fractured. Six depth charges and a shell were lost overboard as seas swept the quarterdeck, the securing eyebolts, wooden chocks and one fixed chute being pulled bodily out of the deck. The 16ft skiff was smashed beyond repair.

The *Ceres* reported that her 32ft cutter, port 23ft whaler and starboard skiff had been swept away. In the *Dragon* all electrical fittings exposed above the upper deck had become waterlogged, one magazine was partially flooded, and seas entering the main wireless office had temporarily put out of action the main transmitting set. The captain of the *Cardiff* reported that with the ventilation of the messdecks already inadequate for the number of men borne, when battened down ventilation became virtually non-existent, as the intakes were exposed to the weather, and ventilation trunks flooded. 'The condensation on these crowded messdecks caused ice to form on the ship's sides, bulkheads and deckheads and resembled a domestic refrigerator long overdue for de-frosting, and at times there were long icicles on the deckheads.'

Comments by individual members of the crews of different ships add emphasis to the official reports of commanding officers. 'The weather was almost constantly atrocious, and nearly every moveable object on board was unshipped; the guns had to be trained round every half-hour in bad weather to make sure that they could move;' 'Over my years of service the weather was the worst I have experienced — blinding snow blizzards and decks iced over.' 'It was extremely uncomfortable; too rough to send away boarding parties — too rough to man the guns. We slept in our hammocks (always slung) "fully booted and spurred" in oilskins, watchcoats and seaboots. Always the lower decks were awash.' And, 'apart from the endless gales, the U-boat threat was always present.'

But while we were short of ships for the job there was to be little respite for them, although the arrival of the first AMCs helped to ease the situation. The fuel endurance of the latter enabled them to remain at sea for longer periods, and they could ride out the weather more comfortably and remain dry between decks. But they were very vulnerable to submarine and air attacks, and Horton considered it to be only a matter of time before U-boats began to take their toll of them.

> Any patrol line designed to intercept neutral merchant shipping on well known tracks must inevitably be readily found by enemy submarines. As an old submarine officer there is nothing I should like better than to find my target reappear in a few hours after I had failed to get in my first attack.

Fortunately at that period the Germans had fewer than forty U-boats operational, and as these were being conserved for future campaigns, there were no more than eight or ten at sea at any one time. Thus the ships of the Patrol were able to keep going effectively.

The trials of 'C' and 'D' class cruisers were not confined to the weather. As already mentioned, following the sinking of the *Royal Oak* and the temporary abandonment of Scapa Flow as the main Home Fleet base while its defences were being strengthened, the cruisers of the Northern Patrol had been ordered to use Sullom Voe, in the Shetland Islands, as a temporary base.

Situated at the north-west corner of the mainland of Shetland and close to the island of Yell, Sullom Voe is an eight-mile long narrow inlet, or sea loch, flanked by hills which slope gently down to the water's edge. It is also separated by a narrow strip of land from Swarbacks Minn which had been the base for the Tenth Cruiser Squadron of World War I. Near the entrance, which was protected only by indicator nets, was moored a small depot ship to service the Sunderland flying boats of RAF Coastal Command which operated between Invergordon and the Shetlands.

At that time Sullom Voe was a desolate spot whose inhabitants were a mere handful of crofters living mostly on the western side. 'Occasionally a human figure could be seen near one of the cottages or walking across a piece of tilled land, but there was no contact between the ships and the people ashore.' The Voe could accommodate up to five cruisers, but was so narrow that when leaving ships often had to back stern first into Yell Sound, with the ever present fear that mines might have been laid beneath its waters by some enterprising U-boat commander.

> This was a place on the frontier of our existence. We came in for twenty-four or thirty-six hours at the most to refuel and replenish. We cleared up, cleaned up, effected minor repairs and went to sea again. It was a place where we came to the surface to take a long breath before plunging back again into the Atlantic.

Information that once again the warships of Britain's northern blockade were using a base in the Shetlands soon brought snooping enemy aircraft over Sullom Voe. After making a number of such reconnaissances the enemy concluded that there were no fixed air defences, although on one occasion a cruiser had opened fire on one of the snoopers. On 13th November the Luftwaffe staged its first raid on the place when three aircraft showered bombs on and around the Voe. Although the only casualty on this occasion was a luckless rabbit, it became clear to Admiral Horton that his smaller cruisers would not be able to obtain adequate rest there, and their base was accordingly shifted to 'Port A'.

This was Loch Ewe, which lies on the west coast of Scotland. It was also being used by ships of the Home Fleet, but had little more to offer in the way of rest and recreation than Sullom Voe. The loch itself is a large sheet of water surrounded by high rugged peaks and hills, with a small island squatting off its northern shore. The Northern Patrol cruisers usually anchored behind this where they were sheltered from the entrance. The nearest village, boasting at that time fewer than 500 inhabitants, was called Aultbea, the initial letter of which obviously provided the 'A' for 'Port A'. A wet canteen had been built close to the pier, and ships' companies were given afternoon leave until six p.m. Since there was little else to do on shore except to go hiking, the great majority of the hundreds of sailors who poured ashore in the converted herring drifters used as liberty boats, made straight for the canteen. They were subsequently conveyed back to their ships by the same means 'in every sort of condition ranging from the strictly sober to the outright insensible'.

The trawlers attached to the Northern Patrol as armed boarding vessels found Kirkwall, which was their particular base, to be a miserable place. In normal times a not unattractive little town with its cathedral of St Magnus, one distillery and small pleasant harbour, it appeared thoroughly inhospitable in those wartime days. The trawlers along with the ships they had brought in for examination were forced to anchor in the nearby bays. Because of the prevailing bad weather with its sudden violent squalls, they always had to keep anchor watches; coaling was delayed and boatwork frequently impossible. But at sea, reported Admiral Horton, they reaped a rich harvest of neutral ships.

November 11th was a particularly violent day at sea. In the forenoon the *Delhi*, on patrol south of Iceland, intercepted a merchantman which identified herself as the Dutch ship *Hoogkerk*. Reporting this to Horton, Captain Hamilton added that she appeared to be German-built and asked if she should be escorted into Kirkwall. In fact the *Hoogkerk* had indeed been built in Germany, in 1911 for a Dutch firm which was engaged in trading to the Far East, but at that time she should have been at the other side of the world. The intercepted vessel was nearly 2,000 tons larger and was in fact some ten years younger. Hamilton was convinced that she was German, and ordered her to lower her boats.

This instruction appeared to have been misinterpreted, for the vessel suddenly hoisted the German flag and her crew began to crowd into two boats which they lowered. They then started to pull across to the British cruiser, but in the full gale and mountainous seas running, hauling them to safety inboard was a hair-raising business. Each individual had to wait his chance and jump for it as the boats were swept up to the level of the *Delhi's* decks. After they had all been rescued, dried out and fed, they were confined below under guard while the *Delhi* sent a prize crew over to their ship, which was now known to be the 7892-ton Hamburg-registered *Mecklenburg*.

But they found it was impossible to board the vessel as she was riding high out of the water and there were no ropes or ladders available for them to climb up. They were therefore reduced to trying to persuade the German master who, after opening her sea cocks, had remained on board with the intention of going down with his ship, to change his mind and jump for his life. He did eventually plunge overboard with a heaving line round his body, and with considerable difficulty was hauled aboard the cutter suffering from exposure and a dislocated shoulder.

Described as 'a Nazi bastard who looked the type who would like to have been employed as a .guard in a concentration camp or in the Gestapo', he was unwise enough to spit in the face of one of the Royal Marines standing by on deck to take him into custody. The marine's automatic reaction was to floor the man with a straight left, for which he was subsequently reprimanded.

The *Delhi* then used the scuttled vessel for a 6-inch target, scoring a number of direct hits and setting her ablaze before she finally sank, the master, livid-faced and seemingly on the verge of apoplexy, being made to stand on deck and witness the destruction of his ship. He had, however, reported his interception by wireless, the message being picked up and obligingly passed on by the Norwegian Admiralty to the German naval authorities by telex, with the information that the crew were taking to the boats.

On 12th November the Norwegian steamship *Tyrjfjord* was brought into Kirkwall under armed guard. The contraband control officer went on board, but it was not until he had completed his examination and was about to leave that he was told confidentially by her master that a week earlier his ship had been stopped in the North Atlantic by the *Deutschland*. Yet although the armed guard had been on board since the 10th none of the Norwegian officers and men had given the slightest hint that anything out of the ordinary had happened. Presumably they feared that their ship might be mentioned in an Admiralty AZ message, and they would not dare to sail in her again for fear of German reprisals.

In their efforts to return to the Reich, German merchantmen did not hesitate to use among others the flag of their Soviet partner. At dusk one day the 6,000-ton Hamburg-Amerika Line's *Parana* was intercepted by the cruiser *Newcastle*, disguised as a Russian vessel with the name *Iama* painted on her bows. She was scuttled and set on fire by her crew before an armed guard could be put on board, but, unknown to the *Newcastle*, one of her boats had got away in an attempt to reach Iceland. It was picked up by the cruiser several hours later. Of the 57 men on board the *Parana*, nearly half were non-members of the crew.

In another part of the patrol area the cruiser *Colombo* intercepted the German ss *Henning Oldendorff* which had attempted to disguise herself as the Russian *Dniester* from Odessa. This name, unknown to Lloyd's Register, had been painted over her own, and she flew a home-made Russian flag. She was in fact the former Dutch *Leersum* which had been purchased by the Germans

as recently as April 1939. Although all 29 of her crew were
enthusiastic Nazis, they were retained on board to work the ship,
except for the Second Engineer who had struck the CHIEF
OFFICER after the latter had accused him of failing to keep up
sufficient speed during the night, and was thus responsible for her
capture. In charge of a prize crew, she safely reached Kirkwall
with her cargo of 5,000 tons of iron pyrites.

While the *Parana* had managed to get off a wireless message
reporting that she was scuttling herself, the fate of the *Henning
Oldendorff* remained unknown to the Germans. It was at about
this time, as related in Chapter 1, that the German ss *Borkum* was
captured by the AMC *California* and subsequently attacked and
set ablaze by a U-boat while on her way to Kirkwall.

The Reich Ministry of Transportation now issued instructions
to all German merchantmen intending to make for home to
follow a false course for a few days if possible, and reiterated that
if while at sea escape was impossible they were to scuttle their
vessels, adding comfortingly that 'to date the British have always
picked up the crews from their boats'. Because recent losses could
be ascribed to the fact that vessels were sailing too near the coast
of Iceland, they were warned that on the homeward passage
through the North Atlantic they should keep west of 30 degrees
west longitude if possible and make for the southern tip of Greenland. They should then hug the Greenland coast until reaching
approximately latitude 69 degrees north, then make for Norway.
'Stronger enemy patrols are definitely to be anticipated north and
south of Iceland, but passage through the Denmark Strait, keeping
as close to the ice as possible, still offers the best chances of slip-
ping through unnoticed.'

Although recording that since 3rd September, 89 merchant
ships had returned home, the Ministry of Transportation now
noted rather sombrely that the monthly cost of German ships
lying in foreign ports totalled, 1,300,000 Reichsmarks in foreign
currency. 'This fact makes it clear that all possible means must be
tried to bring home all ships lying in foreign ports because they are
wasted abroad, and if sold to neutrals will almost certainly be
turned over to the enemy merchant tonnage, or else sooner or
later the enemy will purchase or commandeer them.'

During this period 93 merchantmen were sighted by the Patrol,
57 of them eastbound, and 50 were sent into Kirkwall.

German vessels continued their efforts to get through. On 20th
November while on patrol in the Denmark Strait the AMC *Chitral*

(*Left*) Ice floes in the Denmark Strait. (*Right*) Captain H.G.L. Oliphant, RN (Ret) commanding HMS *Circassia*, and 'friend'

Winter in the Denmark Strait

Looking out for German landings in Iceland

chased and caught the 4,000-ton *Bertha Fisser*, registered in
Emden. She had the name *Ada* of Bergen and the Norwegian flag
painted on her sides, the job obviously having been done at sea.
After being stopped, her crew abandoned ship, and by the time
the British armed guard got on board, the engine room and stokehold were half full of water, the condenser cover and inlet valve
having been deliberately fractured. Although during the chase the
Chitral tried to jam the German's wireless, the latter managed to
get off an SOS giving the ship's position and adding: 'We are
sinking. Chased by men of war (sic). May the Führer and Greater
Germany be victorious!' The message was picked up and passed on
to naval headquarters by the German Consul in Reykjavik. The
Bertha Fisser was shelled and set on fire by the AMC, but next
morning was found to have run aground and broken in half east of
Horne Fjord, in Iceland.

On the night of the 21st the 5,000-ton Hamburg-Amerika steamship *Tenerife* was intercepted by the AMC *Transylvania* in bad
weather. The suspect signalled that she was the Swedish ship *Gunor*,
but there was no such vessel listed in Lloyd's Register. On the
following morning the ship was heard using her wireless and was
ordered to stop. The *Tenerife* then scuttled herself, having successfully got off a message reporting her capture. But the weather was
still so bad that the Germans had to be hauled bodily out of their
lifeboats. The *Transylvania*'s own boarding cutter, which had been
lowered, could not be recovered and had to be cut adrift.

On the 22nd the AMC *Laurentic*, having left the Patrol for her
base at Greenock, sighted a darkened ship steering north. She
immediately gave chase at high speed, and when no reply was
received to her challenge, opened fire with starshell. Thus illumined,
the stranger was seen to be a merchant vessel. Captain Vivian of
the *Laurentic* now signalled her to stop and cease transmitting by
wireless. He then ordered her to proceed on a southerly course and
warned her that: 'If you sink your ship I will not be able to pick
up boats.' Two rounds of 6-inch were fired across her bows as a
further discouragement. The *Laurentic*'s wireless operators were
ordered to jam any transmission by the suspect, and except for
two words they succeeded.

The crew of the merchantmen then abandoned ship in a large
lifeboat. But because of the heavy swell running and the compara-
tive inexperience of his crew, Captain Vivian decided not to send
a boat away, but to remain in the vicinity and board the ship in
daylight if she was still afloat. Meanwhile the German crew were

embarked and made prisoner. Interrogated by the *Laurentic*'s surgeon, who was a fluent German linguist, they revealed that their ship was the 3,000-ton Hamburg-Amerika *Antiocha* disguised as the Dutch *Flora* of Amsterdam, and had newly painted Dutch colours on her sides.

The master and all his 32 crewmen were Germans. The latter said that he had left Hamburg on 8th August for the West Indies loaded with cement, fertilisers and a general cargo. On the outbreak of war he had been ordered by wireless to proceed to the Azores. After lying at Ponta Delgada for two months, he had been instructed by wireless to return to Hamburg with his cargo, and was on the eleventh day of his homeward voyage when stopped. He blamed his slow speed on the marine growths which had accumulated on the ship's bottom during his long stay in port. He added that he had received no definite order to scuttle, but had heard that other German ships were doing this — a remark considered to be untrue.

In the early hours of the following morning the *Antiocha* was seen to be settling in the water. Accordingly the *Laurentic* opened fire with her 6-inch guns and scored several direct hits before a snow blizzard interrupted her shoot, and she moved away from her target. When daylight came the sinking *Antiocha* was again approached, when she was seen to be waterlogged and on fire. She sank soon after two more salvoes had been put into her, and the AMC resumed her interrupted voyage to the Clyde.

On the same evening that the *Antiocha* had been encountered the cruiser *Calypso* intercepted the 4,000-ton Emden-registered *Konsul Hendrik Fisser*, which had *Ora*, Norway, painted on her sides, together with the Norwegian colours. Since it was too rough to board, the *Calypso* escorted her charge under the lee of the Icelandic coast. Boarding was just possible on the following afternoon, by which time three Northern Patrol trawlers had come up. The ship was successfully boarded, and her German master volunteered to work his ship to Leith, where she duly arrived safely in charge of a prize crew. The master said that he had not tried to scuttle his ship as he could not lower his boats in the rough seas prevailing. In fact it was found that he had made no scuttling arrangements, but had, however, managed to get off a wireless message reporting his capture.

The master of the German ship *Ludolf Oldendorff*, a 2,000-tonner of Lubeck registry, made a better job of disguising his vessel. On 24th November in a very strong north-easterly gale he was intercepted west of the Faeroes by the cruiser *Sheffield*. After circling the merchantmen several times in order to ascertain her name and nationality, the warship's captain was satisfied that she was a harmless neutral, and the *Ludolf Oldendorff* was allowed to proceed. The Reich Ministry of Transportation recorded with some satisfaction that two-thirds of Germany's mercantile fleet was now safely home.

CHAPTER TEN

Running the· Gauntlet

Early in December 1939 Sir Cecil Dormer, British Representative in Oslo, reported that at a meeting of the Norwegian War Insurance Club, its members had decided to draw up a document in the following terms to be handed to British boarding officers by the masters of all Norwegian vessels taken in to contraband control ports:

> To the best of my belief and knowledge there is no reasonable ground to suspect that my vessel is employed in any kind of unlawful service. I therefore protest against the capture as being inconsistent with the law of nations. The capture may expose my vessel and all on board as well as the cargo to various and very serious direct and indirect risks, and I must reserve for my owners and my underwriters as well as for the owners of the goods and all others interested in the successful completion of the voyage their rights to claim compensation for any consequential loss or damage.
>
> The ship is now in your care and under your command and you have the sole and full responsibility for what may happen to her and all and everything on board.
>
> Any information given or any assistance rendered by myself or my crew in handling or nagivating the vessel or otherwise shall be considered as rendered and given in your service, and my owners undertake no responsibility whatever for errors or negligence in connexion therewith.

The Admiralty informed Horton, however, that this did not in any way limit Britain's belligerent rights or increase her liability as captor. Boarding officers were to be instructed to accept the document without comment, but not to use any expressions which might be construed as accepting its terms, nor was a receipt to be given. In a confidential order it was also laid down that a neutral crew could not be compelled to work a ship for the benefit of a belligerent, and that the prize officer was responsible for her navigation.

Subsequently, as mentioned earlier, a War Trade Agreement was signed by the British Government with Denmark, Sweden and Norway which put an end to these difficulties.

Following the loss of the *Rawalpindi*, the AMC *Chitral*, accompanied by a Northern Patrol trawler from the Faeroes, had been ordered to search for any survivors. Ten men were picked up from a boat left by the *Scharnhorst*. Except for the *Montclare*, which had put into Scapa, the rest of the AMCs were back in the Clyde. After concentrating as ordered by the Commander-in-Chief, the 'C' and 'D' class cruisers, along with all available units of the Home Fleet, were scouring the waters between the Shetlands and the Norwegian coast with the object of intercepting the enemy force which had sunk the *Rawalpindi*. This — fruitless — operation continued until 1st December, when the Commander-in-Chief, Home Fleet, ordered normal shipping movements to be resumed. Superior German intelligence had enabled Admiral Marschall to slip safely homewards, passing undetected within a hundred miles of the British cordon.

Six Northern Patrol AMCs therefore left the Clyde on 30th November, and next day took up their patrol lines, five to the south of Iceland and one in the Denmark Strait, where they remained for the next seven days, except for a brief period when they were ordered by the Admiralty to steer south on account of a D/F bearing of an unknown enemy having been reported.

The 'C' and 'D' class cruisers, now ordered to use 'Port A', duly arrived there on 2nd December. Unhappily the closely guarded secret that Loch Ewe was the temporary base for the Home Fleet had become known to the enemy, and a number of magnetic mines laid in the approach channels by a U-boat. Thus it was that when on the 4th Admiral Forbes decided to call in at the loch to refuel his destroyers, his flagship, the battleship *Nelson*, detonated and was severely damaged by one of these specimens of Hitler's 'new' secret weapon.

Magnetic mines had already made their appearance in our port approaches and estuaries farther south, and counter-measures were being hurriedly devised. But until the latter became available and its approaches cleared, 'Port A' had to remain closed for several days, effectively locking in the Northern Patrol cruisers.

The fact that the patrol lines were left unguarded for most of this disturbed period doubtless had its effect on the results, but this was not as marked as might have been expected, since the Northern Patrol trawlers continued to intercept a good many vessels. As a measure of the prestige of the Patrol the number of ships voluntarily coming in to Kirkwall was also increasing steadily. Thus in the period from 24th November to 7th December, of the 56 ships sighted, 40 of them called in voluntarily.

Gales were again prevalent for most of the time, that of 26th November being particularly fierce. Officers and men of the trawlers returned to harbour completely exhausted during this period, since the violent motion of these little ships entailed their crews having constantly to hold on.for support to stanchions and other fixtures, and denied them adequate rest.

On 8th December, the channels having been reported as swept clear, the Commander-in-Chief, Home Fleet, ordered the 'C' and 'D' class cruisers to leave 'Port A' and resume patrol. But next day the AMCs were again withdrawn, and the two Home Fleet cruisers stationed in the Denmark Strait moved to positions south of Iceland. By the 10th six cruisers were on patrol between Iceland and the Faeroes, and three to the south of the Faeroes.

Then, on the 13th, the submarine *Salmon*, patrolling in the Heligoland Bight, sighted three German cruisers and five destroyers in the North Sea steering west. This brought about another temporary dislocation of the Northern Patrol, the Home Fleet cruisers being disposed to meet a possible enemy attempt to break out of the North Sea; while the 'C' and 'D' class cruisers were ordered to concentrate west of the Faeroes. But the enemy sortie had in fact been made for the purpose of laying mines off the Tyne. While they were on their way back to harbour the *Salmon* torpedoed and damaged two of the enemy cruisers.

Normal patrols were resumed on 15th December, and two days later the AMCs were ordered out again following an Admiralty warning that a number of enemy merchant vessels might attempt to reach home. Admiral Forbes also took his heavy ships to sea in case the enemy should be tempted to repeat the foray which had resulted in the destruction of the *Rawalpindi*. During the whole period trawler patrols were maintained north of the Faeroes, north of Rona, and to the north-west of the Orkneys. Of the 60 merchant ships arriving at Kirkwall, 36 came in voluntarily.

Yet again gales raged on eight out of the fourteen days; that on the 10th was so violent that the Home Fleet cruisers *Edinburgh* and *Glasgow*, supporting a Scandinavian convoy east of the Orkneys, were compelled to heave to. These convoys had been started in October 1939, and consisted chiefly of iron ore ships from Narvik. Later on, covered by ships of the Home Fleet, they were run from Bergen to Methil. U-boats were sighted twice, and on 14th December while being taken up the Clyde by a tug, the AMC *Scotstoun* went aground and lost a propeller.

Changes were now in the air. The cruisers *Caledon* and *Calypso* left the Northern Patrol to join the Mediterranean Fleet. The *Dunedin* and *Cardiff* were despatched to the Clyde to give leave and refit, while the *Dragon* was sent to Chatham, the *Diomede* to Devonport, and the *Delhi* to Belfast for the same purposes. Not all would rejoin, but those that did found their base was to be Scapa Flow, which had now been made fully secure. On the 20th Admiral Horton was relieved in command by Vice-Admiral Robert Raikes, to become Admiral (Submarines).

The period from 22nd December to 4th January 1940 was comparatively uneventful, and even the weather showed a temporary improvement. Eight patrol lines were maintained, including coverage of the Denmark Strait. The AMC *Laurentic*, which shared this patrol with a Home Fleet cruiser, reported that during her 15-day stint she had not sighted a single ship.

On 21st November 1939 new economic measures, to come into force from 1st January, had been announced in the House of Commons in retaliation for the German breach of International Law by laying magnetic mines, and this meant more work for the Northern Patrol. The export of German goods of foreign or German manufacture could no longer be tolerated, and the Admiralty ordered that all westbound ships which could not be boarded at sea to check if they had certificates of origin or export passes, were to be sent in for examination. Up until then, scrutiny of ships' manifests to discover whether any part of the cargo had come from Germany had been sufficient.

In the early hours of 28th December a British fishing trawler was sunk by U-boat in the North Rona area, but unfortunately the latter's presence remained undetected by Northern Patrol trawlers in the vicinity. Later the same day the battleship *Barham*, which had been brought back from the Mediterranean Fleet to strengthen Home Fleet escorts for Canadian troopships coming in to the Clyde, was torpedoed. Although she did not sink, she was so severely damaged as to be out of action for three months. Further U-boat sightings were reported, indicating that more than one German submarine was prowling in the area.

On the enemy side, the Germans recorded that their merchant ships were continuing to arrive from overseas. Thus on 8th December two steamers with valuable cargoes reached home waters from Vigo. On the 10th two more reached home, one from as far afield as Pernambuco and the other from Vigo. Two days later the 51,000-ton liner *Bremen* arrived safely, the hundredth German vessel to elude the British blockade. This liner, which was known to be on her way home from New York at the outset of the war, had been hunted by the Home Fleet during its North Sea sweep on 3rd September, but by then she had already reached Murmansk. In November a force of one cruiser and two destroyers was detached to search for her again, but when the *Rawalpindi* was sunk their hunt was called off.

German jubilation that the pride of their merchant fleet had successfully eluded the British Navy was, however, tempered by the loss of another fine vessel. This was the 32,950-ton Norddeutscher-Lloyd liner *Columbus*. On her way home from Vera Cruz she was escorted for part of the way by two American destroyers. Hopefully trailing her was the British destroyer *Hyperion*. As soon as the *Columbus* had been shepherded clear of American waters, the *Hyperion* closed in, and the *Columbus* scuttled herself.

In a review of German merchantmen which had left the Spanish ports of Vigo, Cadiz, Huelva, and the Canary Islands for home since the start of the war, the Reich Ministry of Transportation claimed that seven of the sixteen which had sailed from Spanish ports reached home waters, five reached Norway, one was sunk, and three seized. Of the four which sailed from the Canary Islands, one reached home, one reached Norway, and two were seized. German ships abroad were now warned that British warships were sending out fictitious SOS messages purporting to come from German vessels and giving positions, with the object of deterring enemy ships from passing through certain sea areas such as the Denmark Strait. According to a report by the British Ministry of Economic Warfare, German contraband so far seized totalled 510,000 tons, while the French had seized 360,000 tons.

Because of other naval operations the number of Home Fleet cruisers available to augment the Northern Patrol was reduced to two from 8th January to the 18th. Nevertheless the average number of ships on patrol numbered 17 daily, this figure being only one less than for the previous period, which was a record. Traffic came in waves, and the weather, reported Admiral Raikes, was probably normal for the time of year, gales being experienced on some seven days out of fourteen. During one Force 9 blow on 10th January the *Scotstoun* had to heave to as she was rolling as much as 41 degrees to port and 38 to starboard.

One 8-inch gun Home Fleet cruiser and one AMC patrolled the Denmark Strait. The method of patrolling in this area had now been changed. Instead of being given patrol lines parallel to the probable tracks of German vessels returning home, each ship was allotted an area and told to sight the Greenland ice and the coast of Iceland on alternate days so as to cover the area efficiently.

On 18th January the cruiser *Norfolk* experienced a remarkable accident, although this was not due to exceptionally heavy rolling. A huge sea struck the starboard torpedo tubes, which were trained on the beam, and although they weighed 18 tons, unshipped them. With difficulty the tubes were unloaded and secured.

During the opening week of the New Year the first drafts of Newfoundland ratings began to arrive in the AMCs. They had been asked for by Winston Churchill, then First Lord of the Admiralty, as they were 'the hardiest and most skilful boatmen in rough seas who exist'. It was intended that they should form boarding boats' crews as they had done in the First World War. This time, however, it was found that only a proportion of them were seamen, the rest being miners, land-workers, etc. But they were all enthusiastic and willing to learn.

Navigational difficulties occasioned by wartime conditions continued to be experienced by the AMCs. On 6th January the *Laurentic* went aground south-west of Islay, and four days later the *Canton* grounded on the west coast of the island of Lewis. Although both were badly damaged, they managed to get off without assistance.

In the late afternoon of 18th January the Northern Patrol trawler *Northern Duke* was escorting the Swedish motor vessel *Pajala* to Kirkwall when the latter was torpedoed and sunk. Soon afterwards the *Northern Duke* sighted a U-boat on the surface and opened fire at it with her 4-inch gun. The first round was thought to have hit, and certainly the second. The trawler then tried to ram the U-boat, but at the last moment the latter crash-dived, and the *Northern Duke* rode over it although without doing much damage. She then reversed course and picked up the survivors of the *Pajala*. A few minutes later a patch of oil and bubbles was spotted some distance away from the wreckage of the *Pajala*, and into it the trawler dropped a total of four depth charges.

Forwarding the trawler captain's report of this attack to the Admiralty, Admiral Raikes considered that the U-boat had probably been destroyed, but, alas, this was never confirmed. As in the First World War, U-boats were able to absorb a great deal of punishment before being finally put out of action. This was the seventh close U-boat contact made since December and, commenting on the attack, the Admiralty thought that it had become deliberate enemy policy to torpedo neutral ships in the vicinity of our contraband control bases.

It was now that Admiral Raikes felt compelled to complain

TSS *Letitia*

TSS *California*

again, as had his predecessor, about the behaviour of certain Norwegian ships of the Norske-Amerika Line. On Christmas Day 1939 their 4,000-ton motor vessel *Randsfjord* was intercepted by the AMC *Montclare*, whose master declared that he was not carrying mails. The boarding officer inspected the ship's manifests and found that all the cargo was apparently covered by navicerts. The *Randsfjord* was accordingly given the 'flag of the day' and allowed to proceed.

Next day, however, she was again intercepted, this time by the AMC *California*, and despite her having been given the flag of the day, Captain Pope, RAN, of the *California* sent her into detention in Kirkwall as she was on a list of ships to be sent in. There it was found that she was carrying 370 bags of mail, and that her whole cargo was not covered by navicerts.

When on 10th January the 11,000-ton *Bergensfjord* of the Norske-Amerika Line was sighted by the Northern Patrol trawler *Kingston Onyx* 40 miles off the Faeroes proceeding eastward at high speed, she ignored signals to stop until two warning rounds had been fired by the trawler. Because the weather was unsuitable for boarding, the *Kingston Onyx* then signalled: 'Follow me to Kirkwall', to which she replied: 'I refuse.'

After signalling that it was too dangerous owing to the weather and the fact that he had 700 neutrals on board, the master of the *Bergensfjord* continued: 'I have orders from my underwriters not to go to a British port unless a British officer of ability takes responsibility.' At that time the Northern Patrol trawlers were commanded by professional seamen of the Royal Navy and RNR up to the rank of commander.

After a further exchange of signals the master of the *Bergensfjord* finally agreed to proceed direct to Kirkwall. En route she was met by the cruiser *Colombo* who escorted her in. It was noted by Raikes that when intercepted the *Bergensfjord*'s course took her along one of the patrol lines just vacated by the *California* and thus temporarily uncovered, from whence she had altered course to the north-west to clear the Patrol area.

The 6,000-ton Norske-Amerika's *Tanafjord* was sighted steering west at mid-day on 14th January by the Northern Patrol trawler *Northern Duke*, then patrolling in the North Rona area. When instructed by signal to go to Kirkwall she replied: 'No.' The *Northern Duke* then signalled: 'Stop or I fire!' whereupon the Norwegian ship obeyed. After a great deal of signalling the *Tanafjord's* master eventually agreed to call at Kirkwall, but demanded a responsible officer to navigate her there. When the *Northern Duke* requested that she send a boat for him, the master replied: 'No. From this moment all navigational risks are your responsibility.'

After a total delay of three and a half hours the *Tanafjord's* master allowed his ship to be escorted to Kirkwall. There she was detained by order of the Admiralty and warned regarding her future conduct.

Raikes reported that it was evident that the policy of this shipping company was not only to try to avoid the patrols, but also to obstruct and mislead them when intercepted. It also appeared that a number of other Norwegian ships had received instructions from their underwriters to refuse to accept any responsibility for the safety of ship and cargo if sent into Kirkwall. Even as late as March 1940 an increasing number of neutral ships, including Danish, were refusing to proceed to Kirkwall. They were therefore detained at sea by the Northern Patrol warships which had intercepted them until they agreed to work their ships in. In the opinion of the Foreign Office, however, refusal to navigate a ship was not a 'penal resistance to search.'

It was during January that the last of the small cruisers left the Patrol. They were the *Delhi, Dunedin* and *Diomede*. Their efficiency, reported Admiral Raikes, was a tribute to their design and construction. The 'D' class cruisers were in fact slightly larger than their 'C' class sisters and more seaworthy. All eight of them went on to perform distinguished service in other theatres of the war, only one being lost — by U-boat torpedo.

*

The first fortnight of the New Year found the greatest number of AMCs thus far at sea on the Northern Patrol — twenty all told. This was possible only because no enemy action occurred to disorganise normal routine. But bad weather speedily returned to bedevil their work. Thus when towards the end of January the AMCs *Derbyshire, Circassia* and *California* each intercepted a neutral merchantman which was required to be brought in for examination, it took as much as two to three days to escort them through raging seas and gale-force winds to the trawler rendezvous off the Faeroes. It then took the trawlers and merchantmen another four days to make Kirkwall. Not unnaturally the efficiency of the blockade was reduced when patrol lines had to be vacated for so long.

In the Denmark Strait the Home Fleet cruiser *Devonshire*, temporarily attached to the Northern Patrol, reported that her wireless aerials had been carried away by the weight of ice which had formed on them. Lumps of ice as big as a man's head falling from masts, bridges and rigging made working on the upper deck dangerous. During her patrol period a north-easterly gale of Force 10 — up to 65 miles an hour — was experienced. Because of the ferocious weather conditions sights could not be taken for days on end, adding to her navigational difficulties.

Three more AMCs now joined up. They were the *Letitia* on the 14th, *Carinthia* on the 18th, and *Patroclus* on the 22nd. Now the Luftwaffe appeared to increase the hazards of daily life. Farther south Heinkel fighter-bombers operating in pairs had been regularly attacking our minesweeping trawlers in the North Sea. Towards the end of January, German aircraft began to attack Northern Patrol trawlers at Kirkwall and off the east coast of the Orkneys. Up to then these vessels did not carry Lewis guns, and had to be hastily equipped with these close-range weapons which were effective in repelling low-level attacks.

During the same period German Naval Headquarters decided that the return of German merchant ships overseas, of which 240 were known to be in neutral ports, had become 'a matter of urgency and must be expedited.' They were therefore to sail for home as soon as possible with or without cargoes. Approval was given for certain vessels abroad to be sold to Spain, Italy, Russia and Japan, and South American countries subject to conditions such as for use in local trade only. But it was urgent that those in South American ports should sail as they had the longest voyages to make.

On 9th January the 8,000-ton Hamburg-Sud Amerika steamship *Bahia Blanca* wirelessed that she had collided with an iceberg in the Denmark Strait and was slowly sinking. The Danish coastguard vessel *Aegir* left Reykjavik to go to her assistance, and picked up the crew after the ship foundered. 'A British radio report on 30th December that the *Bahia Blanca* had been taken in prize by a British cruiser,' ran an indignant note in the German Naval War Diary, 'was therefore a barefaced fabrication intended to scare German ships from returning home.'

New instructions regarding the return of German merchantmen were sent to German representatives in Buenos Aires, Montevideo and Rio de Janeiro by the Reich Ministry of Transportation. 'All ships to return home regardless whether cargoes complete or not.

Blockade zone to be traversed by end of March at latest. Moment for putting to sea to be selected so that as near as possible ships put out simultaneously.'

Unfortunately, because of the continuing paucity of our naval intelligence the British Admiralty remained unaware of these instructions. But at the beginning of February two Admiralty messages warned the Northern Patrol that U-boats were expected to operate with the object of assisting German merchant vessels to break for home. Two vessels in particular, the 3360-ton Nord-deutscher-Lloyd *Arucas* and the 2500-ton *Rostock* were said to be escorted by U-boats. On 7th February a patrolling aircraft reported a U-boat near Sule Skerry, and on the following day a Fleetwood fishing trawler reported that a U-boat was escorting a large merchantman south-west of that point on an easterly course. Steps were taken to intercept, Home Fleet destroyers being detailed to co-operate with the Northern Patrol.

The AMC *Circassia* duly intercepted the Norwegian *Solferino* in a position which suggested that she was probably the vessel referred to in the trawler report. No U-boat was sighted, however, and the *Solferino* was turned over to a destroyer which brought her in to Kirkwall for examination. But no evidence came to light that she had been working with a U-boat or had even sighted one.

Just after midnight on 10th February, and again a few hours later, the Northern Patrol trawler *Northern Isles* sighted what she took to be a U-boat in the Fair Isle Channel, and dropped a depth charge on the spot in which the latter was thought to have dived. Three separate reports of U-boat sightings by aircraft in the vicinity tended to confirm the trawler's sighting. If so, her attack had obviously failed, for next day a merchantman was torpedoed north-east of the Shetlands. Two days later the 8,000-ton Norwegian tanker *Albert E. Ellsworth* reported that she had been torpedoed a few miles to the west of the previous sinking. The crew abandoned ship, but later returned to their vessel and found that she was undamaged! It is probable, however, that the submarine, which had managed to sink four ships in this area and survived the attack of the *Northern Isles* was *U-53*. On the 23rd she was found and sunk by the Home Fleet destroyer *Gurkha*.

On 13th February the Commander-in-Chief, Home Fleet, launched 'Operation WR'. Its object was to intercept ten German merchant ships which were known to be at sea and were believed to be trying to break home through the patrols, probably with a crop of U-boats as escorts. To reinforce the Northern Patrol,

Admiral Forbes detached nine of his destroyers and the Tenth Anti-Submarine Striking Force. But although the operation continued for thirteen days only one German ship was intercepted.

In the afternoon of 21st February the destroyer *Kimberley*, in company with the cruiser *Manchester*, sighted an eastbound ship a hundred miles south-east of Iceland. Visibility was down to about a mile, a strong easterly wind was blowing and a rough sea running. At first the merchantman altered course away, but when the two British warships approached, she stopped, lowered two boats, and hoisted the signal letters of the German ship *Wahehe*, a 4,700-ton vessel belonging to the Woermann Line of Hamburg, and the signal: 'I am in a sinking condition.'

The *Manchester* fired a few rounds of pom-pom near the boats, which immediately returned to the *Wahehe*, one being emptied of men and set adrift, but the other hoisted by a derrick as the stewardess in it lacked the strength to climb the ship's side. Since the Germans had experienced a great deal of difficulty in returning on board, it was considered impracticable to send over a prize crew, and the *Kimberley* began to escort the enemy ship towards the Orkneys.

On the following afternoon the destroyer *Khartoum* joined up, when the *Kimberley* hove to and sent over a prize crew of two officers and 16 ratings to the *Wahehe*. They found no sign of any attempt to scuttle, the master explaining that although he was ready to open the sea cocks, he refrained from doing so as he was not prepared to expose his unarmed crew to the gunfire of British ships. He seemed convinced that the *Manchester*'s pom-pom fire had been intended to hit his boats. The prize crew immediately turned in all the *Wahehe*'s boats and removed the turning handles and locked them up together with all lifebelts, except one for the stewardess. But the German crew continued to work the vessel and carried out all orders satisfactorily. Their behaviour was exemplary except that, to their mortification, one fireman who had managed to get hold of some gin, staggered up to the bridge and asked the British officer in charge of the prize crew for a cigarette!

In his report of the capture of the *Wahehe*, which had sailed from Vigo on the 10th, the Vice-Admiral Commanding the 18th Cruiser Squadron, who was flying his flag in the *Manchester*, reported that 'she was distinctly unlucky in being sighted in such bad visibility. If other German merchant vessels were attempting to pass the patrol lines on that date, they stood every chance of doing so without difficulty'.

Once again it was the inclemency of the weather that dominated all else. There were ten days of bitterly cold easterly or north-easterly gales; visibility was very poor and at times down to less than half a cable (100 yards). Conditions in the Denmark Strait were even more severe. A north-easterly gale with frequent snow blizzards raged for more than three days. Although there were no German air attacks on Northern Patrol ships, the anti-submarine trawler *Fifeshire*, in company with her sister ship *Ayrshire*, was bombed and sunk east of the Orkneys. The *Ayrshire* managed to fight off her attackers.

Admiral Raikes reported that: 'It seems probable that voluntary entries [into Kirkwall] will decrease as the dangers in the vicinity of the Orkneys increase, and ships which have not obtained navicerts or clearances will be more likely to try to evade patrols.' But in spite of the bad weather, he thought that only 10 out of 71 eastbound ships were not intercepted.

It was during this period and the early part of March that a strong German effort to get some of their merchant ships home coincided with an Allied naval attempt to capture them. At the end of January the Commander-in-Chief, Western Approaches, planned a special operation to intercept six German merchant vessels which were expected to sail from Vigo. To take part in the operation the Commander-in-Chief, Home Fleet, detached the battle-cruiser *Renown*, the aircraft carrier *Ark Royal*, the cruiser *Galatea*, and several destroyers. Also taking part were a number of French warships working with Western Approaches Command, and aircraft of Coastal Command, all of which took up patrolling positions off the Iberian coast.

The Germans soon got wind of the operation, and instructed their representative in Madrid to warn the masters of the merchantmen of the watch being kept on ports and along the Spanish coast, and added that their only chance of a breakthrough was during poor visibility. *U-41* was also despatched to make hit-and-run attacks on the French warships patrolling off Vigo.

On 10th February German Naval Headquarters ordered the vessels in Vigo to break out at all costs, and six of them did so. They were the *Wahehe*, whose fate has already been recorded; the *Wangoni*, a 7,800-ton vessel also belonging to the Woermann Line; *Orizaba*, 4,350 tons, of the Hamburg-Amerika Line; *Morea*, a 2,000-tonner belonging to the Deutsches Levante Line; *Rostock*, 2,500 tons, registered in the port of the same name; and *Arucas*, 3,369 tons, of Norddeutscher Lloyd. The names of both the latter have turned up before, having been reported to be escorted by U-boats.

The *Rostock* was captured by French warships next day just outside Spanish territorial waters. On the following day the *Morea* was successfully intercepted by the British destroyer *Hasty* off the Portuguese coast. In the evening of 22nd February the *Wangoni*, which had passed through the Northern Patrol lines at about the same time as her sister ship *Wahehe*, and whose master was doubtless congratulating himself on safely reaching Norwegian waters, was intercepted by the British submarine *Triton*, patrolling off Kristiansund, in the extreme south-west of Norway. But when the submarine fired two warning shots to bring her to outside territorial waters, the gun flashes in the darkness temporarily blinded everyone in the conning tower, and the *Wangoni* made her escape in the confusion. She was the only one of this batch of blockade-runners to reach home.

The *Orizaba* also managed to get past the Northern Patrol unseen, but ran aground on the Norwegian coast fifty miles north of Tromso and eventually sank. The Norddeutscher Lloyd's *Arucas*, sixth and last of the batch, met her end under somewhat dramatic circumstances.

While on patrol in the morning of 3rd March, just south of Iceland in a gale-force wind and rapidly deteriorating visibility, the cruiser *York*, temporarily attached to the Northern Patrol, sighted a merchant vessel at a distance of eight miles, and altered course to intercept. As the cruiser closed in, the merchantman turned away with two signals flying: 'Am on fire,' and 'In danger of sinking.' At the same time she was seen to be flying the German ensign, and a boat containing about 25 men was lowered.

Passing round her stern, the *York* fired several bursts of machine-gun fire wide of the boat and across the ship's bows to discourage further attempts to abandon her. She then found that another boat with some twenty men in it had been lowered but capsized. The first boat was ordered back to the merchantman, on board which other members of her crew could be seen. The cruiser then signalled: 'Do not use the radio. Stop the leaks', and fired a round of 4-inch astern of her.

Efforts were then made to rescue the men clinging to the capsized boat. Because the wind and sea made it impossible for the *York* to lower her own boats, the cruiser had to be manoeuvred on to the capsized craft, a number of survivors being rescued at each attempt. Five were, however, washed away and lost. During these manoeuvres the first boat managed to get alongside the warship, where it was immediately stove in by the heavy seas, but its occupants were hauled to safety.

Three hours had now elapsed since the merchantman — identified as the *Arucas* — had been intercepted. She was now heard using her wireless to send out an SOS and her position. Another round of 4-inch was fired by the *York* and the signal: 'Do not use radio' repeated. But the *Arucas* again began to transmit the message, which was then jammed by the cruiser, who now transmitted a signal on the same frequency as if from the *Arucas* stating that help was no longer required.

Six men were seen on the vessel's upper deck, and signals were made to them in German warning that if the ship sank they would not be picked up, that several of their men had already been drowned, and ordering that the leaks be stopped immediately with mattresses. The Germans were then seen to go below, and presently a futile attempt was made by them to lower an object, which looked like a mattress, over the side presumably to cover the condenser inlet. Replies to questions put by signal from the *York* were unintelligible.

By 1500 a full gale was blowing. The *Arucas* had taken on a heavy list to starboard and was settling by the stern. It was evident that she would not last the night, and those on board were ordered to abandon ship. About a dozen men appeared on deck aft, and five of them plunged into the sea wearing lifebelts and clinging to lifebuoys and planks. With considerable difficulty all were picked up. The remaining seven then jumped, but only two of them could be saved because the other five had lashed themselves together. Among those lost was the master.

By 1900 the *Arucas* was on her beam ends, and the *York* then sank her by gunfire. Her crew numbered 53, of whom 43 were saved, but three of these died from the effects of their immersion. When they were buried next day, their comrades all gave the Nazi salute.

According to the ship's chief officer the *Arucas*, with a cargo of hides, ore, and sardines in oil, had been waiting off Greenland for favourable weather to slip past the Patrol. He said that the master had not intended to scuttle the ship in the prevailing weather conditions, but the chief engineer lost his head and destroyed the sea cocks. Attempts were made to stop the inrush of water, but all failed. The crew were surprised and grateful to have been rescued and then treated as human beings. Many said they expected to be shot or left to drown!

More German merchantmen from farther afield were also making for home around this time. They were the 7,414-ton *La Coruna* of the Hamburg-Sud Amerika Line, which sailed from Rio on 3rd February; the 6,200-ton *Wolfsburg* of Bremen registry, which left Pernambuco on the 4th; and the 5,846-ton Hamburg-Sud Amerika *Uruguay*, which put out from the same port on the 10th. Three more had sailed earlier from South American ports. They were the 4,100-ton Hamburg-Sud Amerika Line's *Bahia*, which left the port of that name on 5th January; the *Consul Horn*, 7,772 tons, which sailed from Aruba in the West Indies on the 9th; and the 6,000-ton *Santos*, also of the Hamburg-Sud Amerika Line, which left Rio on the 13th. All were carrying valuable cargoes of sugar, cotton, chrome ore, coffee and tobacco.

Of these six ships, HMS *Berwick*, another of the Home Fleet cruisers which were temporarily attached to the Northern Patrol from time to time, accounted for two within the space of three days. While the ship was being swung for compass correction some thirty miles off the North Cape of Iceland on Sunday, 2nd March, her lookouts sighted smoke away to the north-west. For once the weather was fair, and the sea slight with long slow swells. Visibility was good, which meant that the cruiser had probably been seen at the same time as she spotted the newcomer.

As she closed at high speed, flying the flag signals: 'Do not use your radio,' and 'Do not lower boats,' the merchantman was seen to be a 6,000-ton vessel steering north-west as fast as she could go. The name *Aust* with 'Norwegian' and two Norwegian flags were painted on her sides. After a brief chase she stopped and began lowering boats. A round of 4-inch and bursts of pom-pom fired across her bows had no effect, and at the same time the ship began sending an SOS, using her normal call sign. When this was identified as that of the German *Wolfsburg* her signals were jammed. But the SOS had been picked up by the German Consul in Reykjavik.

Smoke was now issuing from the vessel's holds and she was down by the stem. By the time the *Berwick* had closed and lowered a cutter, all the *Wolfsburg's* boats were clear of the ship and fully manned. Ice was now sighted ahead, and it became evident that the German vessel had actually been steaming along only a few hundred yards from the ice pack which covered the Denmark Strait to within sixty miles of the coast of Iceland.

The officer in charge of the cruiser's boarding party now signalled that the *Wolfsburg's* engine and boiler rooms were flooded, and that the forward and after holds were burning furiously. All books and papers had been destroyed. The party was accordingly taken off and the vessel sunk by gunfire. The *Wolfsburg's* boats were brought alongside, the Germans taken on board and their boats hoisted.

From the prisoners it was learned that on her homeward voyage the *Wolfsburg* had steered direct to Cape Farewell, then skirted the ice through the Denmark Strait, but had been badly damaged below the waterline by contact with the floes. Most German ships, they said, were advised to make use of the Denmark Strait when trying to get home. They were able to hide in the ice pack by day and creep along its edge at night. Only the fastest ships were to attempt the passage south of Iceland. The *Wolfsburg* was the first enemy merchantman known to have steered direct for Cape Farewell and then skirted the ice through the Denmark Strait. But up to then, the instructions given them by the German Naval Staff to do this were of course unknown to the Northern Patrol.

Three days later, in the evening of 5th March, while patrolling to the north-east of the Denmark Strait, the *Berwick* intercepted a signal from the Hull fishing trawler *St Wistan* addressed to: 'Any British man of war. American cargo vessel sighted 66 degrees 30 minutes north, 23 degrees 30 minutes west bound for the north of Iceland.'

The cruiser immediately altered course and increased to full speed with the intention of trying to intercept the vessel before it became dark, but the latter's position could only be estimated. Visibility remained clear to the west, but deteriorating to the south-east with snow starting to fall. By 2200 nothing had been sighted, and course was altered so as to be east of the merchant vessel by dawn.

Sunrise brought fine and clear weather. Course was reversed, and the *Berwick's* aircraft catapulted to search to the north while the cruiser covered the area to the south. At 1000 the aircraft sighted and reported an American merchant ship steering north, with the name *Argosy*, Philadelphia, on the stern. There was no ship of that name in Lloyd's List, and Captain Palmer of the *Berwick* suspected that she was in fact the German *Uruguay*.

The aircraft was recalled and hoisted in, although this meant temporarily losing touch with the *Uruguay*. Her last reported position was then closed at high speed, and the aircraft made ready to fly off again to find and shadow the vessel. But now a snowstorm blotted out everything, and the air search had to be called off. The *Berwick*, however, continued to quarter the area, and at 1615 sighted her quarry.

As soon as the oncoming cruiser was spotted, the vessel, identified by the aircraft pilot as the one he had reported earlier, stopped and began lowering her boats. Painted on her sides in white letters were the words: 'MacCormack Lines' and two American flags. She now started to send an SOS using the call sign of the *Uruguay*. This was jammed by the *Berwick*'s operators, but not entirely successfully, the message being picked up and retransmitted by Reykjavik wireless station. When the latter asked for further information, the *Berwick* transmitted a signal using the *Uruguay*'s call sign stating: 'No further assistance required.' Admiral Raikes thought this a good idea, which could be generally adopted throughout the Patrol in similar circumstances.

The German ship had already begun to settle, and flames and smoke were pouring from her holds. Bursts of Lewis gun fire over her and near her boats were ignored, and the *Berwick* had to turn and make a lee in order to lower her own boarding boat. By the time it reached the *Uruguay*, three of the latter's boats had got clear, and the fourth was just shoving off. When the boarding party left the sinking ship, bringing the master with them, the engine room was flooded, and fore hold and superstructure well ablaze; thus salvage was out of the question. 14 German officers and 40 crew members were taken on board the cruiser, and the *Uruguay* finished off with gunfire.

Since leaving Pernambuco the merchantman had made no landfall until she reached the north-west corner of Iceland, thus following a different policy from that of the *Wolfsburg*. It was apparent that the crews of both vessels had been well drilled in abandon ship procedure once a firm decision had been taken to scuttle.

The *Uruguay*'s carpenter was shown by his papers to be a Gestapo agent, and the majority of her crew were ardent Nazis. All her officers were convinced that the war would be won by Germany by the autumn, and spoke of their 'marvellous secret weapon.' When the *Berwick*'s bulldog showed a marked interest in the dachsund bitch the Germans had brought with them from their ship, she turned on him and he was compelled to beat a hasty and undignified retreat!

The skipper and crew of the trawler *St Wistan* duly received a financial reward for their original report which led to the inter-

An AMC's concert party

ception of the *Uruguay*. To their discerning eyes the vessel had looked more German than American, and it seemed that the name and colours had been newly painted on her sides and were high out of the water, clear indication that they had been painted at sea.

Three of the enemy merchantmen which had sailed from South America, however, managed to elude the Patrol and arrived safely at Narvik before making the rest of their way home in Norwegian territorial waters. But two had narrowly escaped capture. Disguised as a Russian ship, the *Consul Horn* was stopped by the cruiser *Enterprise* in mid-Atlantic on 27th January, and ordered to make for Kirkwall as the weather was too bad to allow her to put a prize crew on board. The other was the *Santos*, which was disguised as the Norwegian *Rygja* bound from Capetown to New York. Off the Cape Verde Islands she was stopped and interrogated by the French AMC *Charles Plumier*. After failing to penetrate her disguise and giving her permission to proceed, the Frenchman circled round her and ordered her to dip her ensign to the Tricolour! Yet so certain was the master of the *Santos* of being bowled out that he had her boats already prepared for lowering.

The *Bahia* also made it safely to Narvik, but the *La Coruna* fell victim to the AMC *Maloja*, which had just joined the Patrol. At 1000 in the morning of 12th March, when south of Iceland, the latter sighted a large merchant vessel emerging from a snowstorm.

The newcomer was flying Japanese colours and gave her name as the *Taki Maru* of Kobe. Captain Dane of the *Maloja* considered, however, that she was German, but as the weather was too bad for boarding, ordered her to steer for the trawler rendezvous off the Faeroes.

Later on, when the weather had moderated somewhat, he ordered her to heave to, and prepared to send a boarding boat over. Almost immediately the crew of the merchantman were seen to be falling in abreast their lifeboats, and at the same time she began to use her wireless. A shot was fired across her bows, but she continued to man and lower her boats. As these touched the water there were a series of explosions at each of her main hatches, smoke gushed from the ventilators, and she began to settle. By the time the *Maloja's* boat got alongside her upper deck rails were already under water. She was hastened on her way to the bottom with several rounds of 6-inch.

Eighteen officers and 50 crewmen were taken on board the AMC, and it was then ascertained that she was the *La Coruna*. From the diary of her chief officer, who appeared to be a Gestapo agent, the *La Coruna* had already passed through the Denmark Strait and reached 67 degrees north latitude when she ran into so much ice that she was forced to turn back. Retracing her route down the Strait, she turned for home south of Iceland.

Commenting on the fact that the four German merchantmen intercepted by the Northern Patrol scuttled themselves successfully, Admiral Raikes, as had his predecessor, emphasised the difficulty of preventing this if masters were sufficiently resolute and their plans well laid. On three occasions the enemy vessels had ample warning; on the fourth, since the weather was bad, there would have been plenty of time to perfect arrangements, although in fact that ship (the *Arucus*) was apparently scuttled by accident. He now asked that all ships of the Northern Patrol should be provided with photographs and descriptions of all German ships which might attempt to return home.

Despite hardships and disappointments, he added, the spirit of the crews of the AMCs remained high. One captain had written:

> The morale of officers and men continues to be excellent. Although about seventy-five per cent of them have never been to sea before, they are now working exactly as a seasoned ship's company should work, and are very keen for an engagement with the enemy or the taking of a prize so as to show their worth to the Navy and the country.

CHAPTER ELEVEN

Some Got Through

Despite the increased number of AMCs on station on the Northern Patrol during February, and their reinforcement by cruisers of the Home Fleet, the continuing bad weather enabled one specially sought-after enemy vessel to give them the slip.

Ever since the destruction of the German pocket battleship *Graf Spee* in December 1939 following the River Plate battle, the oceans had been searched for her principal supply ship, the 12,000-ton tanker *Altmark*. Information had reached the Admiralty to the effect that the latter was carrying on board confined as prisoners the crews of the British merchant ships sunk by the *Graf Spee* during her successful foray.

For nearly two months the *Altmark* skulked in the lonely wastes of the South Atlantic while her master, Captain Heinrich Dau, waited for the hue and cry to die down. At last, on 22nd January, the tanker began to head for home. Unsighted by any Allied warship or aircraft during her long voyage northwards, the *Altmark* sailed steadily on, the captured British sailors languishing in wretched conditions below decks, since she had not been fitted with any special accommodation for prisoners of war.

Then, taking advantage of the severe weather conditions prevailing, Dau took her undetected between Iceland and the Faeroe Islands and headed across the North Sea. On 14th February he broke radio silence to report to German Naval Headquarters that he was about to enter Norwegian territorial waters off Kristiansand (North). In the evening of 15th Admiral Forbes received information that she had passed Bergen.

On the same day that the *Altmark* arrived in Norwegian waters, a small force of British warships, consisting of the cruiser *Arethusa* and five destroyers, the latter commanded by Captain Philip Vian in the *Cossack*, left Rosyth with orders to sweep up the Norwegian coast from the entrance to the Skagerrak to Narvik with the object of intercepting enemy merchantmen. At the suggestion of Winston Churchill, the First Sea Lord now told Forbes that the principal object of the searching force was to 'arrest the *Altmark* in territorial waters should she be found'. The order was duly passed on to Vian together with two reports of *Altmark* sightings by aircraft of Coastal Command.

But because the latter differed as to the exact position of the tanker, Vian split his force into two. An hour later, however, she was sighted off Egero Light escorted by two Norwegian destroyers. She refused to stop when challenged by two of Vian's destroyers, and their attempts to board her were frustrated by the Norwegians. She then entered Jossing Fjord and anchored.

When he arrived on the scene Vian took the *Cossack* into the fjord and demanded of the senior Norwegian officer that British prisoners on board the *Altmark* should be handed over to him. In reply he was told that the German ship had already been examined at Bergen, that she was unarmed, and that she had permission to use territorial waters. Vian reported the situation to the Admiralty, and now Churchill intervened directly. Vian was ordered to offer to escort the *Altmark*, along with the Norwegian warships, back to Bergen; otherwise he was to board.

At ten o' clock that night Vian re-entered the fjord and informed the senior Norwegian officer of his orders. The Norwegians, however, refused to co-operate, and the *Cossack* was then laid alongside the tanker, which had got under way and in attempting to ram the *Cossack* had gone aground. After a short, sharp fight, during which four Germans were killed and five wounded, the prisoners were liberated to the heartening cry of 'the Navy's here!' Far from being unarmed, the *Altmark* was found to be equipped with two pom-poms and four machine-guns. In all, 299 British merchant sailors were released and brought back to this country. The fact that the *Altmark* had been able to sail undetected through the 240-mile passage between Iceland and the Faeroes gives some idea of the needle-in-a-haystack situation faced by the Northern Patrol in bad weather.

Renamed *Uckermark*, the *Altmark* met her fate at the end of December, 1942 when she blew up and sank at Yokohama.

Throughout the first fortnight of March the weather continued foul, with gales and snowstorms prevailing. Relentless battering by heavy seas frequently fractured the degaussing coils fitted around the hulls of the AMCs so that they crackled and sparked like a 5th of November firework display. Devised as a form of protection against magnetic mines, the degaussing coil was a girdle of heavy electric cable wound completely round the outboard part of a ship's sides. When the current was switched on, the girdle reduced the intensity of the vessel's own magnetic field.

There were two U-boat encounters at this time. On 2nd March, at 0130 in the middle watch, some eighty miles west of the Orkneys, a U-boat suddenly appeared on the surface and opened fire on the Norwegian steamship *Belpamela*, which was being taken to Kirkwall in charge of an armed guard from the AMC *Scotstoun*. The Norwegian crew immediately panicked and started to abandon ship. In their haste to get away, one boat was prematurely lowered and lost. The armed guard, who were the last to leave, were therefore left with no boat, but managed to find a raft on which they got away.

While this was going on, the U-boat went off to intercept the Swedish steamer *Lagaholm* which had appeared. After giving the Swedes half an hour to abandon their vessel, the U-boat then opened fire on their ship. Some 35 rounds set her ablaze and she was soon burning furiously, watched apprehensively by the crew of the *Belpamela*. But for some unknown reason the U-boat did not return to finish off her first victim, and when daylight came the Norwegians went back on board.

That afternoon they picked up the armed guard from their raft, and also one of the boats from the *Lagaholm*. But the survivors in the second boat, which included her master and twelve crewmen, said that they preferred to sail to safety, although the nearest land was some eighty miles away. They duly arrived at North Ronaldshay, in the Orkneys, in the afternoon of the following day. The *Belpamela* also arrived without further incident at Kirkwall, the armed guard, however, suffering somewhat from exposure.

In the early evening of 8th March, while on duty between the Orkneys and Shetlands, the bridge staff of the Northern Patrol trawler *Northern Reward* suddenly saw to their surprise a U-boat on an opposite course barely twenty to thirty feet away. Although a strong wind was blowing, with moderate visibility, they could see some four feet of the submarine's periscope, and in the troughs of the waves, the clear outline of her conning tower. The officer of the watch immediately sounded the alarm, yanked the engine room telegraphs over to full speed, and sped aft to let go a depth charge. But by the time this exploded the distance between submarine and trawler was about 250 feet and rapidly increasing. The trawler was quickly brought about and three more depth charges let go, but by then the startled U-boat was safely out of range.

In his report for the period Admiral Raikes drew attention to the fact that although very little traffic normally passed between the Faeroes and the Orkneys, more than half the number of ships sent in were now doing so. The inference was therefore that the chance of evading patrols had become so small that if ships' cargoes were not fully covered, their masters considered it better to pass reasonably close to the Orkneys to avoid having to make long diversions if caught. Nevertheless, he thought it probable that a higher percentage of ships were getting through the patrols between the Faeroes and the Orkneys than through the AMC and cruiser lines, because of the greater navigational difficulties experienced by the trawlers. After a prolonged period of bad weather the latter got off their lines, and thus gaps were left. Yet it was known that only eight eastbound ships had passed without being intercepted.

At about this time a sudden flash of resentment was shown by the hitherto seemingly compliant Norwegians against the continuing pressure of Nazi Germany on neutral nations to cease trading with Britain. In the *Storting* the Norwegian Foreign Minister declared that it would be an un-neutral act to stop Norwegian shipping sailing to Britain. 'Even if the British authorities force Norwegian shipping to put in to a control port,' he added defiantly, 'this still would not justify the Germans sinking Norwegian ships.' The maintenance of trade with Britain was of vital importance for Norway.

A few days later came another straw in the wind, when the Danish steamer *Venus* was intercepted and a British armed guard put on board to take her to Kirkwall. The master refused to proceed without an escort — which could not in the event be provided as there were at that time no trawlers available. But the attitude of her master appeared to reflect a change of heart, because Danish ships had previously declined the protection of Allied convoys.

In fact, like the Norwegians, the Danes were averse to co-operating with the Northern Patrol in order to preserve their neutrality. A recent article in a Danish periodical had pointed out the possibility of evading British controls by sailing well to the north. The costly loss of time involved in the detour was considered to be more or less equal to the disadvantage of the non-neutral procedure of voluntarily putting in to control ports. There was also the added danger of mines off British coasts.

That something sinister was brewing was hinted at by a note in the German Naval War Diary that the Naval Staff were now occupied with preparations for *Weserubung* (or Weser Exercise). What this portended was soon to be made known to the world.

Meanwhile on 7th March the Reich Ministry of Transportation

instructed the German Embassy in Madrid and the German Consul at Las Palmas to 'send home no more ships which are ready to sail. Return home probably not until fall. Order about perishable cargo follows.' This message followed advice received from the Naval Staff that they did not consider it advisable under present circumstances to have German merchantmen sail from ports overseas.

After bleakly recording the capture and/or scuttling of the *Wolfsburg, Arucas, Uruguay* and *La Coruna*, the Transporation Ministry informed the Naval Staff of the disposition as at that date of German merchantmen. Thus in home waters were 579 vessels of over 1,600 tons, or sixty-eight per cent of the total merchant fleet; in neutral ports were 219 ships, or twenty-five point eight per cent; two were at sea homeward bound. 114 had returned to date, and 49 had been lost.

There were reports in the Spanish press, it noted, of increasing refusals by the crews of neutral ships to sail to Britain, despite the very high wages offered. Many ports in Spain, Portugal and other countries were said to be filled with sailors on strike. (Indirectly, however, the Germans themselves assisted the Northern Patrol by discouraging neutrals from carrying anything but a fully certified cargo lest they should be brought into the dangerous area around the Orkneys.)

The latter half of March was marked by a recrudescence of enemy air and U-boat activity. The Northern Patrol was not directly affected by the former, except that the cruiser *Norfolk*, intended to reinforce the AMCs, was damaged by a bomb just as she was about to leave Scapa to join the Patrol.

Earlier on, the Home Fleet had begun to return to its main base, whose sea and air defences had been considerably strengthened. But the latter were first tested by sending in two dummy battleships on 1st March to be moored in the main fleet anchorage. The *Hood* and *Valiant* arrived on the 7th, and two days later the Commander-in-Chief himself in the *Rodney* with the battle cruisers *Repulse* and *Renown*. The First Lord also arrived to make a personal inspection of the newly completed defences. Soon after he left for London, however, 15 German bombers raided the base, during which the *Norfolk* was hit. Sensitive to the air threat, the Admiralty told Forbes to take the Fleet to sea for the next seven days while the moon was high.

The U-boat threat affected the Patrol more directly. In the morning of 20th March, the armed boarding vessel *Discovery II*, while on patrol north of the Orkneys, sighted a ship, and on closing found her to be the 3,200-ton Danish steamer *Christiansborg*, which had the whole of her forepart from the bridge forward blown away. In the vicinity were two lifeboats which contained all her crew except one seaman believed to have been killed by the explosion. The vessel had sailed from Kirkwall on the previous day, and when off Sumburgh Head she was torpedoed without any warning by a U-boat, which was afterwards seen on the surface. The *Discovery II* sent over a boarding party to examine the crippled ship, but as her engine and boiler rooms were flooded it was decided that salvage was impossible, and she was sunk by gunfire.

In the forenoon of the 23rd, a few miles from the spot where the *Christiansborg* had been attacked, the trawler *Northern Reward* sighted a surfaced U-boat about three miles distant. The trawler at once increased to full speed and went in pursuit. The chase continued for about twenty-five minutes, but on the surface the U-boat could outpace her pursuer, and finally disappeared into a rain squall, hastened on her way by a couple of rounds from the trawler's foremost gun. Unfortunately no hits were observed, and because she was not fitted with asdic the *Northern Reward* had no chance of regaining contact.

Three days later a sister ship, the *Northern Sky*, on patrol came across three lifeboats full of survivors from the 3,700-ton Norwegian motor vessel *Cometa*. The latter had been intercepted on the 25th by the Northern Patrol trawler *Kingston Peridot*, which had put an armed guard of one officer and four ratings on board to take her in to Kirkwall. Shortly before midnight the *Cometa* had been stopped by a U-boat, which first opened fire on her and then sank her by torpedo after crew and passengers had abandoned ship. Among the latter were three women, a child and a baby in arms.

On the night of 28th March the *Kingston Beryl*, another of the Patrol's trawlers, was on station off Westray Firth, at the northwest corner of the Orkneys, when her lookouts spotted a faint glimmer of light lasting for only a matter of seconds. Two minutes later, as the trawler was moving towards the spot to investigate, the light appeared again. Then it vanished, but all on deck heard a sound resembling a muffled foghorn. Two depth charges were dropped on the approximate position where the lights had been seen, and the trawler continued to circle the area for twenty-four hours, but nothing further was seen or heard. A U-boat had probably been in the vicinity charging her batteries, but it was considered unlikely that she had sustained any damage from the

The North German Lloyd liner *Bremen*

The ships of Force 'W' at anchor in Scapa Flow

trawler's depth charges.

In the morning of 29th March the AMC *Transylvania*, patrolling in the Denmark Strait, sighted a ship some fifteen miles away and closed at full speed. But when she came up with the merchantman the latter was seen to be stopped and on fire with her boats already in the water. As the vessel was soon completely enveloped in flames, Captain Miles of the *Transylvania* decided that it was useless to send over a boarding party or order the boats in the water to return to their ship. Accordingly the 41 German crewmen were picked up, when it was learned that their ship was the 4,000-ton motor vessel *Mimi Horn* of Hamburg. The Germans said that careful preparations had been made for scuttling and setting fire to their vessel if they should be stopped by a British warship. The AMC sent her to the bottom with 20 rounds of high explosive shells fired at short range.

The Germans did not learn of the fate of the *Mimi Horn* until the British announced on 2nd April that she had been stopped in northern waters and that she had been scuttled and set on fire by her own crew. She had therefore failed to get off the usual signal to German Naval Headquarters. The *Mimi Horn* had left Curacao for home on 4th March.

Nine AMCs out of the total of 22 available to the Northern Patrol at this time were out of action for various reasons. The *Asturias* and *Montclare* were in dockyard hands in Belfast for refit and completion of equipment. On the 21st the *Cilicia* arrived there for repairs. A few hours earlier, while on passage from the Clyde to resume patrol, she had collided in thick weather between the North Channel and the Minches with the *Carinthia*, which was inward bound from patrol to the Clyde. Although both ships made harbour safely, the *Cilicia* had sustained serious damage, some thirty feet of her side plating being torn away.

In the Clyde for the repair of grounding damage was the *Canton*; the *Circassia* was also in dockyard hands there for rectification of engine defects, and the *Forfar* to load buoyant ballast. The *Chitral* was at Liverpool for refit and completion of equipment, and it was to that port that the *Carinthia* now put in for the repair of her collision damage. The normal routine for the AMCs on completion of a spell on patrol was three days in harbour for ships of short and medium endurance, and four days for those with long endurance. When in the Clyde they usually anchored at Tail o' the Bank, and more than once in bad weather had grounded through dragging anchor.

The shortage of ships during this period made it necessary to increase the distance apart of the AMCs and cruisers on the main patrol lines from the usual 20 miles to 25 miles. 138 merchantmen were sighted, but only 13 had to be sent in. Eighty per cent of eastbound traffic was intercepted, above the average for the first seven months of the war. 17 were believed to have got through the patrols without being sighted, but a certain number were always expected to get through during bad weather — and the latter had shown no sign of improvement, gales and blizzards predominating for the greater part of the time. Besides this, the denser the traffic the more ships could slip through the gaps left while the patrolling warships were boarding.

One important prize which successfully eluded the Patrol around this time was the 13,589-ton *Antonio Delfino*, one of the crack ships of the Hamburg-Sud Amerika Line. She left Bahia on 21st February, crossed the Atlantic unsighted, and put into Trondheim on 23rd March. There, however, one of our agents started a rumour that British forces had been sent out against her. The German Naval Staff speedily reacted and radioed a message to her in code to remain in Haugesund or return there, and await further orders. The same message was also sent to the German Embassy in Oslo, the Consul at Haugesund, and the Vice-Consul at Kristiansund (North) and Naval Group West. The Ministry of Transportation was similarly advised with the added footnote: 'Other Norwegian traffic to carry on.'

Then, around midnight on the 24th, apparently fearing a repetition of the *Altmark* incident, the Naval Staff ordered the *Antonio Delfino* to be moved round to Kopervik, in a nearby fjord. From there she was cautiously taken down the coast 'helped by the Norwegian Government', and finally ended up at Gothenburg, in Sweden.

CHAPTER TWELVE

Operation *Weserubung*

On 3rd April the Admiralty informed the Vice-Admiral, Northern Patrol that a War Trade Agreement[1] had been signed with Denmark. Following those already signed with Sweden and Norway, a most important stage in the economic offensive against Germany had therefore been completed. It was due to the untiring efforts of the Northern Patrol that the Allies owed the successful conclusion of negotiations, and the message ended with the thanks of their Lordships to all concerned.

Unhappily any benefit was to prove of short duration.

Before going on to the next phase of the war, which was to bring to an end the normal work of the Patrol, mention must be made of another example of the impossibility of maintaining an impenetrable blockade by sea against a determined enemy.

It was earlier stated that as part of his war strategy Admiral Raeder intended to convert a large number of merchantmen into armed surface raiders. In the event, however, fewer than a dozen were sent out. The first of these, named *Atlantis* but designated for reasons of communications security as 'Ship 16', was ready by 11th March and, having sailed from Kiel, spent the rest of the month training and exercising in the Baltic.

The former 7,860-ton freighter *Goldenfels* of the Hansa Line, built in 1937, diesel-engined and with a top speed of 18 knots, she was armed with six 5.9-inch guns concealed behind collapsible steel ports and a number of smaller weapons, four torpedo tubes, carried mines and a reconnaissance seaplane. She was also equipped with searchlights, rangefinders, and smoke generators. She would therefore have made a formidable adversary to be tackled by one of the Northern Patrol AMCs.

On 31st March, disguised as a Russian ship bound for Murmansk, she left home waters and steamed northwards through the Norwegian Inner Leads, escorted for part of the way by a U-boat. Having reached the latitude of the Lofoten Islands she turned west, then headed down the Denmark Strait into the North Atlantic without sighting or being sighted by any patrolling vessel.

[1] See Chapter 7

The *Atlantis* remained at large for over nineteen months, sank or captured twenty-two merchant ships, and was herself finally sunk in the South Atlantic by the British cruiser *Devonshire* in November 1941.

Very early in the war Winston Churchill put forward the proposal that Britain should lay mines in the Norwegian Leads — the 'covered way' for the enemy, as he phrased it — to interrupt the transport of Swedish iron ore from Narvik to Germany. The British Government was also well aware that enemy merchantmen returning from overseas which had managed to slip through the Northern Patrol cordon were using the 'covered way' to complete their homeward voyages in safety. Political considerations, however, prevented the suggestion from being adopted.

Churchill continued to advocate this measure, and eventually his persistence bore fruit, for early in April 1940 the Cabinet approved the plan. Dubbed by its originator 'Operation Wilfred' after the cartoon character of a rabbit named Wilfred in the *Daily Mirror* because it was 'so small and innocent', minelaying destroyers screened by Home Fleet warships laid a minefield in the early morning of 8th April off the entrance to Vestfjord, the channel to the port of Narvik. In case this action might provoke a German retort, it had been agreed that British and French forces should be despatched to deny certain Norwegian ports to the enemy.

Hitler, however, to whom Admiral Raeder had urged the seizure of Norway as early as October 1939, now authorised the activation of Operation *Weserubung*, which had been planned in January. As recorded in the German Naval War Diary: 'Thus commences an operation ranking as one of the boldest in the history of modern warfare.' For on 9th April the Germans invaded Norway and proceeded to occupy Denmark.

While the Home Fleet was fully engaged to the east in coping with these startling events, the immediate object of the Northern Patrol became the interception of all Norwegian and Danish[1] ships to prevent them from falling into enemy hands and to be diverted to our use. Patrols continued normally during the first week of April. Then on the 7th came reports of the movements of heavy German naval units in the North Sea. That evening all AMCs on the patrol lines south of Iceland were ordered to steer to the south-west at their best speeds, the two AMCs patrolling in the

[1] Owing to the German control of Denmark all Danish ships became technically enemy ships, and were to be seized in prize if met, but their officers and crews were not to be treated as enemies.

Denmark Strait also to move to the south-west at top speed, keeping clear of ice and land. Next day the first group of AMCs were ordered to proceed to the Clyde, while the two in the Denmark Strait were instructed to remain west of longitude 32 degrees west, and south of latitude 63 degrees north in order to be clear of any enemy force which might try to attack ships in the normal patrol area.

Then followed a period of confusion, caused by the fact that the German battle cruisers *Scharnhorst* and *Gneisenau* were known to be at sea in support of the enemy landings in Norway. Thus, early on 9th April, the Admiralty ordered the reinstatement of the Northern Patrol, only to cancel this a few hours later, but ordered the two Denmark Strait AMCs to be sent back to patrol south-west of Iceland.

Next day the Admiralty suggested to Admiral Raikes that the Patrol should be re-established well clear of its normal area. The latter, however, proposed instead that as eastbound traffic usually approached the line between the Faeroes and Iceland along the Great Circle track from Cape Race, or headed northward west of longitude 20 degrees west before turning to the north-east in about 60 degrees north latitude, AMC patrols should be established and centred around a position approximately at the entrance to this bottleneck, one patrol line to run north and south across the Great Circle track, and the other east and west to intercept north-bound traffic.

This was approved, but on the 12th before the AMCs had time to reach these positions, the Admiralty ordered the normal Patrol to be re-established since both enemy battle cruisers were reported to be back in Germany. The patrol lines were, however, to keep well to the west. During the whole of this period of uncertainty the trawlers of the Northern Patrol remained on station and were unaffected.

As a result of the new developments a further task was added to the work-load of the Patrol. Control of outward-bound transit mails was now to be enforced, and all westbound ships carrying mails were ordered to be brought in, unless the mails could be removed at sea. Mails carried in westbound American ships, were, however, only to be removed at sea, thus keeping them clear of the Presidential banned zone.

The weather as usual continued at its winter worst, with gales on seven out of fourteen days and poor visibility. There were few reports of U-boats in the area, due largely to the enemy's operations

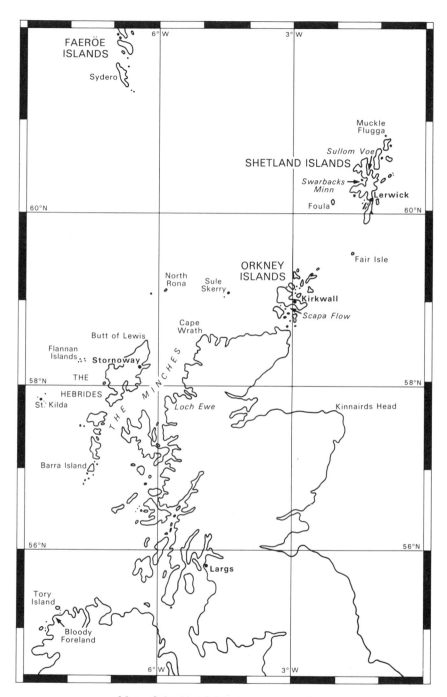

FAERÖE
ISLANDS

Sydero

6° W

3° W

Muckle
Flugga

Sullom Voe

SHETLAND ISLANDS

*Swarbacks
Minn* →

Lerwick

60°N   Foula

60°N

Fair Isle

ORKNEY
ISLANDS

North
Rona

Sule
Skerry

Kirkwall

Scapa Flow

Cape
Wrath

Butt of Lewis

Flannan
Islands

Stornoway

58°N   THE

58°N

HEBRIDES

St. Kilda

Loch Ewe

Kinnairds Head

Barra Island

56°N

56°N

Largs

Tory
Island

Bloody
Foreland

6° W

3° W

Map of the North-Western Approaches

in Norway. But during the night of 9th April two eastbound neutrals were torpedoed just south of the Faeroes. They were the 5,100-ton Norwegian *Tosca*, and the 9,000-ton Swedish tanker *Sveaborg,* the former sinking at once and the latter after having been on fire for several hours. Northern Patrol trawlers picked up a number of survivors from both. The attacks were of special interest, first because a U-boat had not previously been reported in such a high latitude in the Northern Patrol area; and secondly that both vessels were sunk after they had passed through the patrols and after Norway and Denmark had been invaded.

Off Cape Wrath the 7,000-ton British tanker *Scottish American* was torpedoed, and the Northern Patrol trawler *Northern Reward* was sent to her assistance. But the small Q-ship *Looe* had reached the scene first, and after initially inviting attack by the possibly lurking U-boat, took the vessel in tow. The *Looe* was one of three such trap ships fitted out to operate in home waters — there were six larger vessels cruising the broad oceans. The particular function of the *Looe* and her two sisters was to loiter about in the Northern Approaches offering themselves as bait to prowling U-boats whom they hoped to lure to the surface, then attack with their concealed guns. Like the larger vessels, they met with no success whatever. Between them Q-ship and trawler hauled the crippled tanker into Loch Eriboll, and thus saved some 9,000 tons of valuable oil fuel.

Around noon on 28th April, a few miles west of the Shetlands in calm weather and fair visibility, the Northern Patrol trawler *Northern Isles* spotted a periscope some 250 yards away. She promptly dropped two depth charges over the spot, and after the second of these had exploded there came another, very violent, explosion which threw up a huge column of blackish-grey water. The *Northern Isles* quickly moved in and dropped her last two depth charges into the swirling maelstrom, which clearly showed traces of oil, but nothing further resulted. Failing any other explanation of the double explosion, Admiral Raikes considered that the U-boat had been destroyed. Unhappily, none was recorded as having been lost in that area at that time.

Fifty-four merchantmen were sighted during the first fourteen days of the patrol period. One enemy ship which managed to pass north of Iceland unsighted was the 7,600-ton Hamburg-Amerikan motor vessel *Seattle*, which had left Curacao for Germany on 5th March with a valuable cargo. Although she arrived safely at Tromso on 1st April, and was cautiously moved down the Norwegian coast to Kristiansund, she was finally sunk in that port with her cargo by

Luftwaffe bombs!

Another vessel which was on the move at that time and was lucky to escape being caught out by our minelaying force around Narvik, was the second of the German armed merchant raiders. Designated 'Ship 36', she was the 7,000-ton *Orion*, formerly the Hamburg-Amerikan Line's *Kurmark*. Armed in similar fashion to the *Atlantis*, she, too, carried mines and a seaplane. Disguised as the Dutch *Beemsterdijk*, she sailed from Kiel on 6th April without the customary escorting U-boat, and headed northwards along the Norwegian coast. Four days later she intercepted a message which indicated that the real *Beemsterdijk* was in fact in the West Indies. Accordingly Commander Weyher, her captain, altered her disguise to the Russian *Soviet* (a name not, incidentally to be found in Lloyd's Register).

Having been missed by our naval forces farther north she, too, made her way through the Denmark Strait without difficulty since our AMCs had then been temporarily withdrawn from that area, and headed southwards towards the Equator and her designated operational area in the Indian Ocean. Her engines, however, proved to be unsatisfactory, and although she continued her raiding activities until August of the following year — when she reached home safely — her toll of sunk or captured Allied shipping was less than half that of the *Atlantis*.

Ironically enough, it was soon after the *Orion* had sailed that the possibility that enemy raiders might try to break out occurred to Admiral Raikes, although he considered that the time of year was not favourable for this. Since, however, it was to Germany's advantage to bring about as wide a dispersal of our forces as possible, he thought it likely that attempts would be made, the vessels probably being disguised as British, Norwegian and Danish merchantmen. One of the main objects of the Patrol must therefore be the interception of enemy raiders, and he accordingly ordered the AMCs to steam eastward during the day and retire to the west by night, thus reversing the direction of the patrol lines which had been in force since the outbreak of war. Equally important, of course, was the interception of any eastbound Norwegian or Danish ships trying to return home. The results, however, showed a complete stoppage of all traffic to and from Scandinavian ports.

A thoroughly bad winter ended with a spell which several of the AMC captains reported as having been as unpleasant as any former-ly experienced, with north to north-easterly gales persisting for the greater part of the time. During the middle watch on 15th April

Kirkwall itself was struck by the fiercest north-westerly blow of the whole winter. Several trawlers, including Northern Patrol vessels, dragged their anchors and were driven ashore. The worst incident was the sinking at her mooring of the commercial salvage vessel *Disperser* with the loss of all hands. Prior to her arrival at Kirkwall the *Disperser* had been working on the wreck of the former Grand Fleet cruiser *Natal,* which blew up in Cromarty Firth on 30th December 1915.

Except for the weather, however, no special events were recorded by ships of the Patrol. In fact, reported Raikes, there was so little shipping that the AMCs on station complained of boredom. Yet a few hundred miles to the east Home Fleet ships were undergoing a very bad time in support of our expeditionary force in Norway, chiefly because of heavy and continual bombardment from the air.

On the enemy side, as soon as the invasion of Norway was launched, German representatives abroad were ordered by the Naval Staff to warn all German merchantmen immediately of the danger that Allied warships might attack them in neutral ports, that they were to be prepared to destroy themselves, and to be ready to sail on call.

On 13th April an obviously German-inspired broadcast from Oslo radio appealed to all Norwegian ships to make for neutral ports, and on no account to put in to French or British ports. (The Reich Ministry of Transportation noted pessimistically, however, that it was expected that most of the Norwegian tonnage and the greater part of the Danish would join the Allies!)

Next day the Norwegian Association of Shipowners issued a message addressed to all ships under the Norwegian flag, calling on them to put in to the nearest neutral port immediately and to remain there until receipt of further instructions, or to make for a Norwegian port if this was nearer. All ships proceeding to Norway, or were in other north European waters, were instructed to procure the best possible information about new mine barrages for themselves.

But the legitimate Norwegian Government asked the British Government to broadcast a warning to all Norwegian ships that telegrams received from Norway signed by shipowners were transmitted by the Germans. The only authentic orders were those from a Norwegian Embassy or statements by the BBC. The captains of all Norwegian ships were instructed to get in touch with the nearest French or British naval authority, and to avoid putting in to neutral ports except in cases of authentic request.

Norwegian ships abroad, noted German Naval Headquarters, were reported to have painted over their neutral markings and were no longer recognisable as Norwegian. Seven U-boats were now ordered to take up positions around the Shetlands.

It seemed that the boredom complained of in ships of the Northern Patrol would not be of long duration.

Throughout the ill-fated Allied campaign in Norway, the Patrol continued to maintain its unsleeping vigil over almost empty seas. Normal traffic had virtually ceased and apart from fishing vessels and small coasters, only nine merchantmen were intercepted. Of these, two were Danish, two Faeroese, two Finnish, one Icelandic, one Yugoslav and one Russian. All were bound to or from a British port, except the Russian which was outward bound from Murmansk to New York.

The disappointments and disasters of the Norwegian campaign, which resulted in defeat for the Allies on land and heavy losses by sea and in the air, caused profound dissatisfaction at home with the Government. But the final blow, which brought about the resignation of Neville Chamberlain as Prime Minister and the translation to that office of Winston Churchill at the head of a National Government, came on 10th May when the Germans invaded Holland and Belgium. Operation *Gelb*, Hitler's blitzkrieg against the West, had begun, and this compelled the final evacuation of our forces from Norway. 'It was plain to the Cabinet that our naval and air strength were quite inadequate to support a costly overseas campaign in Norway when control of our own coastal waters might at any moment be seriously threatened.'[1]

Even before the German occupation of Denmark, action had been planned to forestall any attempt to land enemy troops in Iceland and the Faeroes. Thus on 7th May the AMC *California* was ordered to patrol off the eastern fjords of the Icelandic coast. Three Northern Patrol trawlers were sent to assist, and board all foreign trawlers to establish their innocence.

On 10th May a force of Royal Marines was landed in Reykjavik from the cruiser *Berwick*, and Iceland was declared to be under British protection. Force 'Fork', which consisted of a marine battalion with a battery of 4-inch guns, a battery of 2-pounders and a naval howitzer battery, remained in Iceland for a month, when they were relieved by army units. Similarly Force 'Valentine', comprising some 200 Royal Marines, was landed from the cruiser *Suffolk* in the Faeroe Islands. They, too, were eventually relieved

[1] Roskill, *The War at Sea.*

by the army.

On the 12th the Commander-in-Chief, Home Fleet directed Northern Patrol trawlers to search all the fjords in eastern Iceland to ascertain if any hostile craft or enemy agents were about, and to establish friendly relations with the local inhabitants. Only one German was discovered, and he appeared to be quite inoffensive. It was reported that no German ships had visited the fjords since the beginning of the war.

Heightened by the bellicose speeches of Mussolini, tension with Italy was mounting, and in the event of war with that country, it was decided to establish a patrol off Vigo and Lisbon to intercept Italian shipping leaving Spanish and Portuguese ports. Although the Commander-in-Chief, Home Fleet complained that the efficiency of the Northern Patrol would thereby be reduced, five of its AMCs — the *Patroclus, Asturias, Carinthia, Derbyshire* and *Cheshire* — were ordered to be detached for this task on 14th May. In fact from now on the Northern Patrol was to be steadily denuded of ships for employment elsewhere as circumstances demanded.

Otherwise no incidents of special importance occurred in the Northern Patrol area at this time. Only fifteen merchantmen were intercepted, four Icelandic, one Italian, one Swedish, one Danish, four Finnish, two British, one Yugoslav and one Norwegian, all of them bound for British ports except two of the Finnish vessels. Gales were less frequent, but fog now became the chief enemy, bringing low visibility. U-boats began to appear and, as will be seen, were soon to take their toll of the vulnerable AMCs.

CHAPTER THIRTEEN

Raiders and U-Boats

Although the Home Fleet suffered grievously during the Norwegian campaign, heavy punishment had also been dealt out to the German Navy. The *Scharnhorst* and *Gneisenau* had both been damaged; the *Lützow* and *Scheer* hit by torpedoes; and the cruisers *Karlsruhe* and *Königsberg* sunk along with ten modern destroyers. Thus Admiral Raeder was left with few ships fit for sea operations. While on land German armoured divisions, spearheaded by Luftwaffe dive-bombers lanced their way through Holland and Belgium, German Naval Headquarters was temporarily preoccupied with efforts to get their third armed merchant raider to sea.

This vessel was the former Hamburg-Amerika Line's *Neumark* of 7,851 tons, built in 1930. Armed and equipped in like fashion to the *Orion*, her sister ship, she was designated 'Ship 21' and given the name *Widder* (Ram). In command was Korvettenkapitän Helmuth von Ruckteschell, an officer of the naval reserve. Although her conversion was completed by the end of November 1939, she experienced so many difficulties during trials that she was not ready to sail until the first week in May 1940.

By then most of the Norwegian coast was in German hands and it was possible to give the *Widder* better cover than had been provided for the *Atlantis* and *Orion*. Yet she ran into trouble almost as soon as she sailed. At the entrance to the Skagerrak a patrolling British submarine fired two torpedoes at her, which she managed to evade. Calling in at Bergen, she disguised herself as the Swedish freighter *Narvik*, and left that port on the night of 8th May. Next she put into Stadlandet, then sailed again after dark, only to encounter in a rain squall the surfaced British submarine *Clyde*, which she mistook for a destroyer. Pursued by the submarine, with which shots were exchanged, she fled back to harbour.

After being provided with air reconnaissance and a trawler to scout ahead, she ventured forth again and this time, aided by thick weather, passed safely through the Denmark Strait and into the North Atlantic which was to be her operational zone. On the 22nd she reported her position to Naval Headquarters as 180 miles south-east of the southern tip of Greenland, having successfully broken through the British blockade.

The *Widder* remained at large for just over five months, during which time she sank or captured some 58,000 tons of shipping, returning safely to Brest in October 1940. Because of his ruthless conduct towards his victims, von Ruckteschell was brought to trial as a war criminal two years after the end of hostilities, convicted, and sentenced to ten years' imprisonment.

Continuing to intercept and decypher much of our naval signal traffic, *B-Dienst* was now able to name the AMCs *Forfar, Asturias, Derbyshire* and *Worcestershire* as on Northern Patrol duties. They also detected that a large number of British auxiliary cruisers were on station in all areas, eight on escort duties in the North Atlantic, and the *Derbyshire* and four more in the area west of Vigo and to the west of Gibraltar, the latter being thought to comprise a possible escort service to Gibraltar and Freetown. German merchantmen and raiders in the Atlantic were duly informed of these dispositions.

On 27th May German Radio Intelligence intercepted 'a very valuable signal which afforded clear insight into the organisation of the Northern Patrol south of Iceland.' The AMCs *Forfar, Andania, Wolfe* and one unidentified auxiliary had received from the Vice-Admiral, Northern Patrol orders for patrol lines to be maintained 160 degrees from Stokkesnes, in Iceland, at distances of 25, 50, 75 and 100 miles. Starting at 2100 on 21st May, the ships were to steer courses of 65 or 245 degrees (roughly north-east and south-west) and turn about every twelve hours. Since the Home Fleet cruiser *Southampton* had also been informed of this order, she was therefore presumed to be included in the Northern Patrol.

Since the last such instructions to the Northern Patrol, noted the chief of the German naval staff, 'we can expect this one to be valid for some time. Our battleships have therefore exceptional opportunities of action from Trondheim.' Two days later *B-Dienst* identified the ships on patrol as the *Forfar, Andania, Wolfe, Laurentic* and *Scotstoun*. Admiral Raikes would have been appalled had he had any inkling that the names and dispositions of his AMCs were so well known to the enemy, although he was at all times conscious of the latent threat to them. Fortunately for him, the German heavy naval units were otherwise engaged at this time, having sallied forth to attack our forces covering the evacuation from northern Norway.

It was during this sortie that the *Scharnhorst* and *Gneisenau* encountered the British aircraft carrier *Glorious*, which was on her way back from the Narvik area with the Hurricanes and Gladiators and their aircrews which had been operating ashore in Norway, escorted by two destroyers, and sank all three. This was a disaster which might have been prevented if a report from one of our ocean-going Q-ships operating off the Norwegian coast which chanced upon a convoy of merchantmen apparently making for Iceland, had not been passed by the Admiralty to the Commander-in-Chief, Home Fleet. Since an enemy attack on Iceland and the unprotected ships of the Northern Patrol was feared, Admiral Forbes despatched the battle cruisers *Repulse* and *Renown*, accompanied by two cruisers and five detroyers, to investigate, thus leaving the carrier and some of the returning troopships almost unguarded.

Meanwhile things were going from bad to worse in the land battles in western Europe. By the middle of May the Dutch were forced to capitulate, and German armoured divisions broke through in the Ardennes, breached the French defences on the Meuse, cut off the Allied armies north of the Somme, and compelled the British Expeditionary Force to withdraw. By the 23rd the Germans had reached the Channel coast, and four days later the Belgians surrendered. By the 26th the Allied northern front had been rolled back and penned into an area around Dunkirk. Cut off from the rest of the Allied front, it was decided that there was no alternative but to evacuate the maximum number of troops from the blitz-shocked BEF.

As disaster followed disaster on shore, the Royal Navy carried out important demolitions, including that of the oil tanks in Amsterdam, and brought the Dutch royal family over to this country. Subsequently a vast fleet of vessels, including destroyers, passenger and merchant ships, and small craft of every kind was assembled under the control of the Flag Officer, Dover to evacuate more than 300,000 British and French troops from Dunkirk, and a few small enclaves to the south.

While these tremendous events were taking place, the ships of the Northern Patrol plodded up and down their patrol lines despite an almost complete absence of east and westbound traffic. An average of eleven AMCs remained on station daily, with one keeping watch in the Denmark Strait. Only eleven merchantmen were intercepted, but of these eight were voyaging to or from a British port, two were Icelandic coasters, and the other was a small Norwegian vessel, which had escaped from that country. As had happened with Norwegian and Danish shipping after the Nazi invasion of those countries, the enemy attack on Holland and Belgium was followed by an order for all Dutch and Belgian shipping to put into British or French ports. German representatives abroad reported that the latter had painted over their neutral markings.

On 6th June the Naval Officer-in-Charge, Iceland informed the Commander-in-Chief, Home Fleet that coast-watchers were again reporting aircraft and suspicious vessels in the vicinity. Next day the army commander at Reykjavik reported strong rumours of a large enemy force landing at Ladmundarfjord. As already mentioned, Admiral Forbes ordered the flag officer commanding the battle cruiser squadron to investigate these reports and take charge of the Northern Patrol to assist in a search.

Later the army commander at Reykjavik reported that two large ships had been sighted off Vestmannaeyar Island. The Northern Patrol armed boarding vessel *Discovery II* was ordered to eastern Iceland to visit all the fjords, find out if there were any signs of enemy activity, investigate and quieten rumours, and visit the military detachment at Seydisfjord. At the same time the *Circassia* was sent to Reykjavik to calm fluttering nerves there. But there was no substance in any of the rumours. The fact was, reported the British Minister, that the Icelanders had become thoroughly jittery because of the occupation, and thought that the British force, to whom they were not overly friendly, was inadequate to hold the island. All German nationals in Iceland had, however, been brought away by the cruisers which had landed the British troops.

During the first ten days of May there had been little U-boat activity. Then the Germans despatched four submarines to operate in the Western Approaches, and a fifth to patrol off Finisterre. In five days the latter sank five merchantmen. On 6th June the Northern Patrol sustained the first of its numerous losses from submarine attack when the *Carinthia* was torpedoed.

The latter vessel, it will be remembered, was one of the five Northern Patrol AMCs ordered on 14th May to patrol off the coast of Spain. Having completed her spell of duty there, she was on her way back to the Clyde at the time via the west coast of Ireland. During almost the entire period of her southern patrol, Captain John Barrett RN her commander, had been confined to his bunk suffering from severe gastritis.

A few minutes after two o'clock in the afternoon of the 6th, the AMC was some sixty miles west of the aptly named Bloody Foreland, steering due east and zigzagging, when she was struck by a torpedo on the port side abreast the engine room. One watch was closed up at the guns, and nine men were on submarine lookout duty, but no one saw anything unusual before the explosion, although a torpedo track was spotted immediately afterwards.

Some minutes later a periscope was sighted crossing astern from starboard to port, and fire was immediately opened at it. Although the periscope was in view for only a minute, four shells burst very close to it. Half an hour later a periscope was again spotted, this time some 1,500 yards off the port bow. Again the AMC's alert guns' crews went into action, and once more several shells were seen to burst very near the target. Then another torpedo track was seen, which passed within a few feet of the ship's bows. The crew braced themselves for further attacks, but no more developed.

The *Carinthia* had, however, been severely damaged. After being hit the ship took a heavy list to port, swung rapidly to starboard and settled by the stern. The engine room was immediately flooded and all but two of the watchkeepers killed. The hatches of No 4 hold, in which the high-angle magazine was situated, were blown off and the whole of the compartment rapidly flooded, as also did No 5 hold. The crew's messdeck was split by the explosion and inundated by sea water. All power and lighting failed at once, but after about an hour it was possible to start up the emergency dynamo on the boat deck, the delay being caused by water damaging the mains. This gave power for steering and a few upper deck lights, but none for pumping.

Using the battery-powered emergency wireless transmitter, a call for help was sent to Malin Head: 'Have been torpedoed by submarine. Remaining afloat. Unable to proceed. Submarine in vicinity. If planes could be sent to keep submarine away,' Captain Barrett added, 'I think ship can be got in.'

Nevertheless it was more than three hours after the attack before a signal was received from the Commander-in-Chief, Rosyth to say that aircraft from Oban were on their way, and that the destroyers *Wren* and *Volunteer* and the minesweeper *Gleaner* and the tug *Marauder* had been ordered to the scene. At 1815 the first aircraft appeared and began to circle the crippled ship.

The *Volunteer* arrived in the early hours of the following morning, and Barrett made preparations for the AMC to be taken in tow. An hour later the *Wren* arrived, followed by the *Gleaner*. At 0700, with the *Carinthia* in tow of the minesweeper, the slow journey to safety commenced. But during the night the water had been steadily gaining and the ship was filling up. At 0950 the situation was such that the crew of the AMC, numbering more than 300 officers and men, had to be transferred to the smaller vessels, a party of volunteers being left on board to tend the towline, although all hands wished to remain.

Then the *Marauder* arrived and took over the tow, the little group of ships heading for Tory Island at 4 knots, with an A/S trawler as anti-submarine screen. That evening, however, a dense fog came down, and speed dropped to a mere crawl. Shortly before 8 p.m., it was considered advisable to abandon the *Carinthia*, but the tug with Barrett on board tried to keep her in sight, which was very difficult in the poor visibility. But the AMC was doomed, and an hour and a half after the towing party had been taken off, she suddenly broke up and sank in a matter of seconds.

At the subsequent inquiry into her loss, the Board thought that if she had been fully fitted out with a buoyant cargo of oil drums she would have stood a good chance of survival. As it was, she carried more than 14,000 'ping-pong balls' on board, but this was below the recommended number.

Her killer was *U-46*, which next day reported her success to Naval Headquarters.

Another enemy armed merchant raider was now preparing to sail. Designated 'Ship 10' and named *Thor*, she was the ex-banana boat *Santa Cruz* of 3,800 tons. She, too, carried an armament of six 5.9-inch guns, seven smaller weapons — which included four light AA guns — and four torpedo tubes. Her oil-fired steam engines gave her a top speed of 18 knots, and she had an operating range of 40,000 miles. Despite her small size, she was to engage at different times during her 9-month cruise three British AMCs, and actually sink one of them.

The *Thor* sailed on 6th June disguised as a Russian merchantman, and was given an elaborate escort of destroyers, aircraft and mine-sweepers to speed her on her way. The farther north she steamed the worse became the weather, much of it fog and snow. Thus although there was almost no darkness in the higher latitudes, this was to her advantage and, unknown to and unsighted by, any Northern Patrol vessel she successfully negotiated the Denmark Strait by keeping close to the ice pack and so reached the open ocean. On the 22nd she reported her position to Naval Headquarters as west of the Azores. Before returning via the English Channel to Hamburg in April of the following year, she sank 11 merchantmen totalling some 83,000 tons and the AMC *Voltaire* off the Cape Verde Islands.

But if Admiral Raikes knew nothing of her passage through his blockade line, the Germans continued to be fully informed about the movements of his ships. Thus on 6th June they knew that the AMCs *Wolfe, Laurentic, Circassia, Letitia* and *California* were on station south-west of Iceland; on the 11th that their patrol line had been moved further west, and that two days later a new patrol system had been put into force. Seven AMCs were to operate this, spaced 20 miles apart from a specified point in southern Iceland, on courses alternating between 240 degrees in one direction and 60 degrees in the other. The ships were to reverse course every twelve hours, so that at 1500 daily they would be steering 240 degrees, and 60 degrees at 0300.

'The exact data on this blockade line,' commented Rear-Admiral Fricke, head of the German Naval Operations Division, 'is extremely valuable for the intended thrust by our battleships into the Iceland area. A speedy raid against these patrols is of great importance for exploitation of this detailed data from the Radio Monitoring Service and for bringing Ship 10 through into the Atlantic. At the same time the Commanding Admiral, Submarines (Dönitz) will send out submarine *U-A* against the auxiliary cruisers.'

It will be convenient at this point to follow through the enemy's intentions as regards raiding the Northern Patrol and see what happened.

On 13th June Fleet Air Arm aircraft from the *Ark Royal* attacked the enemy's units which were in harbour at Trondheim and damaged the *Scharnhorst*. Despite the loss by U-boat attack of one of the British AMCs in the Northern Patrol, Fricke was informed by *B-Dienst* that the patrol system remained the same, except that the most easterly point of their position lines was no longer to be reached at 1500, but at 0300, and the most westerly at 1500. 'There are therefore still possibilities,' he noted, 'for our Task Force *Gneisenau*.' Next day he reported that a thrust into the Iceland-Faeroes area was being planned by the Commanding Admiral, Fleet for the *Gneisenau*. The chief of the naval staff agreed, but thought that the task force should be the *Gneisenau* and *Hipper*, 'which must operate in northern waters. These ships cannot lie in Trondheim continuously, thus completely foregoing the great strategic advantage which possession of the Norwegian coast offers us.'

In the late afternoon of the 22nd, therefore, Admiral Lutjens left Trondheim with the *Gneisenau* and *Hipper* for the 'planned thrust into northern waters'. At the same time the *Scharnhorst*, heavily escorted, started for home. Unhappily for the Germans, however, the departure of Lutjens' squadron was reported. The British submarine *Clyde* which was lying in wait scored a torpedo hit on the *Gneisenau*, and both ships promptly returned to Trondheim, the damage to the flagship putting her out of action for several months. Thus the German Naval Staff's hope of their big ships carrying out operations from Norway for a long time in northern waters and in the Iceland area were frustrated. Raeder was furious, and ordered the *Hipper* to stay in Trondheim.

At this time the enemy was seriously considering the occupation of Iceland. But any such plans they might have been formulating were nullified when, early in July, the British garrisons were heavily reinforced, and defensive measures against enemy assault considerably strengthened.

Four U-boats had been stationed off the Orkneys and Shetlands, and in two successive days two of our Northern Patrol AMCs were torpedoed, one of them by the mysteriously named submarine *U-A*. The latter was in fact the ex-Turkish submarine *Batiray*, a 1,000-ton boat fitted for minelaying. One of a class of three with names ending in 'ay', she was launched at Kiel in 1939 and requisitioned by the German Navy.

CHAPTER FOURTEEN

The Price of Vigilance

Around midday on Wednesday, 12th June the AMC *Scotstoun* left Greenock to return to patrol at the conclusion of a routine three-day spell in harbour. Waiting off the Isle of Arran was a tug and towed target, and the AMC proceeded to carry out a full calibre practice shoot of ten rounds from each of her eight 6-inch guns. When the firings had been completed the tug returned to harbour, and the *Scotstoun* continued northwards at 15 knots towards her designated patrol line south of Iceland.

At 0315 next morning, the 100-fathom line having been reached, course was altered to north-west and the AMC commenced zigzagging. Unknown to Captain Sidney Smyth, her commander, a retired regular naval officer in his fifties, *U-25* was lurking west of the Hebrides hoping for just such a target to appear in her sights.

At 0617 while the *Scotstoun* was swinging on to the port leg of her zigzag and still under helm, a heavy explosion was felt on her port side, and debris seen coming up on the water. The ship's company was at cruising stations with seven lookouts on duty and two of the 6-inch and two 3-inch AA guns fully manned. Normally in less than a quarter of an hour all hands would have been summoned to action stations, but the shrilling of the alarm bells now brought them racing up from below. As soon as manned, guns' crews were ordered to open fire independently at anything they saw. But there was no sign of torpedo track or periscope.

On the bridge Captain Smyth anxiously awaited damage reports from the various departments. The torpedo had struck aft, the explosion causing the port engine to race violently and then stop, indicating that the propeller shaft had gone. The engineers reported the port after tunnel full of water and the steering compartment flooded, although as yet no water had reached the engine room. The starboard engine was still going ahead and the ship turning in a slow circle to port and settling aft. But she was not listing and appeared to be in no immediate danger of sinking.

The explosion had also brought down the rigging and mast stays, and carried away the main wireless aerial feeder. No.7 hold aft was inundated, its covers blown off and some of the buoyant ballast oil drums beginning to surge above the hatchway. The *Scotstoun*'s allocation of these important additions to her damage control arrangements was more than 17,000. The aerial was quickly repaired, and a signal reporting the torpedoing passed to the naval authorities at Scapa. Within minutes the message was acknowledged and Smyth informed that aircraft and destroyers were being despatched to his assistance. Had the enemy attack been broken off at this stage, there was a good chance that the crippled AMC could be got safely back to port. But since she had no anti-submarine screen to protect her, the *Scotstoun* remained a sitting duck.

Having taken up a new position ahead of her target, the U-boat now fired two more torpedoes, both of which however ran erratically and were plainly seen by anxious lookouts in the *Scotstoun*. One went speeding down the starboard side of the AMC from forward to aft, and the second ran in the reverse direction, porpoising badly. Clearly they must have been defective, and both missed.

Two more, which did run accurately, however, were already on their way, and both struck the *Scotstoun* in quick succession in almost the same place on the starboard side aft, their combined explosions giving the impression that a magazine had blown up. Lieutenant-Commander Cookson, the AMC's gunnery officer, who had seen them approaching, reached his control position in time to spot a submarine breaking surface about a thousand yards off the starboard bow. He ordered fire to be opened, and half a dozen rounds of 6-inch forced the U-boat to submerge in haste.

But she had inflicted mortal wounds on her victim. All the engine room steampipes burst, filling that compartment with acrid fumes and scalding vapour, and every light went out. The gyro compass, wireless transmitters and telemotor gear were also wrecked by the explosions. The starboard engine was quickly shut down and engine and boiler room staffs evacuated. When the double blow struck into her vitals the AMC heeled over to starboard, then slowly righted herself and began to settle by the stern. Ship's company discipline was admirable. Guns' crews remained at their weapons, and damage control parties did their best to cope with the situation in the pitch darkness of the 'tween decks.

It was clear that the ship could not now last for long, and Smyth ordered all boats to be turned out ready for lowering. By 0710 these were filled and away, leaving a small party of officers and ratings manning the 3-inch guns in the hope of striking a blow at their attacker. As the *Scotstoun* settled lower in the water and waves began to lap over the promenade deck, these last-ditchers reluctantly launched Carley rafts and floated off, until only Captain Smyth and an engineer officer remained. Then the vessel gave a sudden lurch and a wave washed both men overboard. When Smyth surfaced he was hauled aboard a raft and transferred to one of the lifeboats, but the engineer failed to reappear.

Fortunately the sea was relatively calm, although a long swell was running, and there was a light south-westerly wind. At 0727, just over an hour after the first torpedo struck home, the *Scotstoun* heaved her bows out of the water and slid under, leaving the sea strewn with wreckage. After collecting all the survivors from the rafts, the boats remained in the vicinity of the sinking for about two hours. A head count established that out of the entire complement of more than 350, only two officers and four ratings were missing.

When the wind freshened and the sea began to get up, sails were hoisted and the little flotilla began to make its way eastwards. The first aircraft appeared in mid-morning and started to circle the boats, followed an hour or so later by the destroyer *Highlander* which embarked all the survivors.

Luck favoured the *Scotstoun*'s killer, whose crew might otherwise not have had very long in which to savour their success, for, after disposing of the AMC, *U-25* went on to sink a tanker. During this attack the latter managed to ram the U-boat, but inflicted only superficial damage. Less than two months later, however, *U-25* struck a British mine in the North Sea and went to the bottom with all hands.

Following their identification of five of the seven AMCs on station on the 6th June in the current Northern Patrol system south-west of Iceland, *B-Dienst* was able to establish next day that the sixth vessel was the *Andania*, and two days later the *Salopian* as the seventh. The German naval staff made plans accordingly. For the first time in the war the blockaders were to be attacked by U-boat on their own patrol lines.

At 2330 on 15th June the *Andania* was steering 240 degrees at 15 knots, zigzagging every ten minutes 20 degrees to either side of her mean course, when she was struck by a torpedo on the starboard side aft. In the twilight prevailing at that time of the year visibility was good. Although there was only a slight breeze and a moderate sea, there was also a heavy swell. Captain Donald Bain RN, her commander, had just come on to the bridge.

As was usual, in addition to a proportion of the guns' crews,

seven lookouts were on duty — one at the masthead, one on each
side of the bridge wings, and two on the HA gun platform, yet no
one saw anything out of the ordinary. In accordance with standing
orders two of the HA guns immediately opened fire in the presumed direction of the U-boat, the alarm was sounded, and all
hands were quickly at action stations.

When the torpedo slammed into the AMC she immediately lost
headway, took on a list to starboard — which was promptly
corrected by the alert engine room staff pumping oil fuel from
starboard to port tanks — and settled by the stern. Her rudder had
been put out of action, while the force of the explosion brought
down the main wireless aerials, fouling the emergency aerial on
the way. By the time the tangle had been cleared and a jury
aerial rigged, the main generators in the engine room had become
flooded and put out of action. No attack report could be sent,
therefore, until the emergency dynamo on the boat deck had been
started up.

Damage was severe. The stewards' mess had been blown in, and
the after magazine and Nos 5, 6 and 7 holds completely flooded.
B and C decks had been split open, releasing large numbers of
buoyancy barrels from the holds beneath. Both propeller shafts
were flooded, and water was entering the engine room through the
starboard shaft gland and a fractured bulkhead. All available
pumps were brought into action, but the sea continued to gain.

On deck anxious eyes watching for further attacks spotted a
second torpedo approaching from a point off the starboard bow.
One of these observers, the principal fire control officer, had time
to note as it broke surface that it was hissing and running erratically.
All guns at once opened fire along its track, and the torpedo
missed by 100 yards astern. Twenty minutes later a third torpedo
appeared, which passed from port to starboard, missing the ship
by 50 feet. The port 6-inch guns were able to get off several
rounds at it, as well as at a periscope which briefly appeared off
the port bow.

After half an hour had elapsed yet a fourth torpedo came
arrowing towards the ship's port side, the origin of its track clearly
visible. Fire was directed along this tell-tale marker, apparently to
some effect since no more attacks were made. Captain Bain, who
now got off a second signal: 'Still firing torpedoes at us — three
misses,' thought that the reason for the ship's escape was that her
engines were still edging her slowly ahead, and that the U-boat's
torpedoes had run 'cold' — thus they all missed astern.

The *Andania's* attacker was submarine *U-A*, and when the latter's captain reported having torpedoed the AMC, although adding: 'Sinking not yet observed,' the German naval staff noted jubilantly that: 'The first satisfactory result has been obtained by the planned operation of *U-A* against the British patrol dispositions in the Iceland area on the basis of radio intelligence reports.'

Like Captain Smyth of the *Scotstoun*, Captain Bain also hoped that his ship might yet be saved. Following his report of the torpedoing he had been informed that the armed boarding vessel *Discovery* II had been ordered to the scene from eastern Iceland, the destroyer *Forester* from the Faeroes, and other destroyers from Scapa. The AMC *Derbyshire* on the next patrol line reported that she was in visual contact with her stricken sister — strict orders barred her from approaching closer while a U-boat was suspected of being in the vicinity, a lesson painfully learned from the *Aboukir, Hogue* and *Cressy* disasters of World War I. The AMC *Forfar*, which had intercepted the Icelandic trawler *Skallagrimur*, now persuaded the latter's skipper to go to the *Andania's* assistance, and she, too, was on her way to the scene.

Shortly after one o'clock on the following morning Captain Bain decided to lower the ship's six outer lifeboats to sea level and fill them with personnel not required for fighting the ship. The remaining boats, which were stowed inboard, could then be turned out and made ready, to save time and confusion if complete abandonment suddenly became necessary. As time went on, additional parties were sent to join those in the boats already lowered.

But, despite the utmost efforts of all available pumps and ejectors, the water level continued to rise rapidly. When it became breast-high, making further work impossible, the engine and boiler room personnel were brought up from below. Nevertheless, after consultation with his officers, Bain thought that the ship might last for a further three hours, although after that the rate of sinking would probably accelerate. With this in mind, and in view of the fact that sea conditions were deteriorating, he decided to evacuate the ship completely but remain nearby in case it became possible to re-board. The *Andania* was now down by the stern and beginning to list over to port.

After the boats had been in the water for four hours, the *Skallagrimur* appeared and proceeded to take all the survivors on board, including four injured — the only casualties. The *Andania*

'A giant hand to squeeze a U-boat' — depth charge exploding

The end of a U-boat

sank soon afterwards, disappearing beneath the surface in less than a minute. Escorted by a Sunderland flying boat of Coastal Command and the *Forester*, the weather having become too rough to transfer the survivors from trawler to destroyer until the following afternoon, all arrived safely at Scapa. Captain Bain was full of praise for his crew, whom he reported to be 'cheerful, full of enthusiasm and ready for anything.'

The Board convened to inquire into the circumstances of the loss of the *Andania* recommended once again that more buoyancy ballast should be carried in AMCs — the *Andania*'s quota had been 15,000 oil drums — and also that the type of patrol should be varied.

The Commander-in-Chief, Home Fleet, thought that the attack on her might be an attempt by the enemy to disorganise the Patrol while an armed merchant raider was breaking out. For this reason he reinforced the AMCs in the Denmark Strait with the cruisers *Newcastle* and *Sussex* with instructions to use their aircraft while on patrol. He was of course still unaware that the *Thor* had already broken out, and that yet another raider was standing by to make the attempt. A rumour about the latter may, however, have reached the Admiralty and been passed on to him.

The fifth raider, designated 'Ship 33', was named *Pinguin*, and was the former 7,766-ton *Kandelfels* of the Hansa Line. Armed similarly to her sisters, she carried in addition 300 mines. One of these, which she laid in Australian waters, was responsible for the sinking of the first US merchantman of the war. The *Pinguin* remained at large for nearly twelve months, during which she destroyed or captured 136,000 tons of shipping before being sunk herself in action with the British cruiser *Cornwall* in May 1941.

She began her outward voyage on 19th June disguised as a Russian merchantman bound for Murmansk. Her departure went according to plan, and on the 20th she put in at Stadlandet. Two days later, having been provided with air reconnaissance, she set out again and continued up the Norwegian coast. But because the weather remained unusually clear, she was compelled to go north of Jan Mayen Island and hang about off the southern edge of the Greenland ice pack to wait for suitably foggy and misty conditions. When these finally came down, she was able to slip unobserved through the Denmark Strait and out into the Atlantic.

Although the German naval staff knew that the raider would be unable to break radio silence until she was well clear of the British blockade, they seem to have worried unduly about her, finally noting hopefully on the 27th that: 'Ship 33 must have got through.' That there was reason for anxiety is clear from an entry in the War Diary recording that: 'Ship 37 which left on 23rd April for Trond-heim and from then on no more is declared "Missing"!'

No further details have come to light regarding 'Ship 37', but submarine *U-A* now re-enters the story, for in addition to attack-ing Northern Patrol AMCs on their own patrol lines, she was intended to work farther afield. Accordingly after sinking the *Andania* she made her way into the Atlantic, there to await the *Pinguin* which was bringing out stores, fuel and torpedoes for her. The two vessels duly met at a pre-arranged rendezvous, and after the transfer of supplies had been effected, the *Pinguin* towed the submarine to the latitude of Freetown, off which port the latter was to operate in order to draw off any British patrol craft which might be sent out in search of the raider. The plan failed, however, for *U-A* suffered a machinery breakdown and was forced to return home.

Meanwhile the war was taking a graver turn. On 10th June Mussolini declared war on Britain and France, and Italian bombers raided Malta. On the 17th came the collapse of France and her appeal for an armistice. Britain now stood alone to face the might of the Axis Powers.

As far as the Northern Patrol was concerned, Italy's entry into the war made little difference, as only seven Italian ships had been intercepted since its outbreak. But although the Spanish coast patrol was cancelled at the end of May, the Admiralty decided that four of the five Northern Patrol AMCs which had been detached for the purpose must now remain to reinforce the Freetown Escort Force. Otherwise patrols continued normally, the number of AMCs on station in northern waters averaging eleven daily. For the first time since the Patrol had been instituted not a single mer-chantman was intercepted. The weather had become abnormally bad for the time of year, bringing a succession of gales, alternating with fog or low visibility.

In mid-June the Admiralty ordered that the Patrol was to make every endeavour to intercept the Finnish steamer *Brita Thorden*, bound from Petsamo to New York, and remove from her the pro-Nazi Icelandic Director of Posts and Telegraphs who was on his way back to Iceland. The return of this individual was considered highly undesirable, but local action to prevent it was impossible. The hunt for the *Brita Thorden* provides yet another example of the enormously difficult task of tracking down a single ship in the broad oceans without the help of air reconnaissance and technical aids, such as radar, neither of which were then available.

The Commander-in-Chief, Home Fleet, directed that the search for the vessel was to be based on the supposition that she would proceed from the North Cape either north or south of Iceland, and that one AMC should search along each of these possible routes as far as longitude 5 degrees west, with Northern Patrol trawlers working close inshore along the east coast of Iceland. On the 24th three AMCs were accordingly diverted from their normal patrol lines to begin their sweep.

Four days later the *Laurentic*, one of the searching AMCs, intercepted a wireless message from Reykjavik asking the *Brita Thorden* to report when the Director of Posts and Telegraphs disembarked from the ship, thus indicating that the latter must either have reached harbour or be somewhere near land. Speculation was ended when later the same day the Naval Officer-in-Charge, Iceland, signalled that the Finnish ship had indeed arrived, landed her undesirable passenger, and cleared for America. No one, it seemed, knew just where she had closed the Icelandic coast. The weather, it need hardly be said, had been almost continuously bad with the inevitable gales and poor visibility.

Commenting on this failure, Admiral Raikes wrote that even when the Northern Patrol was at greater strength, fifty per cent of enemy ships homeward bound had been able to get through the patrol lines by choosing periods of low visibility. Somewhat bitterly he added: 'It seemed that to prevent a single ship from reaching Iceland we should have stationed the whole of the Northern Patrol to the east of that island.'

CHAPTER FIFTEEN

Western Patrol

Following the fall of France, Britain was herself threatened with invasion, and strenuous preparations were made to defend these islands against direct assault. The Navy's anti-invasion measures included assembling destroyers and cruisers withdrawn from the Home Fleet and other naval home commands into striking forces poised ready to pounce upon any seaborne expedition. As many small craft as possible, including trawlers temporarily withdrawn from the Northern Patrol, and vessels hastily requisitioned from the fishing industry, were also formed into an Auxiliary Patrol and concentrated round our south and east coasts to keep constant watch close off shore.

Even before these measures were put into effect the Admiralty suggested to the Commander-in-Chief, Home Fleet, that the Northern Patrol AMCs should be moved down to take station along a line running north-westward from the North Channel as a guard against a possible German invasion of Ireland. But Admiral Forbes pointed out that if such an operation should be attempted, the enemy force would also certainly pass to the west of the patrol line, and that the AMCs would be exposed to U-boat attack since German submarines passed through that area on their way to the Western Approaches. Any enemy force bound for Ireland was more likely to be sighted from their usual patrol lines, and could be intercepted by Home Fleet units from Scapa. Also the AMCs would need to be supported by warships to the south, which would involve a further dispersion of our available naval forces. The idea was then dropped.

Throughout this period of extreme tension the possibility of an invasion force attempting to pass through northern waters was kept very much in mind, and a keen lookout and high state of preparedness maintained in the ships of the Northern Patrol.

Early in July it was decided to mine all the waters between Scotland and Iceland, and between Iceland and the coast of Greenland. Although the great northern mine barrage laid by the British and Americans in 1918 stretching from Scapa Flow to the south-west coast of Norway had proved ineffective, the Admiralty felt that any additional obstacle placed in the path of U-boats and enemy surface units was worth the effort.

Laying accordingly began, those parts of the area considered more likely to be traversed by U-boats being mined first. The operation was then extended into the Denmark Strait in order to narrow the passage between the west coast of Iceland and the Greenland ice pack. Moored magnetic mines were used for this area as they could be set deep enough to avoid them being carried away by ice floes in the winter.

Notice of a dangerous area embracing these waters was then given in very broad terms, together with instructions for the safe passage of vessels through the Pentland Firth, and between the Orkney and Faeroe Islands. Incoming merchantmen were advised to proceed to Kirkwall between North Rona and Cape Wrath; outward bound vessels to seek instructions at British consulates in the Baltic or at Kirkwall.

The Germans, however, decided that the purpose of these minefields was merely to force neutral shipping to submit to a British check. They therefore expected the Northern Patrol system to be modified by the withdrawal of the AMCs and the assumption of the role of the latter by reconnaissance aircraft and cruiser patrols. In fact an increased number of AMCs was maintained on station daily. Apart from fishing vessels and British ships, they intercepted three Norwegian merchantmen, one Swedish, one Dutch, one Greek and one Finnish.

On 16th July Rear-Admiral Ernest Spooner DSO took over command of the Patrol with the title of 'RANP', Admiral Raikes having been appointed Commander-in-Chief, South Atlantic. Changes which were to take place in the future disposition of the blockaders necessitated the transfer of Patrol Headquarters from Kirkwall to Largs, a few miles south of Greenock; the move was made early in September.

During the latter part of July the AMCs were able to take more offensive action than had been possible since the invasion of Norway. Four neutral ships were sent in under detention, three Finnish (whose country was now working with the Germans) and one Swedish, all bound from Petsamo to New York. The weather, too, was much improved. Because of our anti-invasion measures all shipping bound for British east coast ports was now passing round the north of Scotland through the Pentland Firth.

On 21st July the Admiralty decided that it was now necessary to extend the blockade to include the Atlantic coasts of France,

Spain, Portugal and French North Africa, and that a Western Patrol was to be instituted. In addition to AMCs and trawlers acting as armed boarding vessels, a number of ocean boarding vessels were to be taken up, armed and equipped. But until the latter became available, six AMCs and four armed trawlers were allocated to the Western Patrol.

The area they were to cover was defined as lying between 39 and 45 degrees north latitude, and 15 and 20 degrees west longitude — a rectangular 'box' roughly equidistant between Lisbon and the Azores — and extending as far north as the middle of the Bay of Biscay. Based on Gibraltar, the armed trawlers would operate inshore off Lisbon, Cape St Vincent and Cadiz. The main object was contraband control, although full export control was also to be exercised. After 31st July all merchantmen would have to obtain ship navicerts, i.e., covering complete cargoes; any vessels not complying would be sent in for examination. As was to be expected, the Spanish Government strongly protested.

Because of the shortage of ships the establishment of the Western Patrol had to be made at the expense of the Northern Patrol; both, however, came under the administration of the RANP. The first two Northern Patrol AMCs to be transferred to the new region were the *Cilicia* and *Cheshire*, which sailed from the Clyde on 29th July. They were joined soon afterwards by the Northern Patrol trawlers *Kingston Jacinth, Kingston Sapphire, Kingston Topaz* and *Kingston Turquoise*.

Although preoccupied with preparations for Operation 'Sealion', Hitler's code name for the invasion of England, which by order of the Führer were to be completed by the middle of August, the German naval staff found time to remind the Reich Ministry of Transportation with some acerbity that prospects for German overseas traffic had materially increased since the defeat of France. *B-Dienst*, however, had obviously failed to obtain information regarding the forthcoming establishment of a Western Patrol, for the naval staff's admonishment to the Ministry went on to point out that German merchantmen coming from overseas to French Atlantic ports were unlikely to be interfered with as there was no British control zone such as that between Greenland and Iceland. Even the breakthrough to Norwegian harbours during the dark winter period was considered easier than before since the British Navy had fewer patrol forces available.

'The British bluff of announcing a declared mining area on 11th July in the vast area between the Shetlands and Greenland indirectly admits this fact. The present control of the Norwegian coast itself is nothing compared to earlier British efforts. Departure from neutral harbours is less dangerous as the enemy has considerably fewer patrol forces since the elimination of French naval forces. As long as Great Britain does not acquire new allies with powerful navies, these more advantageous conditions of sailing from overseas ports will persist.' The Ministries of Transportation and Economics were therefore exhorted to exploit these conditions.

For reasons already mentioned the average number of AMCs which could be maintained on station daily on the Northern Patrol had fallen. In addition, one had been paid off altogether while she was being refitted and re-armed, and three transferred to the America and West Indies Command for Atlantic escort duty. During the first two weeks of August only three neutral vessels were intercepted in northern waters, the remainder being British. Despite the time of year they were still being plagued by gales or misty visibility.

Because of the reduction in the number of Northern Patrol AMCs, the Commander-in-Chief, Home Fleet decided that the armed boarding vessels should be moved to patrol lines north of the Faeroes, leaving the area south of these islands to look after itself. When Admiral Spooner asked the Admiralty for ten more trawlers or corvettes until the ocean-boarding vessels were ready, he was told that no additional ships were available.

He was now about to lose another AMC.

On Friday 9th August the *Transylvania* left the Clyde to return to patrol. A few minutes after midnight, having cleared our own defensive minefield south-west of Ailsa Craig, the ship, steaming at 16½ knots, was altering course and still swinging when she was struck by a torpedo on the port side abaft the engine room. There was no sign of U-boat or torpedo track, but weather conditions at the time were deteriorating, with a strong westerly wind and frequent rain squalls.

The captain, who had just turned in, was back on the bridge within seconds, the hands summoned to action stations, and a signal despatched reporting the torpedoing and the ship's position. Damage reports indicated that the engine room was flooded, and the after part of the ship already awash as far up as C deck, with the depth charges and one of the after 6-inch guns under water. The ship had listed six degrees to port and was well down by the stern.

The first of the aircraft ordered to the scene arrived at 0315 while it was still dark, followed by the destroyers *Achates, Fortune* and *Antelope.* By now the AMC was slowly but steadily settling and her list had increased to twelve degrees. It was obvious that she was doomed, the rate of sinking being retarded only by her buoyant ballast. Captain Miles ordered the boats away, and it was now that casualties began to occur, no one having been killed by the explosion of the torpedo.

In the rising sea one of the boats was accidentally slipped with only five on board, which drifted away in the darkness and was lost. The men who should have completed its complement now clambered into another boat which was already full. Thus, over-loaded, it capsized soon after leaving the ship. A third boat, which was also overcrowded, overturned alongside one of the destroyers, among those who lost their lives in this accident being an officer who fell between boat and destroyer and was crushed to death. The *Transylvania's* was the heaviest casualty list since the sinking of the *Rawalpindi,* and was due entirely to confusion in getting the boats away in darkness and rough seas.

Next day the AMC *California,* also on her way back to patrol from the Clyde, picked up an SOS from the British steamship *Llanfair,* which had been torpedoed west of the Irish coast. Captain Pope found himself faced with an agonising decision to make. On the one hand, his orders were not to risk his vulnerable vessel in a U-boat area. On the other hand, he knew from information received that an RAF aircraft was circling the *Llanfair's* survivors in their boats, and that its presence and the heavy and confused seas running would make a submarine attack difficult. He was also aware of the time that must elapse before any other ship could reach the survivors, if they were still able to remain afloat in the worsening weather. Having made up his mind, he headed for the last reported position of the *Llanfair* at full speed.

Dropping depth charges on arrival as a deterrent to any lurking U-boat, he then proceeded to pick up the thirty survivors from their boats 'with the least possible delay'. Half an hour after quitting the area he received a signal from the Commander-in-Chief, Western Approaches forbidding him from taking the action he had just successfully completed!.

As a result of the loss of the *Transylvania* the Commander-in-Chief, Home Fleet told the Admiralty that he considered the AMCs should be escorted through the submarine danger area in the north-west approaches, and that he proposed to use a reinforced destroyer flotilla based on Greenock for this purpose. But in the event it turned out that no A/S escorts could be made available because they were still retained in the Channel as part of our anti-invasion measures.

During the second half of August an average of only seven AMCs operated the Northern Patrol but no merchantmen were intercepted. Thus because the ships had to be thinly disposed, the many gales, and the loss of trawlers, the Patrol was largely ineffectual. Although it was not yet autumn, the weather continued to be quite extraordinarily bad, with gales raging on ten out of sixteen days, and visibility practically down to zero on the others. Farther south conditions were much kinder for the Western Patrol, which intercepted twenty-six merchantmen of various nationalities, half of them Spanish. But few had to be sent in for examination.

The latter's patrol areas were now designated as 'M' — 300 miles west of Finisterre, and 'O', 300 miles west-south-west of that point. There was also a special Madeira patrol, while the armed trawlers worked off the Tagus, Cape St Vincent and Cadiz. The ships were therefore well placed to intercept traffic between South America and South Africa and Europe, and the bulk of that which was still passing to and from the Mediterranean.

On 16th August, while the AMC *Cheshire* was returning from the Western Patrol to the Clyde for a routine rest period in harbour — there being no safe and convenient port any nearer — she found herself in the role of U-boat hunter instead of, as so often happened, the other way round. When off Bloody Foreland in the afternoon of that day, her lookouts suddenly spotted a periscope a few hundred yards off the port bow. Increasing to full speed, the AMC began to describe a series of S curves along the estimated track of the submarine, dropping depth charges each time she crossed the track.

After the explosion of the second depth charge, the submarine's periscope again appeared some 500 yards off. In the meantime the AMC had sent off a U-boat sighting report, and she was now joined by two destroyers, the *Arrow* and *Achates*, closely followed by two A/S trawlers. While the four began a systematic hunt for the *Cheshire's* quarry, the latter continued on her way to the Clyde. Unhappily no success was reported, the scared U-boat having apparently succeeded in making good her escape.

A day or two later the AMC *Circassia* on the Western Patrol also attacked a U-boat, but again without success. In the evening of 18th August she was steaming along her patrol line just north of

Ponta Delgada, in the Azores, when a U-boat surfaced so close to her that her guns would not bear. She made every effort to ram the submarine, and dropped depth charges at 50-yard intervals. But a passenger liner-turned-warship cannot be expected to manoeuvre like a destroyer, and the AMCs were not fitted with proper depth charge throwers. Shortly afterwards the U-boat broke surface again, then disappeared stern first. Captain Oliphant and his jubilant ship's company had reason to think that they had scored a victory and avenged the loss of the *Transylvania* — but there was no confirmation of this.

In the early hours of the following morning the *Circassia* sighted a darkened ship, and as her signals to the vessel remained unanswered she fired two warning shots, the second across the ship's bows. These, too, were disregarded, and the suspect then made a large alteration of course and opened fire on the *Circassia*. The latter's ship's company was at action stations with all guns manned, and fire was immediately returned. After letting go several broadsides, the *Circassia* again challenged by signal lamp. This was now replied to, when the vessel identified herself as the British steamship *Rowallan Castle* (7,800 tons) belonging to the Union Castle Line. Her master reported that she had been damaged in the shooting but refused to give any details of this or whether she had suffered any casualties. She was accordingly allowed to proceed. When the ship arrived in the United Kingdom and her shaken master reported 'this unfortunate incident', as he termed it, he paid tribute to the accuracy and effectiveness of the *Circassia's* gunnery. The *Rowallan Castle* was by no means the only British ship which failed to answer when challenged by our patrols, and thus risked destruction.

It was now that Hitler announced a total blockade of the British Isles, and gave warning that neutral shipping would be sunk at sight. The battle to cut our Atlantic lifeline by unrestricted U-boat warfare was about to begin.

But *B-Dienst* was also about to be abruptly cut off from its most valuable source of information regarding our naval movements in home waters. On 13th August the German radio monitoring service had for the first time since the institution of the Western Patrol succeeded in identifying by name five AMCs 'working between the west of Ireland and the Canaries.' 'From this,' noted the German naval staff, 'it seems that the British plan to establish a patrol line of auxiliary cruisers and enforce the blockade against France, Spain and Portugal.' On the 16th *B-Dienst* identified by name the AMCs *Worcestershire, Forfar, Laurentic* and *Derbyshire*, and one unknown vessel as operating on the Northern Patrol.

Then on the 20th of that month the blackout came down, for all British naval communication codes and cyphers were simultaneously changed, and a shaken *B-Dienst* warned its masters that: 'Deciphering cannot be counted on for the time being.' Lamented the naval staff: 'This is the most serious blow to Radio Intelligence since the outset of war. The enemy had adhered to pre-war codes and only changed the keys periodically, causing some temporary difficulties. Radio monitoring and deciphering had been greatly facilitated by the capture of numerous enemy documents which afforded at times a complete insight into the enemy's radio service.' The Germans considered it remarkable that we had not changed our procedures after almost a year of war.

B-Dienst thought that it would take about about six weeks to make a new evaluation. But in fact that service was never again to enjoy anything like its previous success; while, on the other hand, our own cryptanalysts were about to break the German Navy's most secret cyphers, which they considered to be impenetrable.

*

The changed conditions of war brought about by the enemy's control of the coasts of Norway, the Low Countries and France, stretching from the North Cape as far south as the Franco-Spanish border, diminished the importance of the blockaders. Its AMCs began increasingly to be taken away for other duties.

Thus during September the number on the Northern Patrol fell to less than seven daily, with five maintaining the Western Patrol. The latter had now become the busiest, intercepting twenty-nine merchantmen in September, while only three were stopped in northern waters. The abnormally bad weather in that area actually brought ice conditions down to within the latitude of the Faeroes, with large bergs being sighted.

During October Western Patrol ships intercepted 40 neutrals, and in November 136. The majority were Spanish, but they also included Brazilian, Panamanian, Greek, Portuguese and Japanese. All were allowed to proceed. The time spent by boarding officers in examining the intercepted ships was greatly reduced since all now carried ship navicerts. In the same period Northern Patrol vessels intercepted 14 merchantmen.

In October and November occurred more sinkings of AMCs.

These disasters were to hasten the demise of a strategy which, in view of Nazi conquests in Europe, could no longer materially affect the enemy's war economy as had the stranglehold exerted by the old Tenth Cruiser Squadron. Although a trickle of contraband goods continued to get through, the Patrol was gradually to fade away, its last few months of active life emphasising the increasing hazards of the war at sea for the vulnerable AMCs.

While she was off the Azores on 2nd October, lookouts in the AMC *Cilicia*, escorting from Freetown to the Clyde the old aircraft carrier *Argus*, which was employed in ferrying urgently needed RAF planes to the Middle East, spotted a torpedo track passing about fifty yards under her stern. A periscope was sighted shortly afterwards, course altered to bring the port guns to bear, and fire opened at about 2,000 yards. Almost immediately a U-boat shot to the surface, only to dive precipitately amid a straddle of bursting 6-inch shells.

Unfortunately no hits were obtained, but the submarine had remained in view long enough to be identified as Italian. Italian U-boats had in fact started work in these waters in August, and by the end of November some 26 were operating in the Atlantic. But they accomplished virtually nothing, and were regarded with little more than contempt by Admiral Dönitz.

A few days later Convoy WS 3, en route from the Clyde to the Middle East, was attacked by enemy aircraft some hundred miles north-west of Lough Swilly, the troop transport *Oronsay* being hit and disabled. The AMC *Salopian*, which was on her way to resume duty on the Western Patrol after a refit at Liverpool, intercepted the *Oronsay's* SOS and altered course to close. But the AMC *Cheshire*, inward bound to the Clyde from that patrol and nearer to the *Oronsay*, was ordered instead to go to her aid, while the *Salopian* took the remaining three ships of the troop convoy under her wing and joined them up with the main body. In company with the cruiser *Cairo*, which also arrived to help, the *Cheshire* brought the disabled troopship safely back to the Clyde.

After her customary three days in harbour for rest and replenishment, she sailed again for the Western Patrol, only to fall victim herself to the enemy. Early on the following evening, when about 70 miles south-west of the scene of the *Oronsay* bombing, she was hit by a torpedo. Fortunately the U-boat did not on this occasion linger to press home a further attack. When the AMC's call for assistance was received, Admiral Spooner despatched the Canadian destroyer *Skeena* and the Flower Class corvette *Gladiolus* to her aid together with two rescue tugs from the Clyde. There now ensued a minor epic of seamanship, courage and determination.

During the night the crippled *Cheshire*, screened by her two escorts, struggled along at between four and six knots in the direction of Lough Swilly. At daybreak, however, she was forced to stop because three of her holds had become full of water and her foredeck was awash. Except for a small steaming party, her company was now transferred to the *Skeena* although they asked to remain on board, and the AMC taken in tow by the tugs.

But she continued to settle lower and lower in the water. By the following morning her draught had increased to as much as 49 feet forward and 16 aft, and her commander, Captain Bernard RN, suggested that a salvage tug should be sent to pump out the foremost hold. This was done, the Liverpool Salvage Association's *Ranger* being despatched to the scene at top speed. At 1230 on 17th October, four days after she had been torpedoed, HMS *Cheshire* was triumphantly beached in Belfast Lough. Although she would be out of action for many weeks, she had been saved by the determined efforts of her captain and crew.

There now occurred a double tragedy which was brought about by the captains of two of the AMCs allowing their humanitarian instincts to override the standing Northern Patrol order which forbade these ships to close the position of a torpedoed merchantman except in very special circumstances.

On the night of Sunday, 3rd November, the AMCs *Laurentic* and *Patroclus* were returning independently from a stint on the Western Patrol, the former having been ordered to Liverpool and the latter to the Clyde. Steaming at 15 knots and zigzagging, both ships had by 2100 reached a position approximately 150 miles west of Galway Bay. The weather was clear with good visibility, and although not then in sight of each other the two ships were not many miles apart. Both received at about the same time a message reporting that the homeward bound ss *Casanare*, independently routed from the West Indies, had been torpedoed. The position given was about twenty miles from that of the *Patroclus*.

Against the advice of his officers, Captain Gerald Wynter DSO RN (Ret) who commanded the *Patroclus*, decided to try to pick up her survivors, and altered course accordingly. After circling the spot where the *Casanare* had been torpedoed until he considered it was sufficiently dark, he came in and dropped two depth charges to scare away any enemy submarine. Boats were now seen in the water, and the nearest hailed alongside. Unknown to Captain

Wynter, it contained survivors, not from the *Casanare* but the *Laurentic*!

Hardly had the boat bumped alongside than a torpedo slammed into the *Patroclus* immediately beneath it. The boat was blown to pieces, some of the men in the AMC killed and others hurled overboard, and her foredeck turned into a shambles. Ten minutes later, while the crew of the *Patroclus* were falling in at their mine and torpedo stations, a second torpedo exploded in No 4 hold. Captain Wynter now ordered the ship to be abandoned, and those of her boats which had not been smashed in the first explosion were got away. In fact the ship could have steamed on after the first torpedo hit, since the engine room, boiler room and bulkheads were undamaged. But she had remained stopped because Wynter refused to sacrifice the men who had been blown overboard, and had actually called away a cutter to pick them up.

Then the ship was hit simultaneously by two more torpedoes, one exploding in the cross-bunker and the other in No 6 hold, blowing one of the 6-inch guns and its mounting bodily overboard. It was after these had hit and all survivors appeared to have got away that Wynter finally left the ship with the navigating officer, exclaiming as they stepped into the water, 'I am the last man off the ship!' He was never seen again.

But because there were insufficient boats and rafts for all, a number of officers and men, including Commander Ralph Martin RN the First Lieutenant, found themselves still on board, and congregated on the boat deck. There they discussed what they should do.

The U-boat, however, had not yet finished with her victim, and at about 0100 she surfaced a thousand yards off and began to shell the slowly foundering AMC. Martin and his companions, who had debated what action to take under such circumstances, now manned the starboard 3-inch high-angle gun and returned the submarine's fire, one of them claiming that they had hit her. Apart from starting a minor conflagration, which was soon extinguished since the ship was almost awash, the U-boat's shells had done no damage. In fact, even after the fourth torpedo hit, the AMC's engines, boilers and pumps were still intact. Ten minutes after the gun action the ship was hit by another torpedo in No 6 hold.

As she continued slowly to settle in the water, Martin and his party paced up and down the boat deck and drank rum and whisky to keep themselves warm. Taking it in turns to keep watch for the submarine's return, they lay down and covered themselves with blankets fetched up from below. They had already discussed the possibility of trying to save the ship, but concluded that it was only a matter of time before she sank, and settled down to wait.

At about 0400 another torpedo hit the *Patroclus* just beneath the bridge, which collapsed completely, the effect of which was to break the ship's back. 'We all laughed,' Commander Martin recounted afterwards, 'because we realised that the submarine had put four torpedoes in almost the same place.' Five minutes later a seventh torpedo struck home in the engine room, and the *Patroclus* began to list rapidly. One by one the party slid overboard, supporting themselves with pieces of wreckage and moveable gear they had collected beforehand.

Martin had a small flask of brandy in his Gieves waistcoat, which he presently passed round and 'revived us a lot'. Then Lieutenant Murchie, RNR, another of the little group paddling about in the water, actually produced a bottle of whisky, and this, too, helped to keep them going. Sadly, Murchie died from exposure half an hour later.

Dawn came at about 0800 and with it the destroyer *Achates*, one of several rescue vessels ordered to the spot. But as Martin was being hauled up her side her asdic operator got a 'ping' and the destroyer surged ahead. He was dropped back into the water and hit on the head by several pieces of wreckage. When he came to the surface again, 'somebody dropped a depth charge' which almost stunned him. It was more than half an hour before he was picked up by another destroyer.

On arrival in harbour he learnt that not only were more than 100 officers and men missing from the *Patroclus*, including Captain Wynter, but that the *Laurentic* had also been sunk. No boats from the *Casanare* had been seen anywhere in the vicinity. It is a measure of the spirit of the crew of the *Patroclus* that many of the men told Martin: 'We wouldn't have missed this for anything.'

What had happened on board the *Laurentic* was that Captain Eric Vivian, her commander, received the signal about the *Casanare* at 2145 and was considering altering course to go to the rescue of her survivors when the AMC was torpedoed. Her engine room was immediately flooded so that she was unable to move or operate her pumps. The boats were turned out and, except for two guns' crews, the men ordered to their abandon ship stations. With the aid of the battery transmitter a call for assistance was got off. Then a submarine was sighted on the starboard bow, and several rounds of 4-inch, including starshell, fired at it before it disappeared. Very lights were then fired as a signal to the *Patroclus* that her consort had been torpedoed.

A second torpedo now hit the *Laurentic*, which blew two of her lifeboats to pieces and damaged a third. As we have seen, one of the undamaged boats that got away managed to reach the *Patroclus*, only to be destroyed alongside her. Concluding that his ship was doomed, Captain Vivian ordered her to be abandoned. When this had been done he personally paddled round the foundering vessel in a Carley raft to make sure that everyone had got away. She was then finished off by a third torpedo. Along with the rest of her survivors Vivian was picked up in due course by the rescue ships.

At the subsequent Board of Inquiry both captains came in for blame; Wynter for having gone to the rescue of survivors and for not going ahead after the first and second torpedo hits on the *Patroclus*; Vivian for not having immediately altered course away from the position of the *Casanare* after he had received the signal that she had been torpedoed. The Board also thought that the *Laurentic* could not have been saved after the second torpedo had hit her. Unhappily, the feeling that he had 'let the side down' preyed on Captain Vivian's mind to such an extent that he eventually developed suicidal tendencies and had to enter a mental hospital.

The villain of the piece was *U-99* commanded by the 'ace' U-boat captain Otto Kretschmer. Before his submarine was rammed and sunk by the destroyer *Walker* while attacking a convoy in the Atlantic in the following March, Kretschmer was to claim yet another of the Northern Patrol's AMCs.

Two days after the loss of the *Laurentic* and *Patroclus* news was received of the destruction of another AMC which, but for a minor accident already mentioned, would herself have become a unit of the Patrol.

On 27th October the German pocket battleship *Admiral Scheer* after a long refit at Gdynia, sailed from Brünsbuttel to carry out a raid in the Atlantic. Because we were still preoccupied with our anti-invasion measures, although this threat was now receding, her passage up the North Sea went undetected by our air patrols. When her captain headed for the Denmark Strait he was fortunate enough to find the weather at its most abominable, with gales and frequent snow and hail squalls. By hugging the edge of the Greenland ice pack, the *Scheer* passed through unseen by the *Chitral*, the solitary Northern Patrol AMC on patrol, although at one stage she came within four miles of the latter. After having two men swept overboard and a third severely injured by huge seas, the pocket battleship safely emerged into the Atlantic, reporting the fact to German naval headquarters on the 1st November.

On the 5th, with the aid of her scouting aircraft, she gained touch with an approaching British convoy, HX 84 inward bound from Halifax. Comprising 37 merchantmen, the convoy's sole escort was the AMC *Jervis Bay* commanded by Captain Fogarty Fegen RN.

When the *Scheer* was sighted and identified, Fegen ordered the convoy to scatter, then headed towards her at full speed. For nearly an hour the weakly armed AMC fought the powerful raider until, ripped to pieces by gunfire and blazing from stem to stern, she finally sank. 190 of her crew of 254, including Captain Fegen, were lost. But except for four merchantmen picked off by the *Scheer*, the *Jervis Bay* had saved the convoy. Captain Fegen was awarded a posthumous VC.

In the expectation that the *Scheer* would attempt to return home after this foray, Admiral Forbes sailed from Scapa with two battleships, a cruiser and four destroyers to cover the Iceland-Faeroes passage. Still patrolling the Denmark Strait, the *Chitral* was withdrawn to Reykjavik, since she would have been no use against a pocket battleship, and the AMCs *California* and *Worcestershire*, on patrol south of Iceland, were ordered to take over the trawler lines close to the Faeroes.

But the *Scheer* was not to be found. Continuing her raiding activities as far as the South Atlantic and into the Indian Ocean, she finally returned to Kiel on the 1st April 1941 after breaking back safely through the Denmark Strait.

CHAPTER SIXTEEN

Final Curtain

The month of December 1940 saw the effective end of the block-aders as originally constituted. On 18th November, following the loss of the *Laurentic* and *Patroclus*, the Admiralty decided to withdraw the AMCs of the Northern Patrol, except for a small number to continue to patrol the Denmark Strait, the passage between the Faeroes and Iceland being left to trawlers and mine-fields. The ships thus made available would be used to strengthen the Western Patrol. But the change was not actually made until the end of the year.

Meanwhile the average number of AMCs on the Northern Patrol was reduced to five out of the eleven remaining in the squadron, with three on the Western Patrol. 15 merchantmen were inter-cepted in northern waters, and 155 by the southern patrol. Only three ships — all from the latter — had to be sent in under armed guard, one of them a Vichy French vessel, since these could now be regarded as suspect.

One German ship made an attempt to get through the Western Patrol to a Spanish port. She was the 5,800-ton Hansa Line's *Klaus Schoke* which had reached the Azores from South America. Late in the evening of 1st December she sailed from Ponta Delgada and headed for Vigo. But she had not got very far when she was intercepted by the AMC *California*. As soon as she was challenged her crew scuttled and abandoned the ship.

Nevertheless the AMC sent over a boarding party, whose officer in charge reported that although the vessel's engine and boiler rooms were flooded he thought that she would remain afloat long enough to get her into port. Accordingly Captain Pope of the *California* asked permission of the Flag Officer Commanding, North Atlantic at Gibraltar to tow his prize either to the Azores or Gibraltar. But he was told that because of the danger of U-boats this was not expedient. Instead he was to put an armed guard on board the merchantman, and a destroyer and tug would be sent from Gibraltar.

Pope duly complied, but the *Klaus Schoke* continued to foun-der slowly by the stern although her foremost holds remained dry.

By the afternoon of the 5th, however, it had become obvious that she would not last much longer, and the armed guard was taken off. The ship sank soon afterwards.

Farther north another Northern Patrol AMC had been lost with a tragically high number of casualties. She was the *Forfar* commanded by Captain Norman Hardy RN. Scheduled to take up duty on the Western Patrol after having completed a refit at Liverpool, she was ordered instead to meet Convoy SC14 in mid-Atlantic and escort it home. The latter had sailed unprotected as no ocean escorts had been available at the time. SC convoys were composed of slow ships whose maximum speed of advance was no more than 8 knots which were periodically sailed from Sydney, Cape Breton Island, in Nova Scotia. Unfortunately for the *Forfar*, Convoy HX90 inward bound from Halifax was nearing the United Kingdom, and four U-boats were gathering to attack it.

Escorted by the Canadian destroyer *St Laurent*, the *Forfar* sailed from the Clyde at noon on 30th November. Just before midnight on 1st December the destroyer was detached to return to harbour by order of the Commander-in-Chief, Western Approaches. Shortly afterwards Captain Hardy was instructed by the same authority to keep south of a U-boat reported to be in position 54 degrees 23 minutes north latitude, 20 degrees 11 minutes west longitude. Action was accordingly taken to skirt the danger area, and the original course then resumed.

It was a dark night with a heavy swell running, and the AMC was steaming at 15 knots and zigzagging. Seven lookouts were on duty, which included one on 'monkey island', one at each wing of the upper and lower bridges, one by the HA guns and one right aft by the depth charges. Besides Captain Hardy, the officer of the watch and another lieutenant, and two midshipmen were on the navigating bridge. At about 0330 a suspicious object was sighted to starboard, but this could not be identified. Hardy decided to take no avoiding action and continued to zigzag.

At 0450 the ship was hit by a torpedo on the starboard side in the engine room. The explosion shook the entire vessel, and all lights went out as the power failed. Commander Ralph Arnot RN, the First Lieutenant, whose cabin was near to the point of impact and who had been flung from his bunk by the blast, hastily donned some clothes — including his Gieves lifesaving waistcoat — and made his way up to the bridge. No one had seen anything of submarine or torpedo track, and as there was some doubt as to whether a signal had been sent reporting the attack, Arnot went aft to the wireless office to make sure that this was done via the emergency transmitter.

Continuing his rounds of the ship to assess the damage, he met the engineer commander who told him that all engines and auxiliary machinery were finished, and the after tunnels and main diesel room flooded. The engine room was also flooding and diesel oil escaping into the boiler room. A few small fires had been started. As part of standard procedure in such circumstances, Arnot ordered the boats to be turned out and Carley rafts cut loose ready to be got away in a hurry. When he returned to the bridge to report on the situation he found Captain Hardy optimistic about their chances. The ship appeared to be in no immediate danger, she had no list, and was rising and falling easily to the swells. Hardy remarked that it was up to them to get the ship back to harbour and said what a glorious thing it would be if they could do so.

Starshells were then seen bursting in the sky some miles away. Believing these to have been fired by the *St Laurent*, Hardy ordered a number of rounds of starshell to be fired from the 3-inch guns, and followed these up with red Very lights.

Arnot then set off to make a further round of the ship, and on going below saw that water and oil fuel had risen to within a few feet of B Deck level. Then a second torpedo exploded on the port side near the engine room. Hastening back to the bridge, he asked the captain whether the ship should now be abandoned. Hardy agreed, the order was piped, and the Commander went off to get everything organised. Then a third torpedo hit on the port side almost in the same place as the second.

After supervising the preparation of the boats and other life-saving gear, Arnot was making his way forward again in the dark-ness and confusion when he suddenly fell through a cavity which appeared in the boat deck. Weakened by the explosions, the entire boat deck had in fact collapsed, crushing to death many of the men who were fallen in at their abandon ship stations on the promenade deck beneath. Before the full extent of this catas-trophe could be realised there came a fourth torpedo hit, also on the port side, which 'crumpled the ship up'. Her back was now broken, and bow and stern began rising up to meet each other.

Most of the ship's boats had been smashed by the repeated explosions, and those remaining badly damaged by being hastily lowered on to the jagged steel plates which had peeled bodily away from the ship's sides. In fact the situation had become such that all attempts to leave the ship in orderly fashion had to be abandoned, and it became a case of every man for himself. Eventually Arnot and two other officers found themselves standing alone on the torn and splintered promenade deck, at which the water was lapping. Since there was no point in remaining, they plunged overboard and swam to the motor boat, which had been blown over the side and was floating waterlogged and empty some fifty yards away. As they clambered into it, a fifth torpedo slammed into the foundering AMC and blew up her forward magazine. The bow and stern portions of the vessel then reared into the air independently and sank, the stern going under first. From beginning to end the entire tragedy had been enacted in fifty minutes.

'I need hardly detail the horrors experienced with so many men in the water absolutely saturated with oil fuel,' the Commander as senior surviving officer later told the Board of Inquiry. He had himself been soaked with oil fuel which fountained over him when he fell through the boat deck. Somehow the survivors got through the night, during which many died from exposure or from injuries sustained in the explosions and the collapse of the boat deck. But they had to wait a long time for rescue to arrive, for nearby Convoy HX90, with its inadequate escort of two destroyers and a corvette, was suffering cruelly at the hands of Otto Kretschmer and his fellow U-boat captains, losing ten ships. It was Kretschmer who had torpedoed the *Forfar* while steering to meet the luckless convoy, and his U-boat had been the 'suspicious object' she had sighted earlier.

One of the ships from the convoy, the British freighter *Dunsley*, which had earlier lost touch with the main body, actually fought off a surface attack by *U-99* with her DEMS gun, although not without suffering damage and casualties. The starshells seen from the *Forfar* had in fact been fired by the U-boat during this action. It was the *Dunsley* which first appeared on the scene of the *Forfar* sinking and picked up some of her survivors before hastily quitting the area. A searching Sunderland aircraft failed to spot others who were frantically waving from their rafts and pieces of wreckage trying to attract the crew's attention. It was not until late in the following afternoon that they were found and picked up by searching destroyers.

Apart from those killed by the torpedo explosions or died of wounds, 37 officers, including Captain Hardy, and 141 of the crew of the *Forfar* were lost. It was the worst disaster to befall the

AMCs of the Northern Patrol since the *Rawalpindi* — but not the last.

Earlier in the month the Germans had managed to pass two more raiders through the Denmark Strait and out into the Atlantic. First to make the attempt was the heavy cruiser *Admiral Hipper*, which left Brünsbuttel on the 1st December. Her presence in that port was actually spotted by our reconnaissance aircraft, but the significance not then realised. Cautiously she crept up the Inner Leads and hung around in the northern latitudes until bad weather grounded our air patrols, then passed through the Denmark Strait while it was temporarily unwatched.

A few days later 'Ship 41', biggest of all the German armed merchant raiders, also left Brünsbuttel to break out via the northern route. Originally she was to have passed through the English Channel, but no surface escorts were available. She was the *Kormoran*, formerly the Hamburg-Amerika Line's *Stiermark* of 9,400 tons. Armed similarly to the earlier raiders, she was fitted with six torpedo tubes, carried two Arado seaplanes and a small motor torpedo boat. She, too, got safely through the Denmark Strait by hugging the ice barrier, reporting her success to German Naval Headquarters on the 13th December. The *Kormoran* was able to wreak a good deal of havoc before being sunk by the Australian cruiser *Sydney*, which was herself sunk in the engagement.

The *Hipper*, however, although perhaps representing the greater threat, actually accomplished very little. 700 miles west of Finisterre, on Christmas Day, she found and attacked Convoy WS5A, which comprised a number of troopships bound for the Middle East. The twenty ships of the convoy were being escorted by the cruisers *Berwick*, *Bonaventure* and *Dunedin*, and the aircraft carrier *Furious*. When the *Hipper* appeared, the convoy was promptly scattered while she was tackled by the cruisers and quickly driven off. Machinery defects and the damage she had sustained compelled her to return to Brest.

Besides the *Berwick*, two of the merchantmen had suffered slight damage, one of the latter being the *Empire Trooper* whom we last encountered as the 13,000-ton *Cap Norte* of the Hamburg-Sud Amerika Line being captured by the British cruiser *Belfast* in October 1939. The AMC *Derbyshire* on Western Patrol was ordered to shepherd her into the lee of the Azores and embark her military personnel. But the transfer was not in fact found necessary, the *Empire Trooper* being permitted to enter Ponta Delgada for

The German heavy cruiser *Admiral Hipper*

An Ocean Boarding Vessel

repairs, after which she was escorted to Gibraltar.

On 21st December the Admiralty issued orders that the AMCs remaining in the Patrol should be transferred to the Rear-Admiral, Third Battle Squadron at Halifax, Nova Scotia. There they were to take over the combined duties of escorting HX convoys and patrolling the Denmark Strait. Thus, after bringing over a convoy, the AMCs would patrol the Strait, refuel and replenish at Hvalfjord, in Iceland, do a further patrol in the Denmark Strait, then return to Halifax. The round trip would last about thirty days, of which twenty-two would be spent in effective service.

Commenting on these arrangements, the Commander-in-Chief, Home Fleet, remarked:

> While these measures were dictated by necessity there could be no gain-saying that our reconnaissance of the important strategic passage between Scotland and Iceland and in the Denmark Strait was more illusory than real. There was a daily average of less than two AMCs in the 300-mile wide Denmark Strait, supported by a minefield of low efficiency and aided by ice in a measure which could only be conjectured. A daily average of four trawlers patrolled to the south-westward of the 240-mile passage between the Faeroes and Iceland, while occasional air patrols supported the incomplete and only partially effective minefields between the north of Scotland and the Faeroes.

In January 1941 the last two AMCs to be employed on the Western Patrol, the *Derbyshire* and *Salopian*, returned to the Clyde. The Halifax Escort Force was increased by seven AMCs, which enabled two to be always on patrol in the Denmark Strait, until this patrol was finally withdrawn in mid-June. Other AMCs released from the original Northern Patrol were transferred to trade routes, joining up with the appropriate escort forces. Four more were to be lost by enemy action, three by U-boats in the North Atlantic and one by fire.

But the British blockade was not to be lifted entirely. The work of the Western Patrol, which had become the most important, although a few vessels were intercepted in northern waters, was carried on by the ocean boarding vessels which began to come forward at the end of the previous September. The first of these was the *Camito*, an ex-banana boat of 6,833 tons owned by Elders and Fyffes. The others were the *Cavina, Corinthian, Crispin, Ariguani, Manistee, Maplin, Maron, Malvernian, Marsdale, Registan and Tortuguero*, all of similar tonnage and background, and with a better than average turn of speed. They were armed with two 6-inch guns and a number of smaller weapons. But by the time the last of these was ready for service, the need for them had fallen, and several were converted into fighter catapult ships for convoy work. Four were sunk by U-boats and one by enemy bombing.

During the first six months of 1941 the ocean-boarding vessels intercepted 177 merchantmen and the armed trawlers 654, most of them being allowed to proceed. Only 13 were sent in for examination. Three Italian tankers and four smaller vessels were captured. But while a minor flow of contraband goods never entirely ceased, most of it carried in small ships in the Mediterranean, attempts to run the blockade from the outer oceans finally died away despite the enemy's control of the entire European seaboard.

Although no statistics covering the work of the Blockaders during the Second World War have been compiled as was done when the Tenth Cruiser Squadron was disbanded in 1917, some idea of the total tonnage of goods denied to Nazi Germany during the first twenty-one months of hostilities can be gained from the figures of seizures to April 1940 when the normal work of the Northern Patrol came to an end. These were 602,370 tons, with a similar total intercepted by the French.

But nothing can detract from the courage and devotion to duty of the crews of the little 'C' and 'D' class cruisers at the outset of the war, and their comrades in the even more vulnerable AMCs backed by the trawlers of the inshore patrols, whose story has yet to be told. They had little to work with, and one of their greatest enemies was the weather. Yet they never faltered.

Bibliography

The Grand Fleet, Jellicoe, Cassell, 1919
From the Dreadnought to Scapa Flow, Vol. II, Marder, O.U.P. 1965
Max Horton and the Western Approaches, Rear-Admiral W.S. Chalmers, Hodder & Stoughton, 1954
Reminiscences, Admiral Sir Reginald Tupper, Jarrolds, 1929
The War at Sea, Vol. I, Roskill, HMSO. 1954
The Second World War, Vol. I, W.S. Churchill, Cassell, 1949
Mines, Minelayers and Minelaying, Cowie, O.U.P. 1949
Economic Blockade, History of the Second World War, Vol. II, Grand Strategy, HMSO
Economic Warfare, P. Einzig, Macmillan 1941
British Intelligence in the Second World War, Vol. I, HMSO 1979
Ultra Goes to War, R. Lewin, Hutchinson, 1978
Very Special Intelligence, P. Beesley, Hamish Hamilton, 1977
Inside S.O.E., E.H. Cookridge, Arthur Barker, 1966
The Orkneys & Shetlands, E. Linklater, R. Hale, 1965
German Naval War Diary
Admiralty documents in the Public Record Office.

Index